IMAGES
of America

DUNDEE

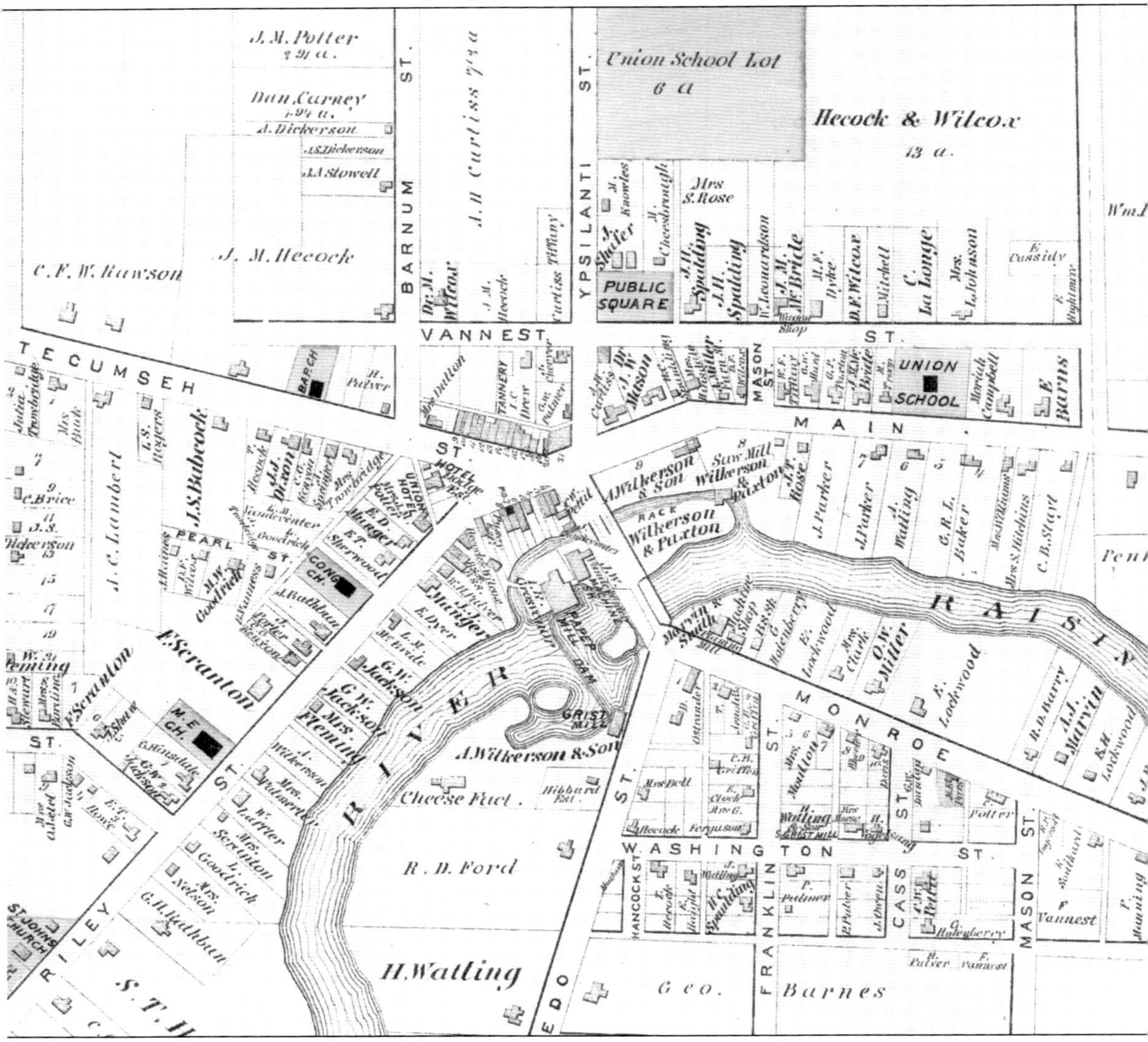

Dundee Village appears in the 1876 *Beers Atlas*. The roads at the center of the town's business district are forming Michigan's only triangular downtown. The River Raisin has determined the layout. Churches, town schools, gristmills, and the author's home (the former W. Penfield house) can be located on this map. (Dorothy R. Heinlen collection.)

ON THE COVER: Israel Drew and his wife, Martha, opened this bakery and grocery store some time after 1875. The store, at 138 Tecumseh Street, was located on Dundee's downtown triangle. Possibly the baker (with the apron) and a barefoot boy join onlookers on the rough plank sidewalk. An 1887 ad indicated Drew's store carried a range of goods, including coffees, imported cigars, baked goods, and fresh oysters. (Courtesy of the Old Mill Museum.)

IMAGES
of America

DUNDEE

Dorothy R. Heinlen
and Martha A. Churchill

ARCADIA
PUBLISHING

ISBN 978-0-7385-8321-1

Published by Arcadia Publishing
Charleston, South Carolina

Printed in the United States of America

Library of Congress Control Number: 2011925047

For all general information, please contact Arcadia Publishing:
Telephone 843-853-2070
Fax 843-853-0044
E-mail sales@arcadiapublishing.com
For customer service and orders:
Toll-Free 1-888-313-2665

Visit us on the Internet at www.arcadiapublishing.com

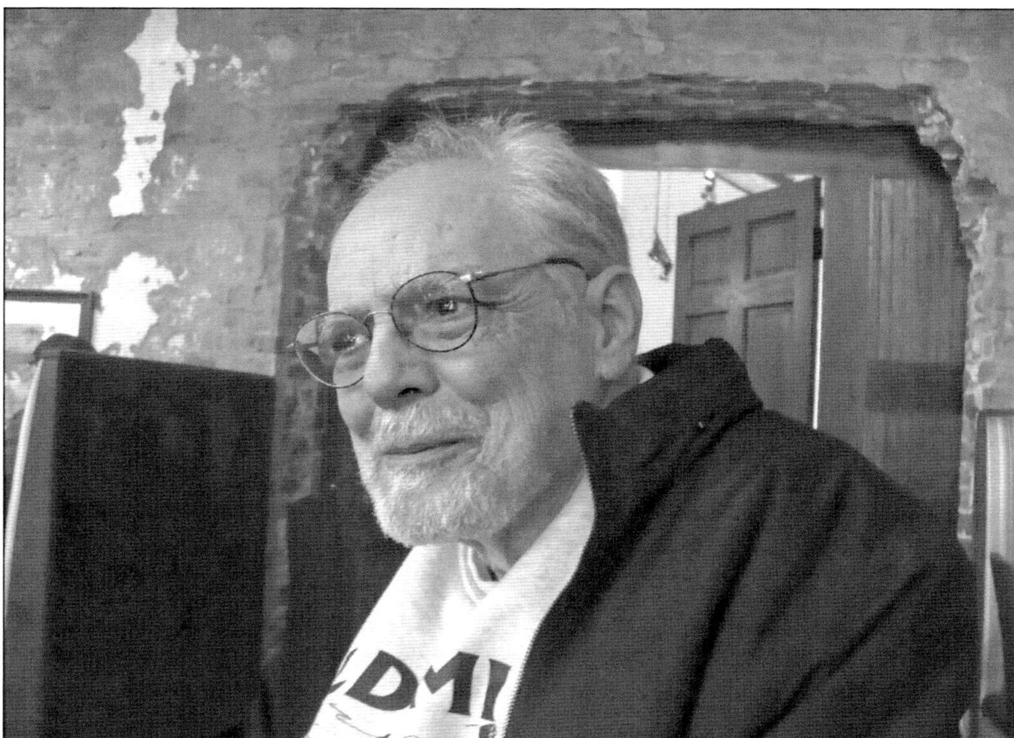

This book is dedicated to Douglas Brown Heinlen, our unofficial editor and "super scanner," and the other wonderful fellow preservationists of the Old Mill Museum. (Dorothy R. Heinlen collection.)

Contents

ACKNOWLEDGMENTS

We are indebted to Jeannette Brockman, Lois Eicholtz, and Robert Helle for sharing with us their extensive historical postcard albums, which form the backbone for chapters one, two, three, and four; this book would not have been possible without their contributions. Their individual pictures are not credited because these generous people have donated digital copies to the Old Mill Museum. Our sincere thanks is also extended to Nancy L. Kanitz, assistant director of the Old Mill Museum, who brought L.T. Harris's negatives to our attention, thus opening up a new chapter. We are very grateful to the many people who helped us indirectly through their previous contributions to the Old Mill Archives; they stepped forward to help preserve Dundee's history. We also thank the following with whom we directly interacted: Allen Berns, Madelyn Berns, Walter Berns, Gary Brockman, Mary Jo Brossia, Marjorie Busz, Henry Burger, Patrick Burtch, Ed Craft, George Croitori, Margaret Dettlof, John Eicholtz, Cynthia Ellis-Stoll, Christine Estereicher, Helen Goetz, Kevin Harris, Mary Hartwell, Doug Jennings, Jim Jennings, Sean McClellan, the late LeRoy Meyer, Rev. Doug Olsen, Darrell Powell, Mary Rehberg, Marilyn Rigel, Carole Smith, Tanya Whitaker, Carol Wiech, and two wonderful archivists: Chris Kull, of the Monroe County Historical Museum, and Randi Kominek, of the Old Mill Museum. We appreciate the encouragement and patience of our editor at Arcadia Publishing, Anna Wilson. We wish to acknowledge three crucial resources, which informed many of our captions. The first was the *Dundee Area Sesquicentennial 1824–1974: A 150 Year Recollection of the Dundee Area.* This book, affectionately known as the "Red Book," was privately published during the village's sesquicentennial celebration. Another resource consulted for chapter five is *Country Schools of Monroe County, Michigan: Teacher Directory 1828–1967* by Arthur V. Meyers and Robert H. Trace. Lastly, we are indebted to the late Otis Gloff and Richard Gloff for their historical chronology of store-by-store businesses in the triangle. Some of their work predates 1900. Blessings to all! Unless otherwise noted, all images appear courtesy of the Old Mill Museum.

Introduction

Native Americans traveled through the area clearing two long-distance trails. Mostly Potawatomi, they were placed on the Macon Indian Reservation in Dundee in 1808. In 1828, they were moved further west to St. Joseph County, and their land became available for purchase to settlers from New York.

In 1825, Riley Ingersoll and George Wilcox built the first cabins in the wilderness that would become Dundee. By 1831, Samuel H. Gale and his brother owned a sawmill on the south bank of the River Raisin. Approximately 11 families lived in the area.

In 1832, Sybrant Van Nest bought the sawmill, founded the village, and platted the land on the north side of the river. One story says that he named the village "Dundee" in honor of his friend Ebenezer Dustin, a native of Scotland.

For whatever reason, Van Nest tried to sell Dundee in 1835. His broadside (flyer) advertised it as featuring "two first rate Sawmills and one small Gristmill in the village, and a large and elegant Tavern House." He further claimed, "About 40 of the lots are sold to actual settlers, who have built houses and stores."

In 1832, the wooden-planked LaPlaisance Bay Turnpike (now Michigan Highway 50) followed the Indian trail along the south bank of the river. Eventually, so many trails and roads crossed in Dundee that, 100 years later, Dundee businessman Arthur M. Ritter dubbed the farming community "the hub of the highways."

The town was incorporated as a village in 1855. In 1868, a railroad magazine boasted that Dundee "contains 500 inhabitants, 15 stores, five millinery shops, two wagon shops, a school, and a Masonic Lodge. A tri-weekly stage plies between Dundee and Petersburg and the fare is 50 cents."

A fire on Christmas Eve 1875 destroyed most of the wooden commercials buildings on the north side of the triangle along Tecumseh Street. A row of uniform brick buildings in the Italianate style replaced them, matching the rest of the business district.

Dundee's historic downtown buildings survive, and the entire district, along with the former gristmill, were placed in the National Register of Historic Places in 1990. Today, the village is home to 4,200 residents. While Dundee looks toward the future, it never forgets to honor its past. *Dundee*, with its emphasis on the early 1900s and the 1950s, offers its tribute to the area's history.

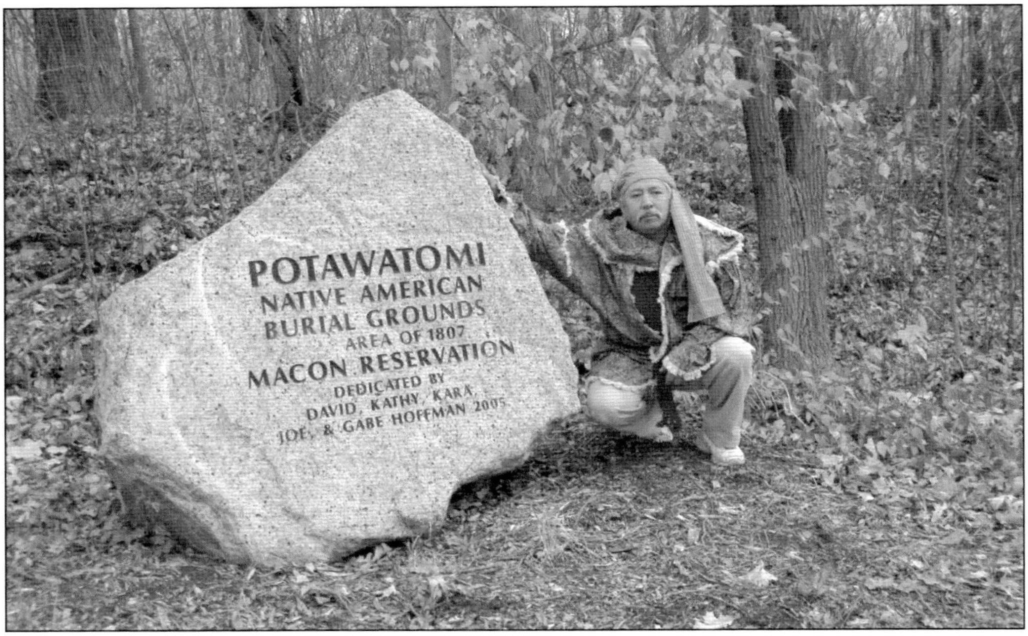

Colin Roderick Reaume of Dundee visits Bone Hill, the Native American burial ground on Bigelow Road east of Dundee. A member of the Ottawa tribe, Reaume feels confident that some of his ancestors are buried nearby with the Potawatomi. Before Europeans arrived, Native Americans traveled along the River Raisin. They used this high bank for burials. The stone marks the heart of the Macon Reservation. (Martha A. Churchill collection.)

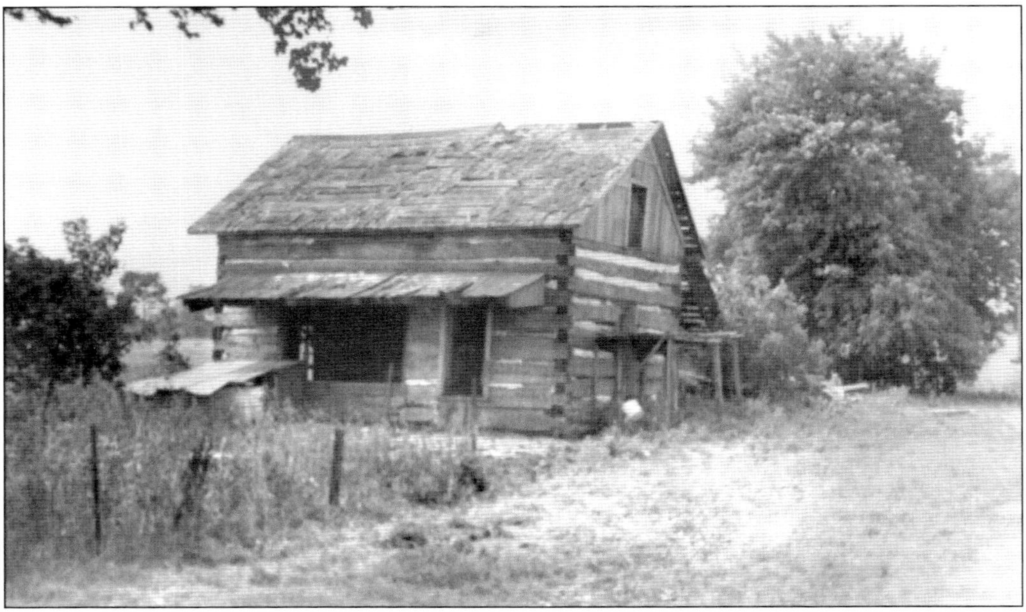

After both his parents died in Lansing, William Coleman II purchased land about two miles west of Dundee in 1866. The trip from Lansing to the Dundee Township farm took three days with Coleman walking every step of the way driving the ox team and wagon. The Coleman homestead was constructed near Rea Road. (Courtesy of Carol Wiech.)

One

Around the Triangle and Beyond

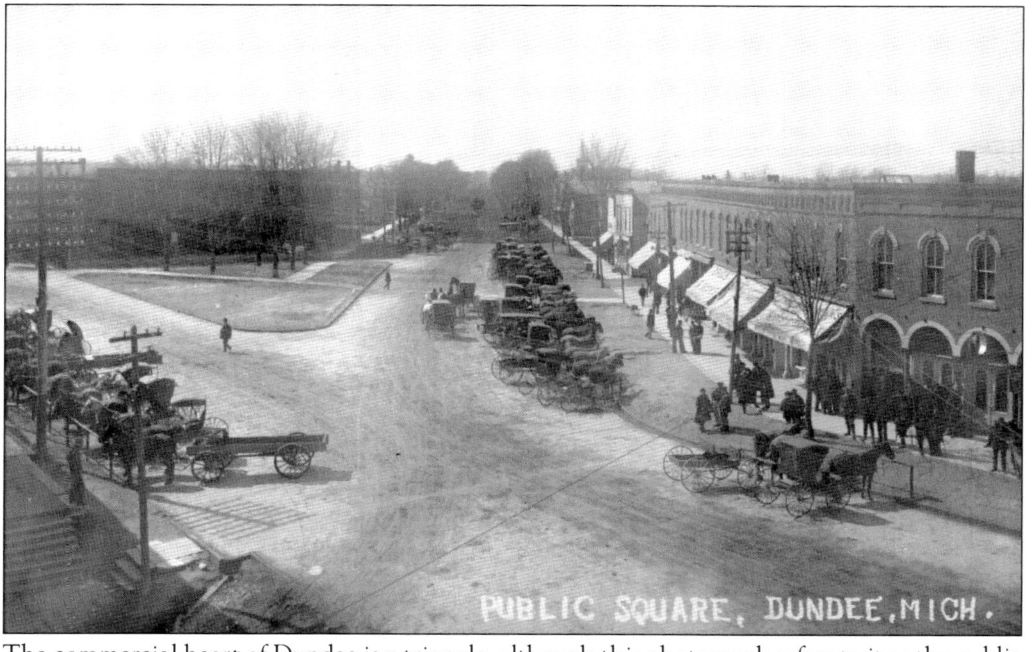

The commercial heart of Dundee is a triangle, although this photograph refers to it as the public square. The picture was taken around 1908 from the National Hotel roof looking west. On the left is the beginning of Riley Street. Across the top of the triangle is Park Place, and Tecumseh Street stretches into the far distance. The visible streets have just been bricked, and the triangle remains bare except for a few trees.

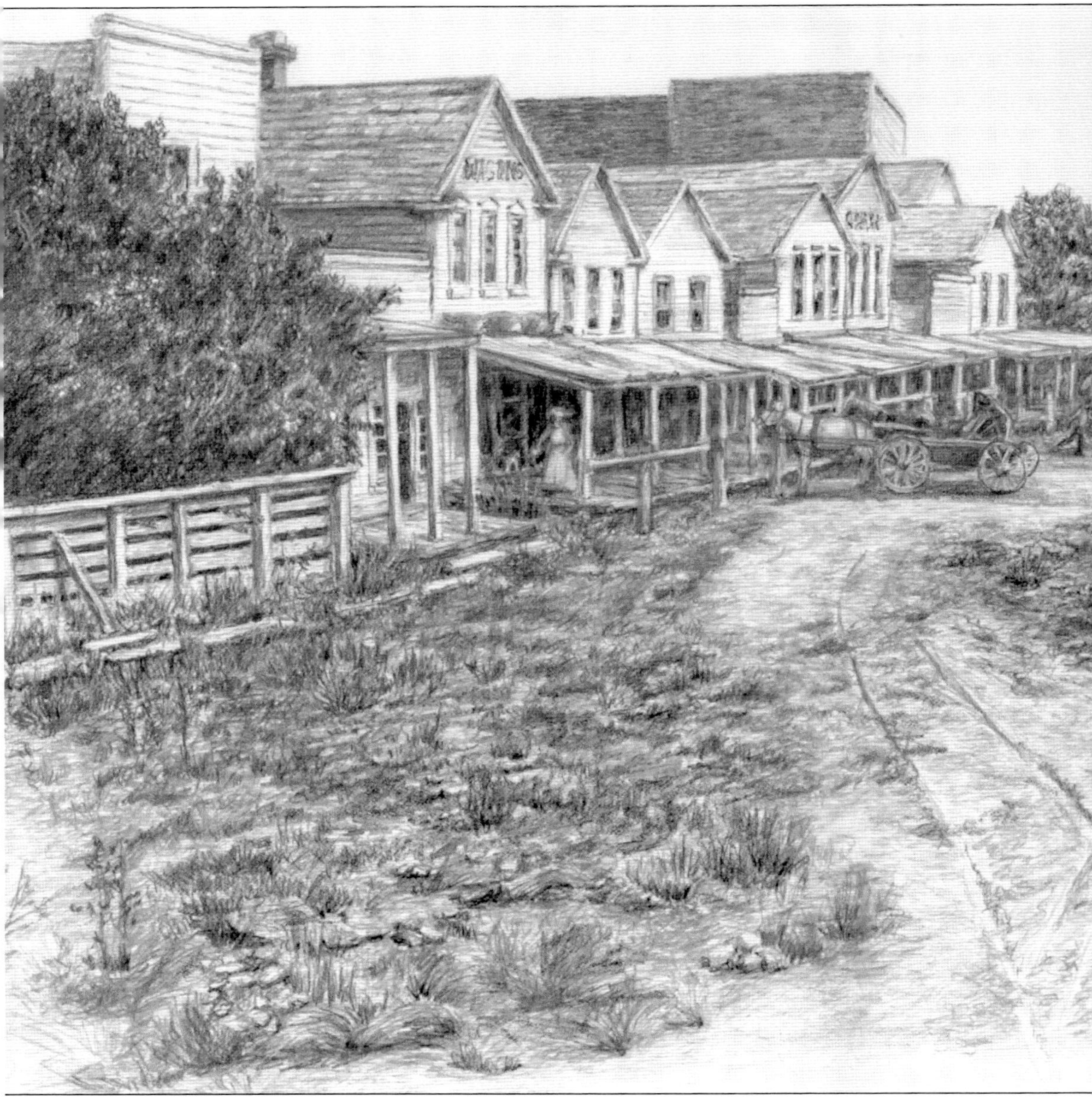

The earliest available image of Dundee, with a population about 500, is shown in an 1872 postcard. Mostly wooden buildings were connected by wooden sidewalks, awnings, and hitching posts. On the left, the Johnson Block is a substantial brick building, with its third floor barely visible above the line of wooden roofs. To the right, another brick building is only about three years old, Dr. George Washington Jackson's office and drugstore. His commercial Italianate style

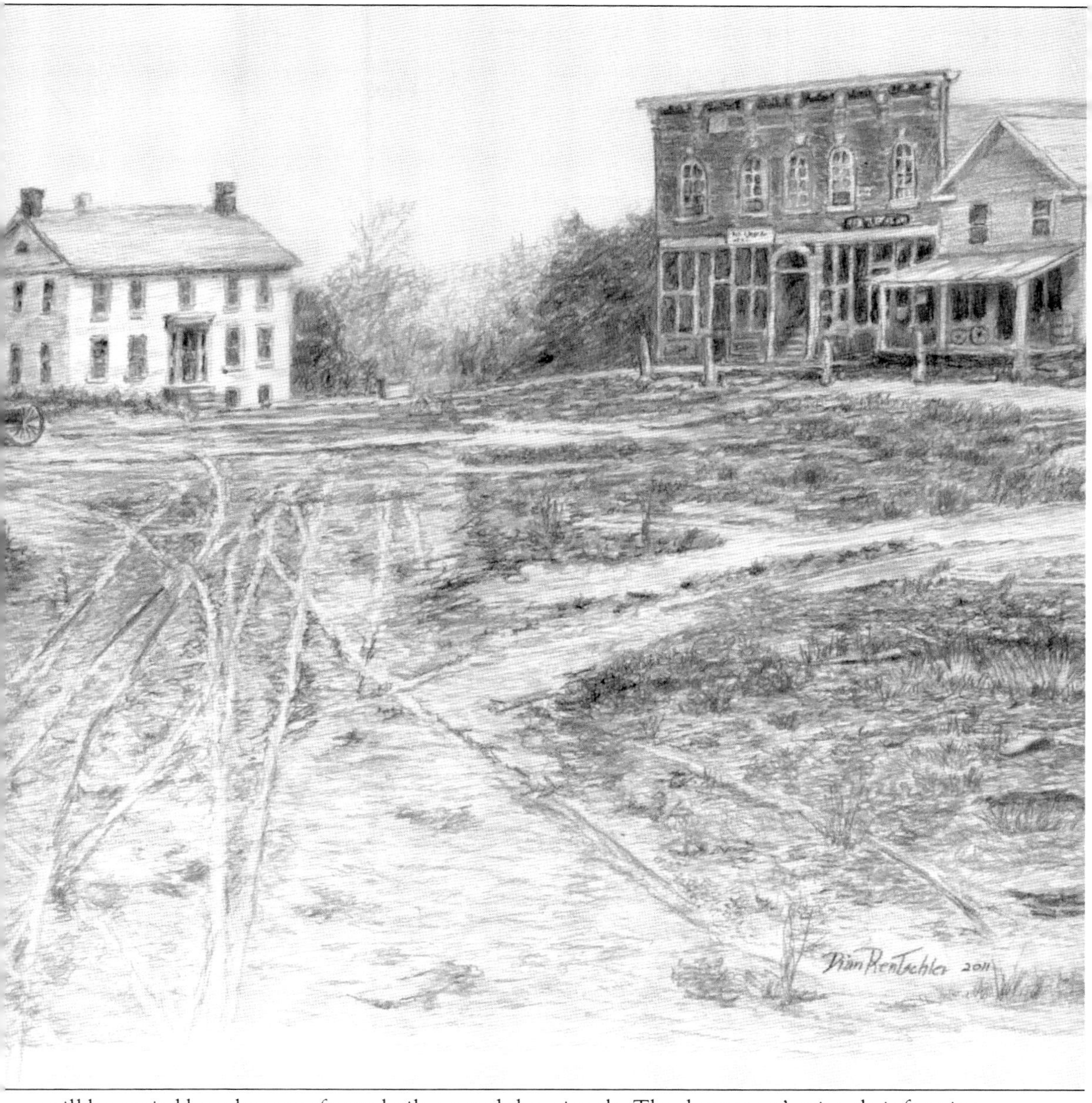

will be copied by other storefronts built around the triangle. The downtown's triangle is forming from the carriage ruts, with Tecumseh Street down the middle of the picture, Riley Street in front of Jackson's building, and Park Place closer and to the right. Fine artist Dian Rentschler of Tecumseh created this pencil drawing from the original photograph.

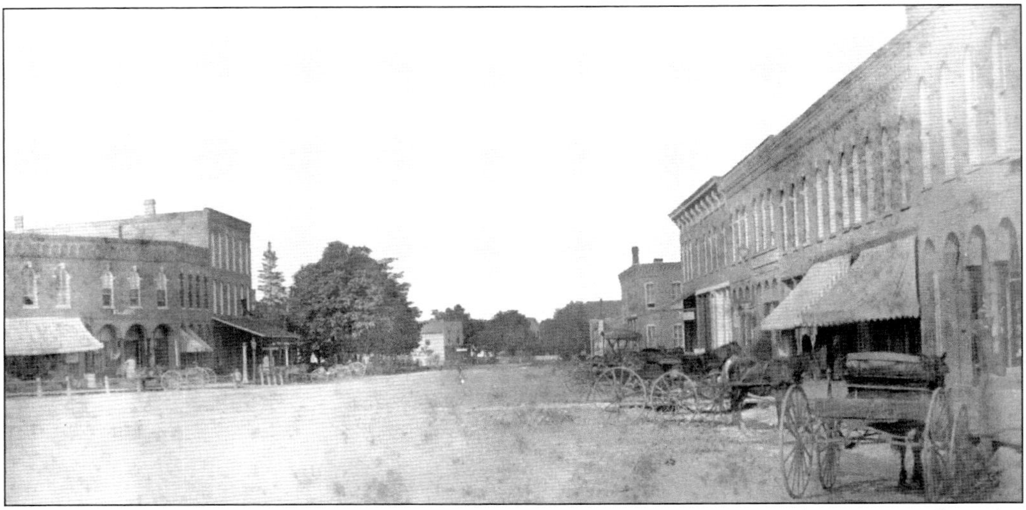

Dundee looked charming in this postcard taken before 1894. No electric poles are seen along the roadside. These businesses were lit inside with kerosene lamps and candles. The Johnson Block, a three-story building on the left, displays a barber pole with two kerosene or oil streetlights near the barbershop. A shoemaker is identified by a boot-shaped sign above the awning.

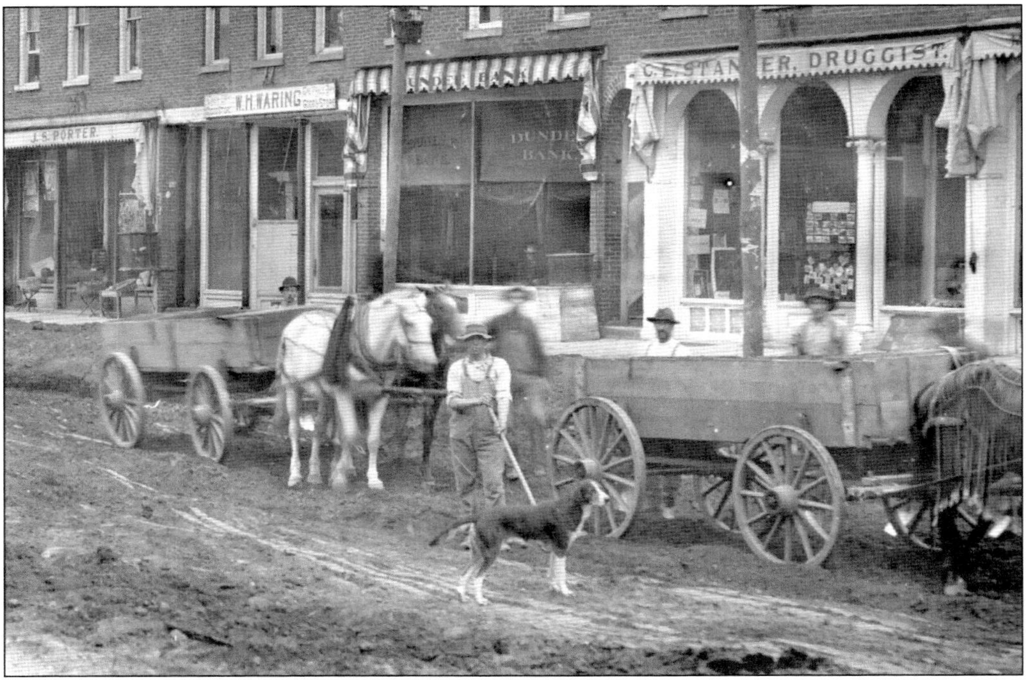

This c. 1905 photograph shows the muddy condition of Tecumseh Street before it was bricked. It must have been a struggle to go any distance in these horse-drawn vehicles in rainy weather. The wagons are parked in front of Stanger's Drugstore and its striped-awning neighbor, the bank. The Porter Store (far left) displays a circus poster and a penny-operated Zeno Gum machine dispensing sticks; produce baskets line its entrance.

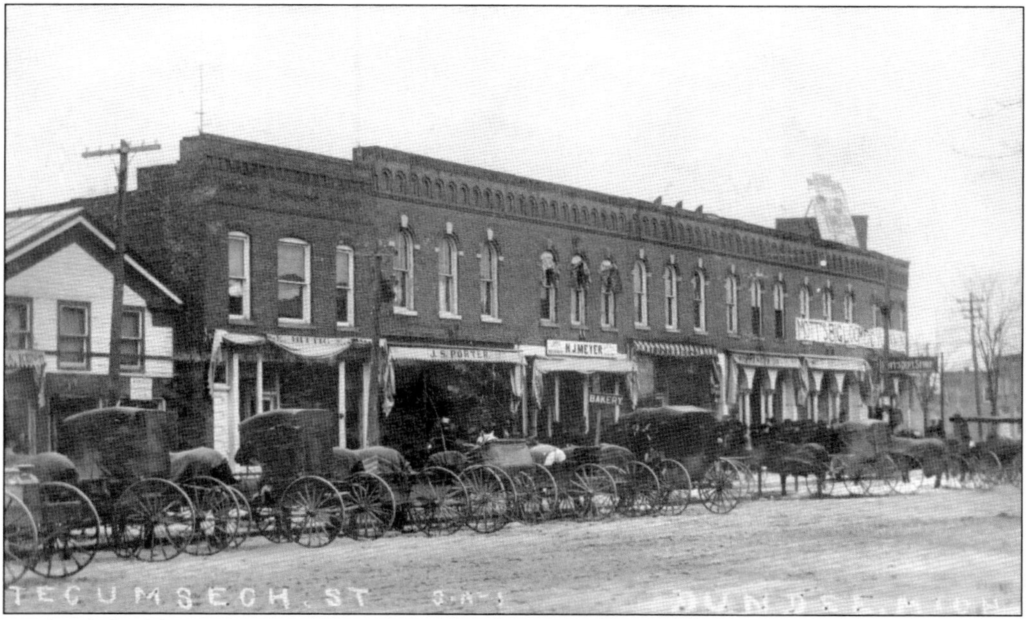

Six brick buildings on Tecumseh Street with the same roofline are shown around 1910. The brick storefronts replaced the wood-framed "old shackling concerns," which were destroyed in the disastrous 1875 Christmas Eve fire. That fire was stopped by throwing salt on the roof of the left-most brick building and dumping water from the river brought by a bucket brigade. The catastrophe prodded the village into purchasing a fire engine.

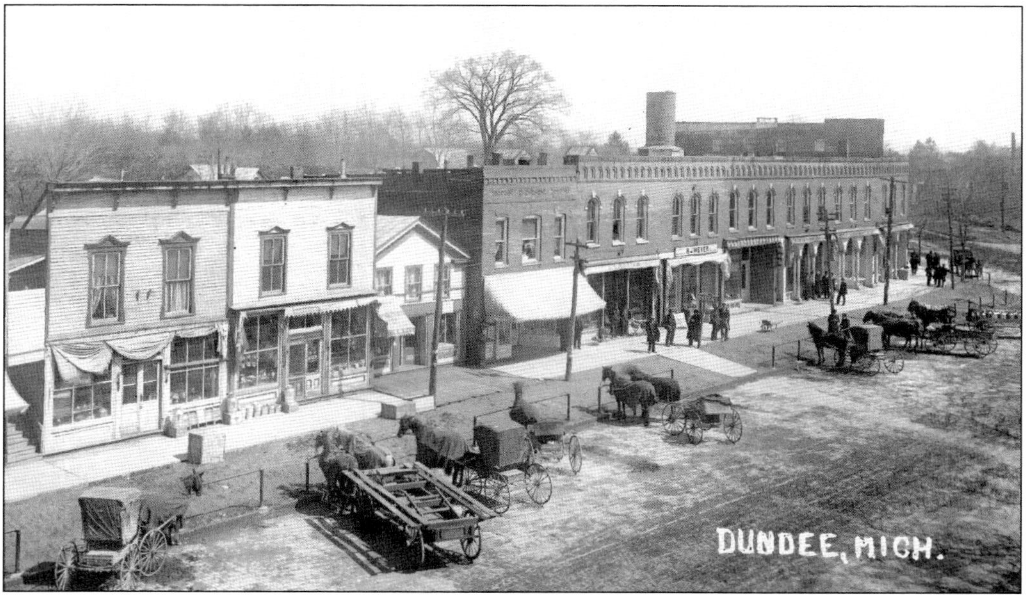

The first wooden building on the left is a dairy. The second building displays a false front covering the former Drew Bakery. The small Greek Revival building houses a millinery on the left and a bicycle shop on the right. The brick buildings are occupied by, from left to right, Hittig Shoes, Porter Grocery, Meyer Grocery, Dundee Bank, Stanger's Drugs, and Mott's Department Store. This image was taken around 1910.

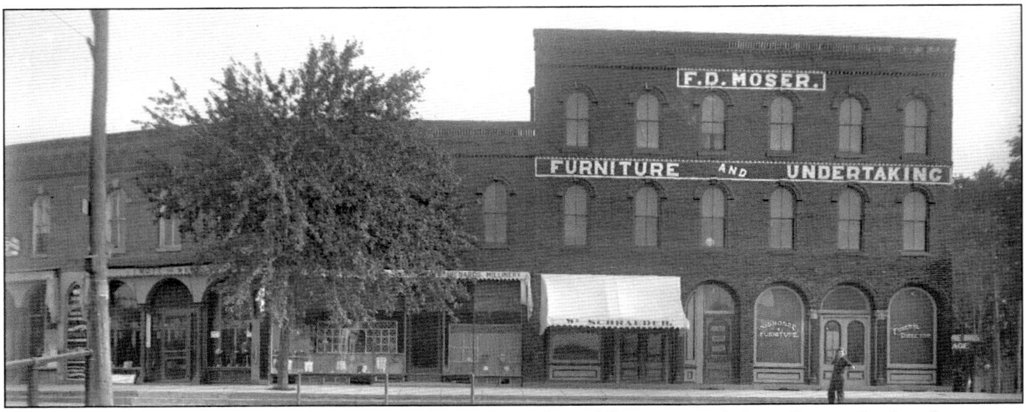

In 1910, Fred Moser purchased the three-story Hotel Pocklington on Main Street for his furniture and undertaking business. A window has been converted into a door to give outside access to the upper floors. Schraeder's Restaurant occupies the left front. Continuing left, Alty Porter and Libby Richards run the millinery store next door, followed by Mott and Waring's Department Store and McAtee's Dry Goods. (Photograph by Virgil Van DeVenter.)

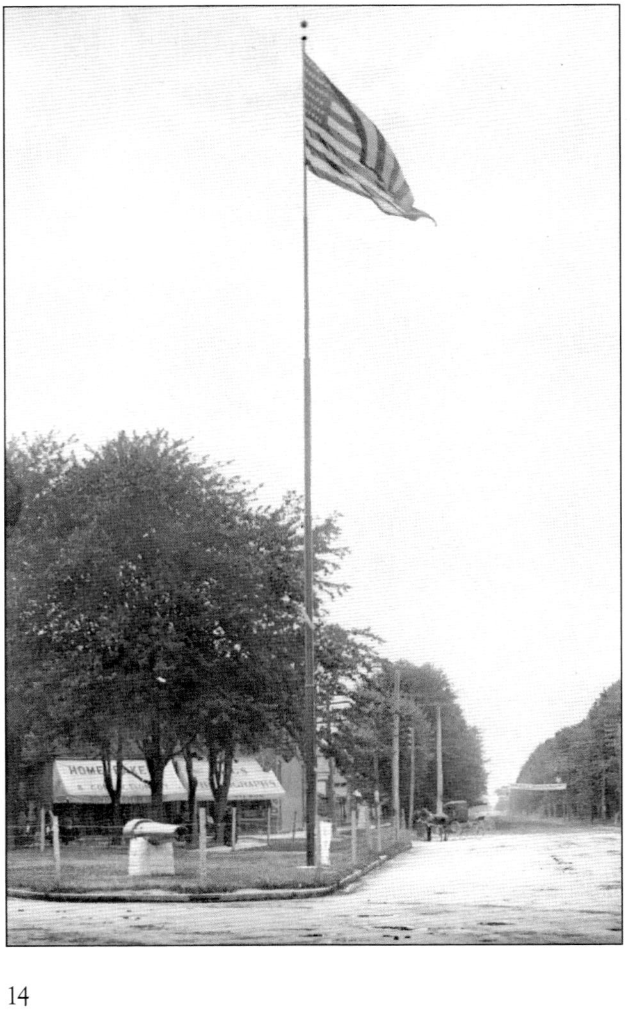

A c. 1912 postcard refers to the Dundee triangle as "Central Park." The Civil War cannon arrived in 1909 and the flagpole in 1910. The triangle is fenced in. On Park Place, awnings advertise A. Morscheuser's Home Bakery and Confectionery as well as Wilson's Drugs and Photographs. In the distance, a banner across Tecumseh Street advertises what is probably a revival meeting.

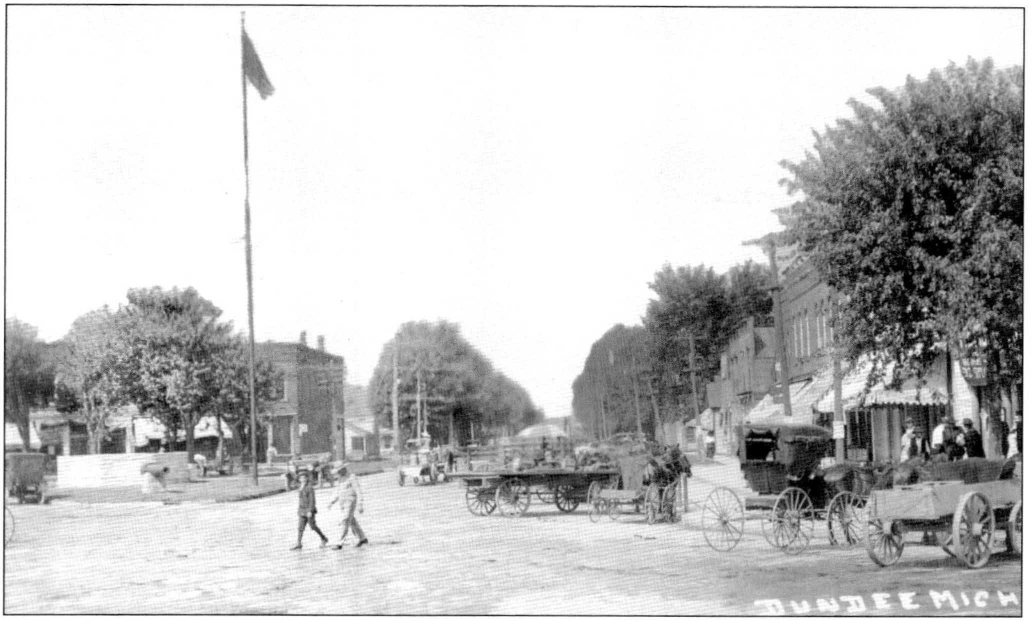

The time is 1912, and a young man in short pants is strolling across Tecumseh Street with an older gentleman, perhaps his father. In the background to the left, the bandstand is being constructed. The bandstand walls are up, but the pillars to support the roof are not yet in place. A wagon with milk cans travels westward. To its left, a roadster is parked on the triangle.

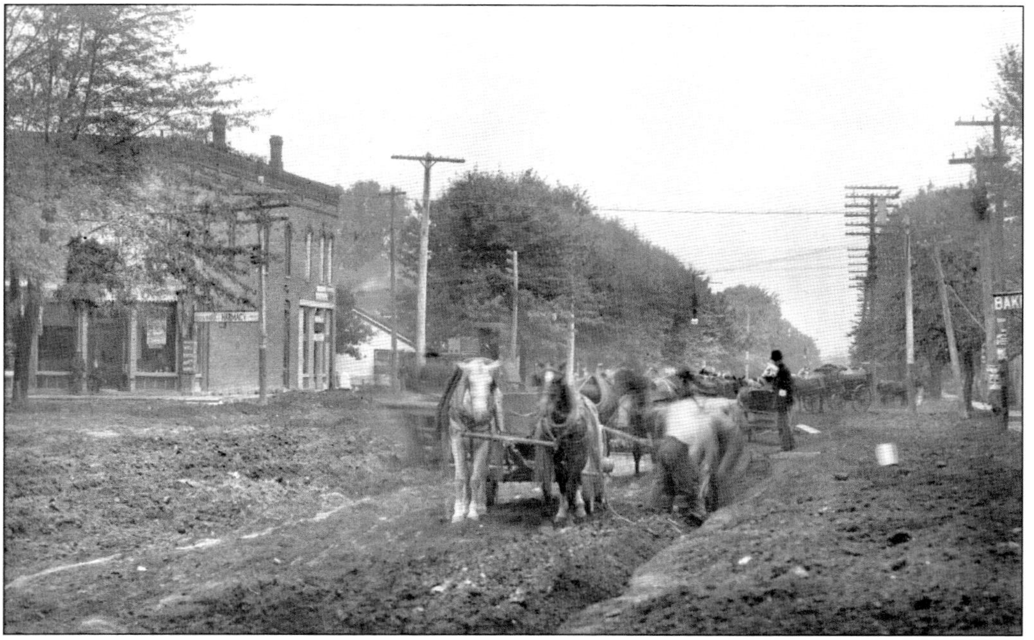

Horses and laborers are hard at work digging trenches down the side of Tecumseh Street around 1907. The trenches, dug by hand, were for curbing in preparation for paving bricks on the street. Park Place starts on the left with D.G. Wilson's drugstore visible on the corner.

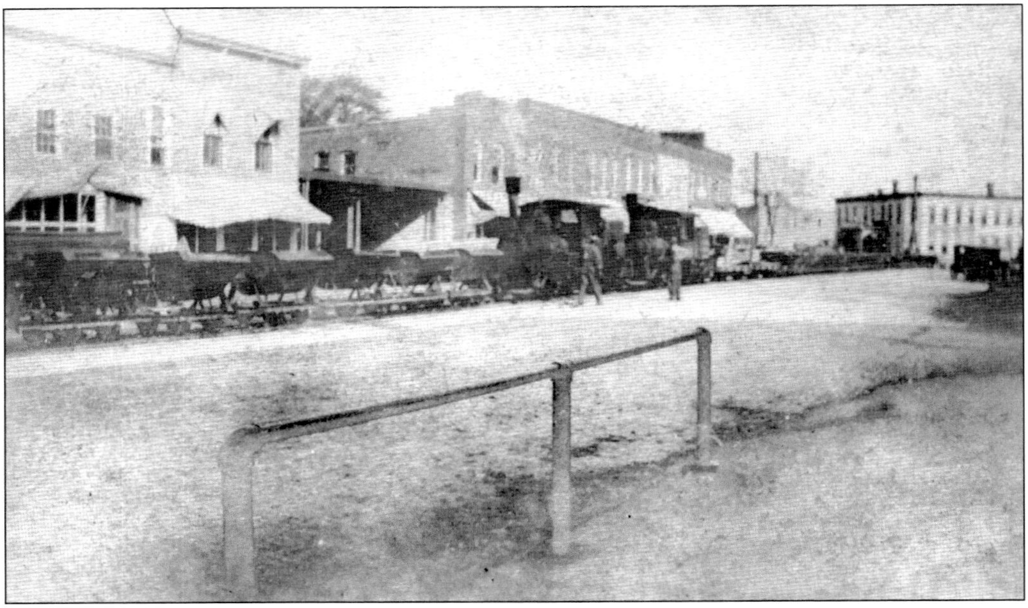

A temporary narrow-gauge railroad is running through downtown Dundee in 1921. The tramcars carried stone to be dumped as the foundation for the new road that was being paved from Monroe to western Michigan. In the background, flatcars and gondolas are seen just beyond the engine. Dundee resident Serge Williams remembered, as a youngster, hitching a ride on this train from west of Dundee into town.

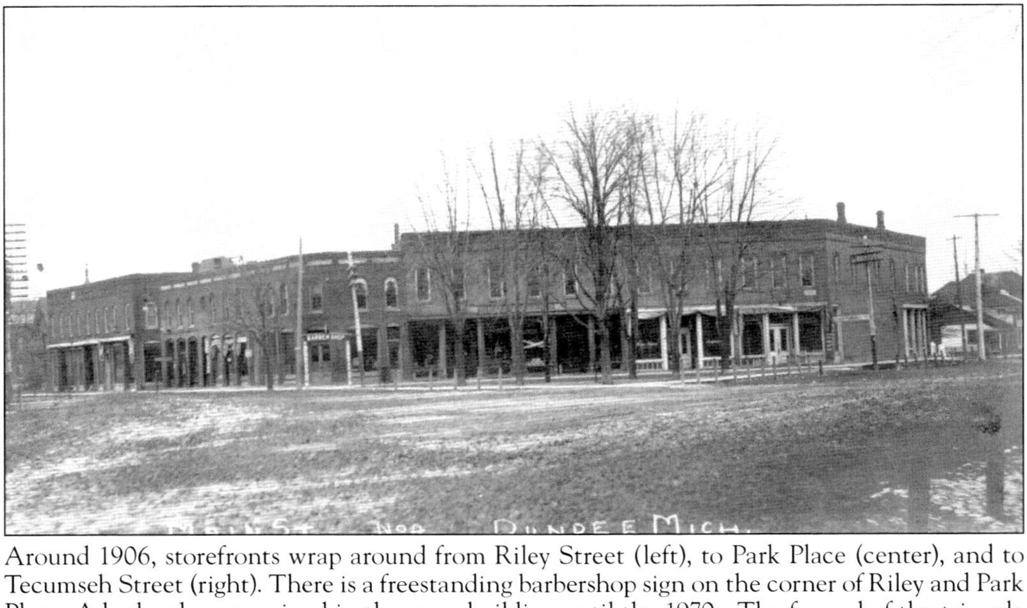

Around 1906, storefronts wrap around from Riley Street (left), to Park Place (center), and to Tecumseh Street (right). There is a freestanding barbershop sign on the corner of Riley and Park Place. A barbershop remained in the same building until the 1970s. The far end of the triangle has wooden hitching posts, sidewalks, and trees.

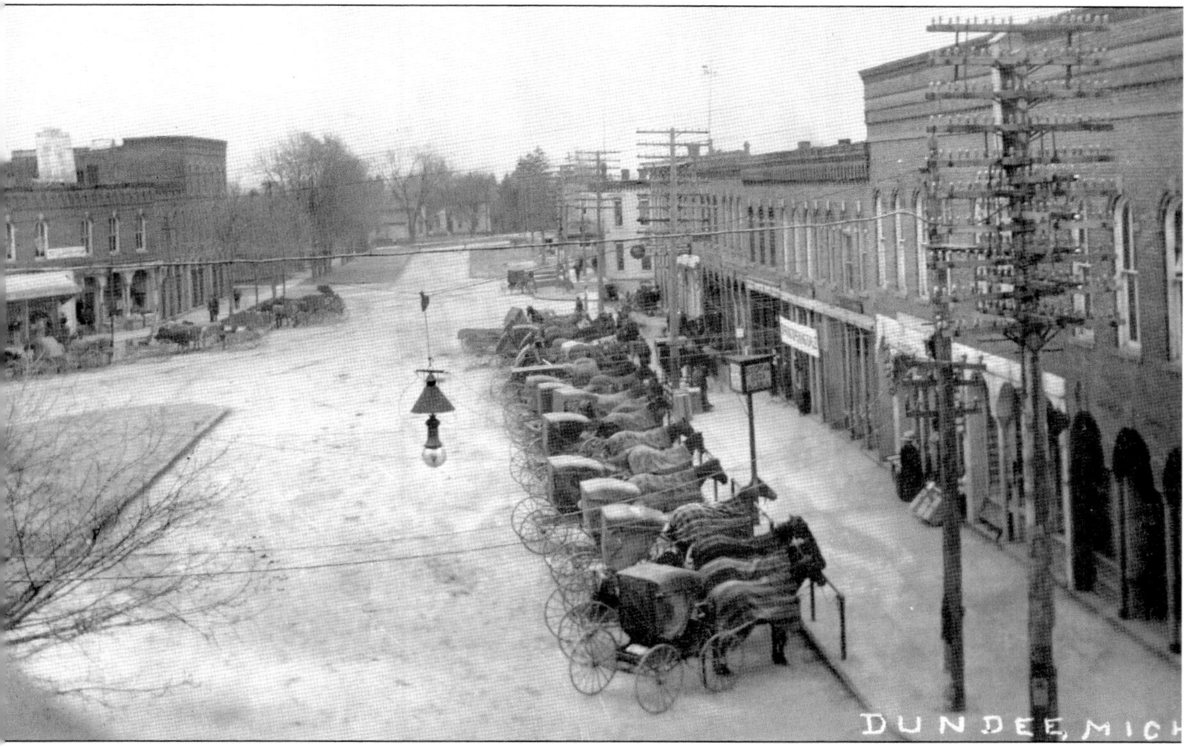

In this bird's-eye postcard, the many buggies attest to the popularity of Dundee's commercial district. It is probably just before 1909, because the Civil War cannon has not yet been placed in the triangle. The triangle is now defined by curbing. Telephone poles and electric lines are prominent features. The streetlight (center) is hanging from a pulley so it can be lowered to change the bulb. Dundee will eventually be known as the hub of the highways because (clockwise from left to right) Tecumseh, Ypsilanti, Main, Monroe, and Riley Streets come together in the center of town. Mott's Department Store (left), on Tecumseh Street, and Jacobs's Fruit and Confectionery (right), on Riley Street, display examples of early outdoor advertising. O.E. Mott has installed a billboard on his roof, and Ellis Jacobs has placed a signpost on his sidewalk.

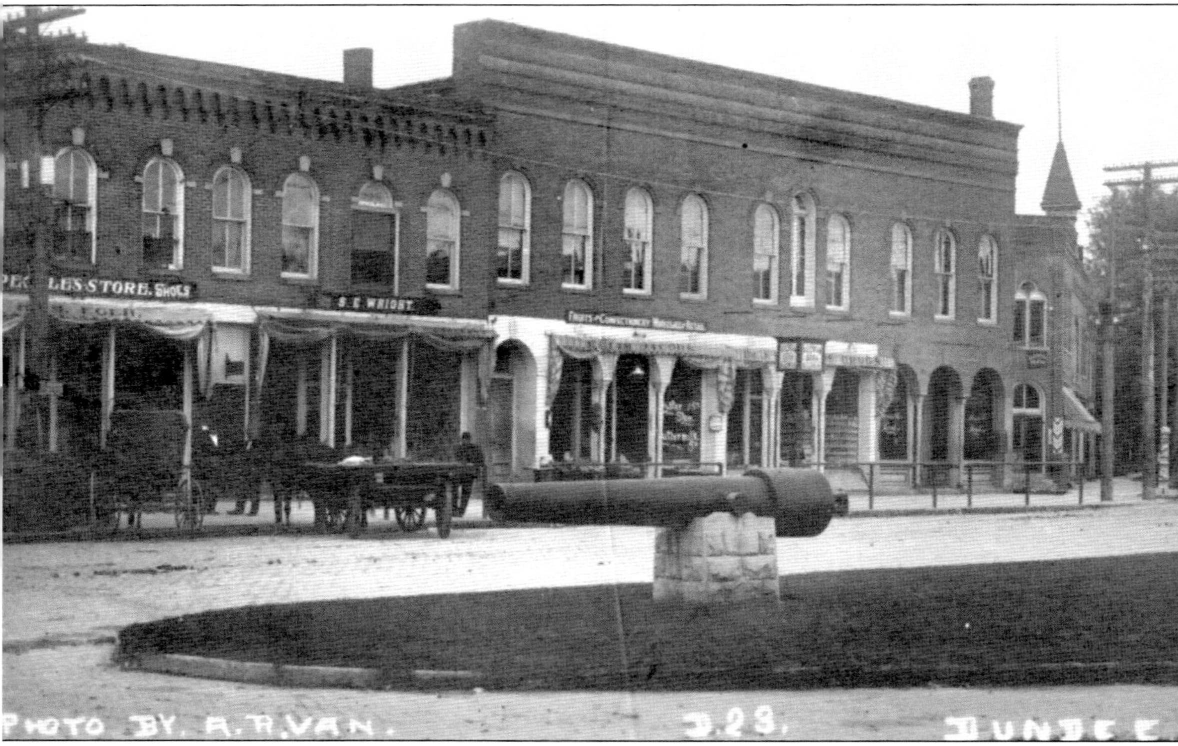

The Parrot gun, known as a Civil War cannon because of its ability to fire a 100-pound shell, dominates this c. 1910 view of businesses on Riley Street. The three-stores-wide opera house occupies the second floor of the building on the right, with an entrance from the sidewalk on the left side. A narrow window-door on the second floor could open to allow someone to stand in it and call out to people on the street, announcing the name of the upcoming performance. Below the opera house, three storefronts are seen in this view: Ellis Jacobs's confectionery (advertising oyster stew as well as bananas), Dr. John B. Haynes's drugstore and office, and the Monroe County Bank; the bell tower over the village building can be seen above the rooftops on the right. (Photograph by Virgil Van DeVenter.)

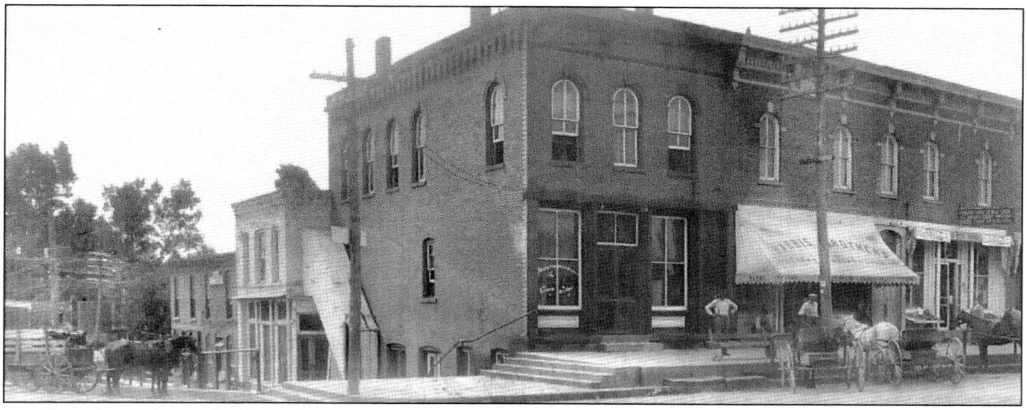

Knabusch Café, with dark frames around the door and windows, leads off the corner of Monroe and Riley Streets around 1900. The café window advertises lunch served all day, and a handy bench sits in front of it. The next stores on the block are Harris Brothers Farm Real Estate and the Dundee Candy Kitchen. Around the corner, on the left, another restaurant occupies the two-story white building on Monroe Street. Cyrus Petitt's harness shop is beyond it.

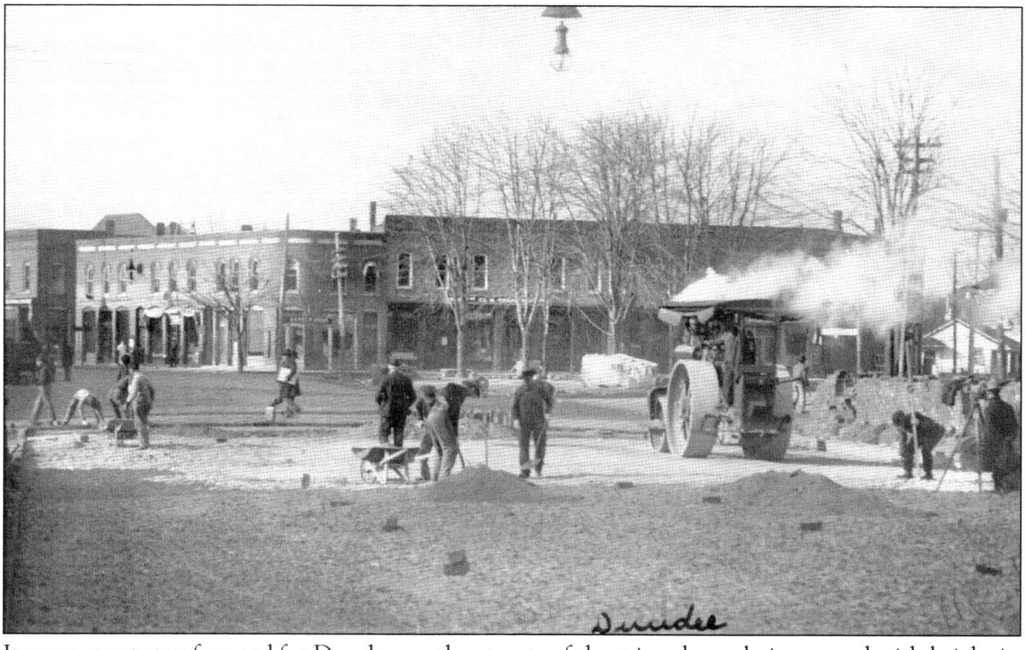

It was a great step forward for Dundee, as the streets of the triangle are being paved with bricks in the early spring of 1908. Park Place and the north side of Riley Street are seen in the background. A steamroller compacts the dirt, and a pile of bricks is stacked to the right. The bricklayers are on the left, and other workers in the center are spreading sand to level the new street.

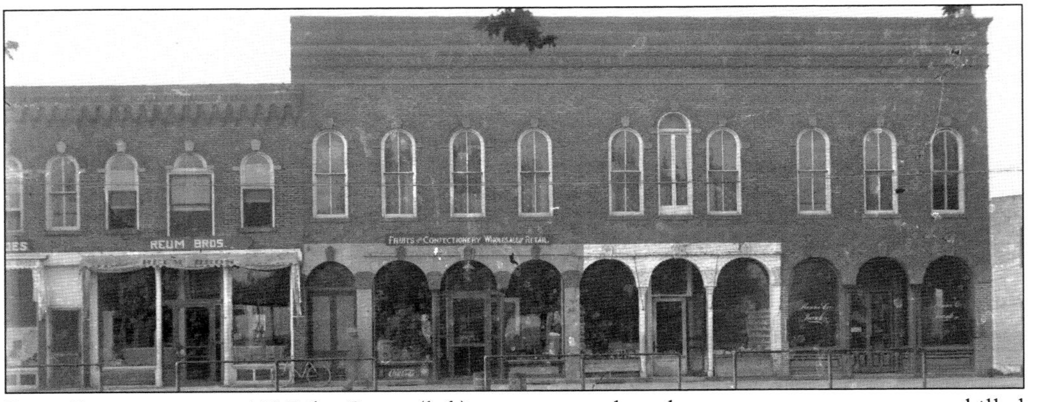

Reum Bros. grocery, at 135 Riley Street (left), was not a cash and carry store; customers were billed weekly. Around 1915, the brothers advertised, "Eat Well, Feel Well, Do Well." They also assured their clientele, "*Hier wird deutsch gesprochen*," meaning German is spoken here, which indicates the strong German influence at this time. To the right are the confectionery, an unidentified store, and the Monroe County Bank. (Photograph by Virgil Van DeVenter.)

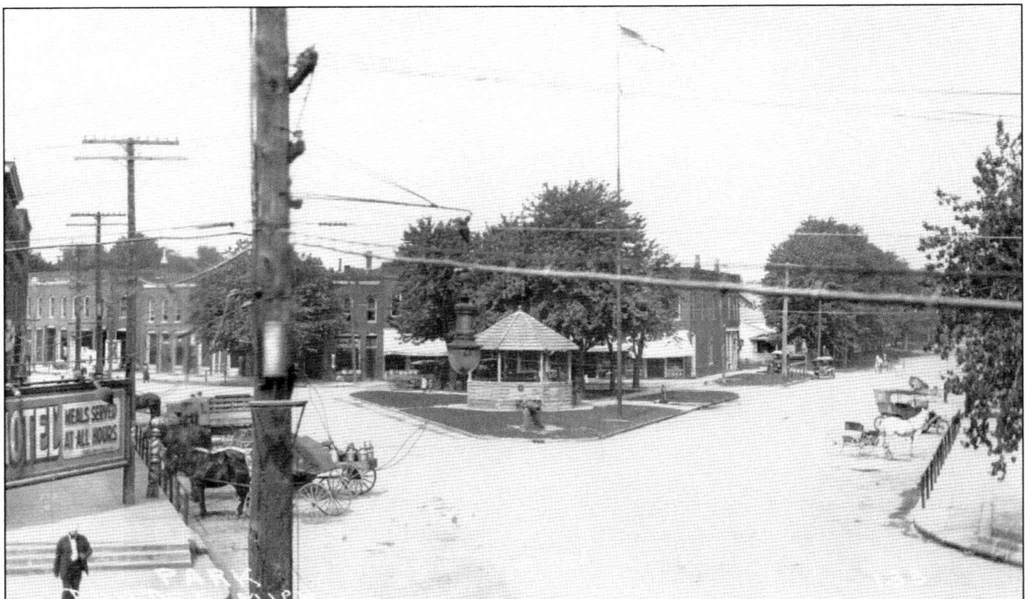

Seen in 1917, the triangle contains its monuments to veterans and a well pump for thirsty citizens. A tall flagpole stands next to the gazebo, and cars, buggies, and wagons are parked on the street. In the rear (left) on Riley Street, three large posters advertise the latest silent film at the Electric Theater. The National Hotel's sign (left) advertises, "Meals served at all hours."

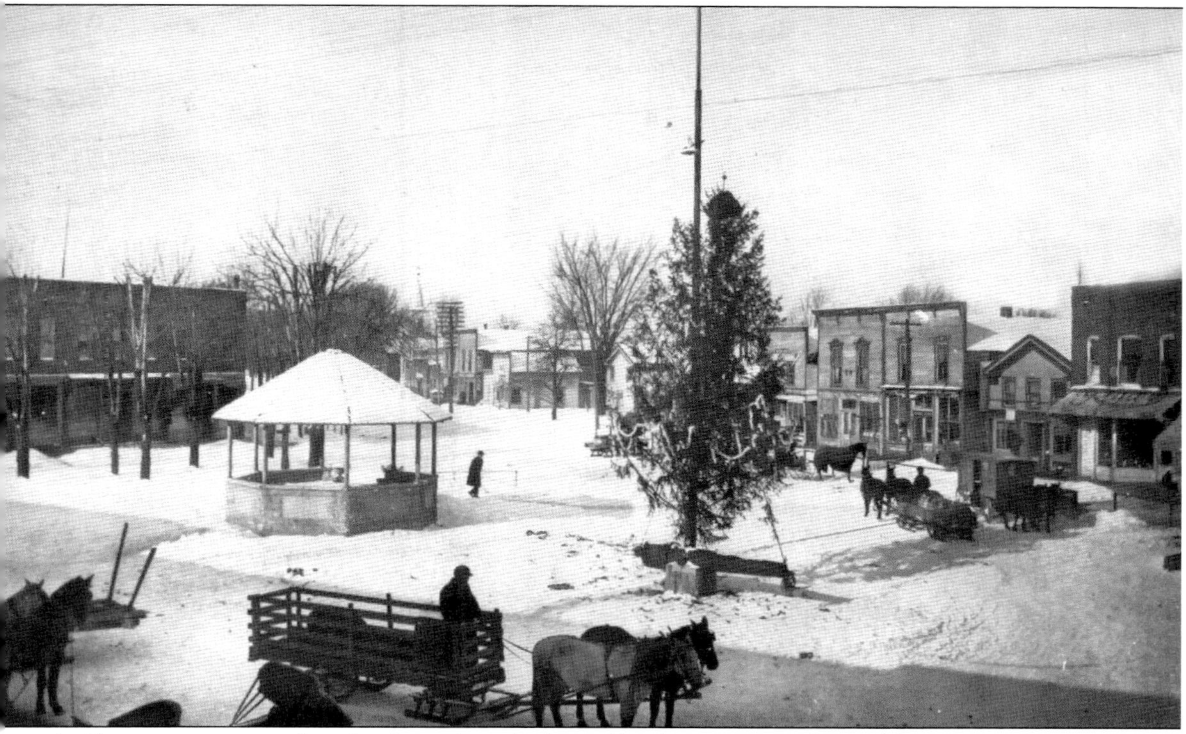

A Christmas tree is tied to the flagpole and admired by shoppers. People would exchange their wheels for snow runners on their wagons for winter weather. A sign behind the bandstand reads, "Ford Cars." At that time, a car dealership could operate from a tiny storefront. An enclosed wagon on wheels, a delivery wagon for Keith Jenne's grocery, is being pulled toward the camera by a team of horses. Beside it, a large awning advertises A.M. Ritter's shoes. It is easy to see the false fronts on some of the stores. All the wooden buildings were gone by the 1980s, having been moved or destroyed by fire. This photograph, from the Earl Stowell estate, was donated one week before the final selection of photographs for the Old Mill Museum's timeline.

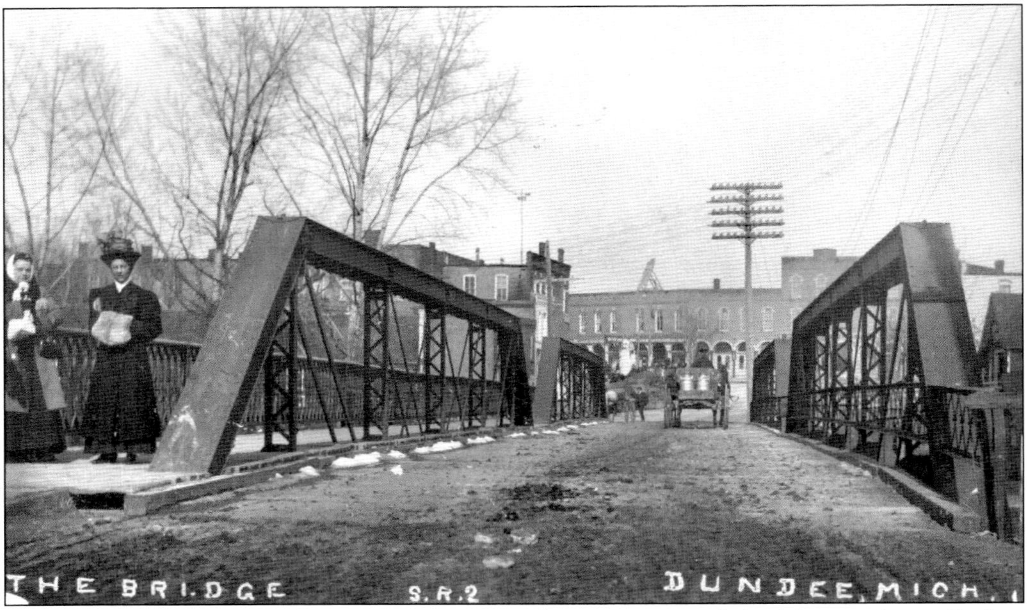

On the left-hand side of the image, two women have just crossed the Monroe Street Bridge, probably after a shopping trip downtown. The one on the left, carrying a grocery bag, appears to be employed by the lady on the right with the muff. A wagon heads across the bridge toward downtown restaurants or grocers with large milk cans. The bridge carried Monroe Street across the River Raisin from 1898 to 1937.

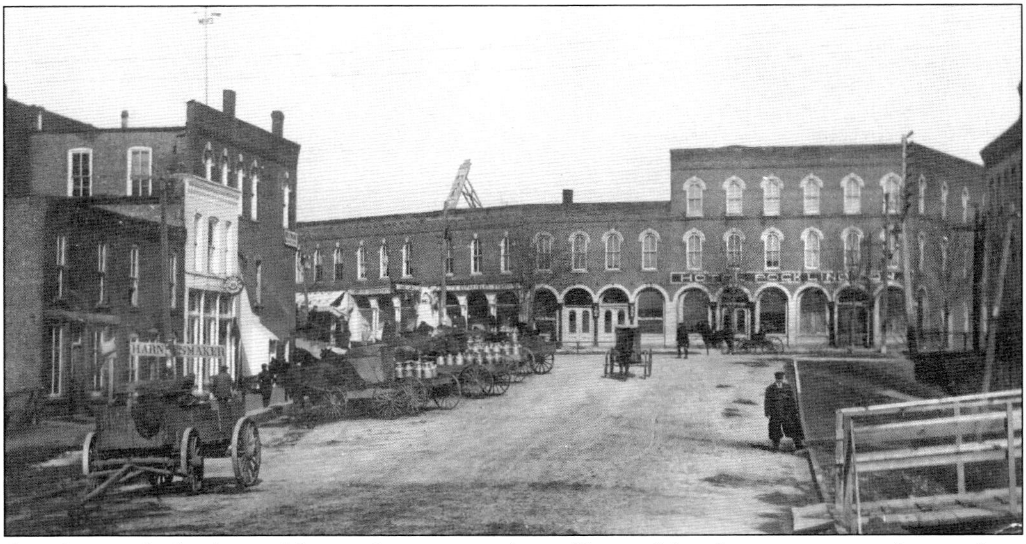

Standing at the bridge and facing downtown, a line of beautiful arches is seen over the windows in the Hotel Pocklington and other buildings on Tecumseh Street around 1910. Petitt's harness shop (far left) displays a large sign over the sidewalk, followed by several restaurants. All the carriages and wagons are horse drawn. Perhaps the drivers parked their wagons while going inside for a bite to eat.

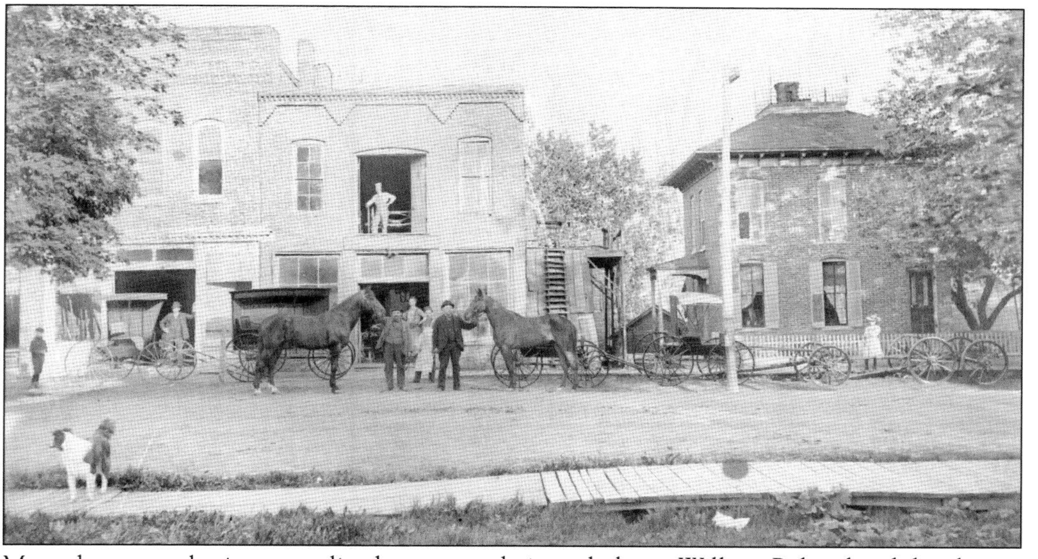

Many downtown businessmen lived very near their workplaces; William Pulver lived the closest. His 181 Riley Street home, pictured in 1901, was next door to William H. Pulver and Son, which manufactured carriages, wagons, and sleighs. Products of Pulver's factory are displayed on the street. The house is brick Italianate with a widow's walk. Both the house and factory were converted into apartments and still stand today.

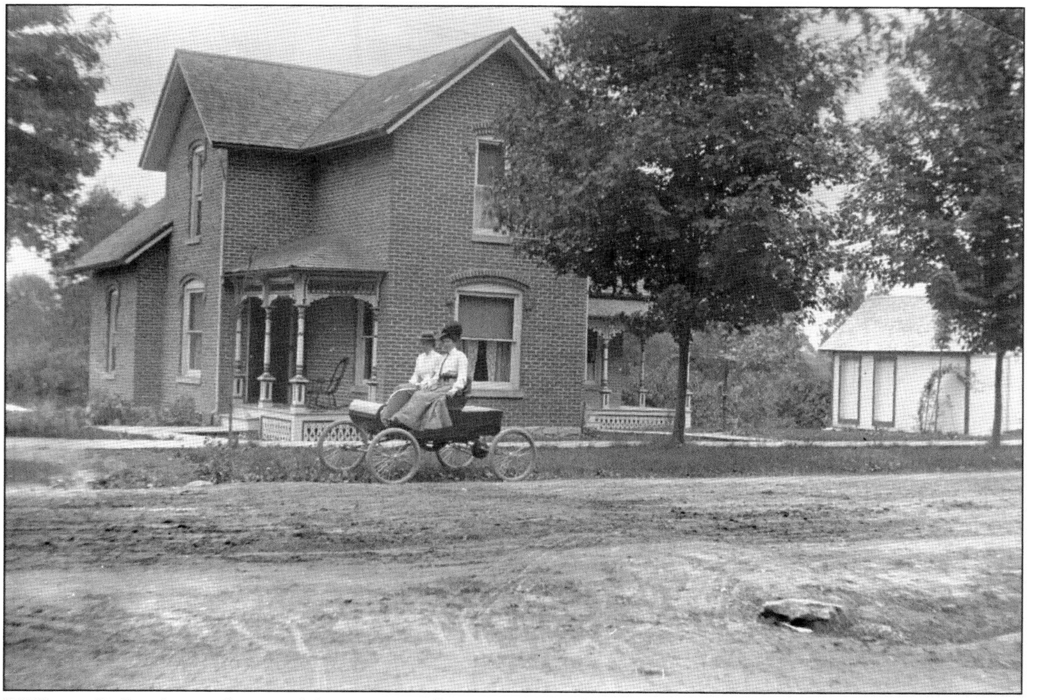

William Pulver's nearby neighbor was William Hittig, whose home was located at 215 Riley Street. Hittig owned a shoe store on Tecumseh Street. His brick home is listed in the 1876 *Beers Atlas* and still survives. It is a type of the Provincial style with Victorian assets. In this photograph, Grace Hittig is seated in their brand-new 1901 R.E. Olds.

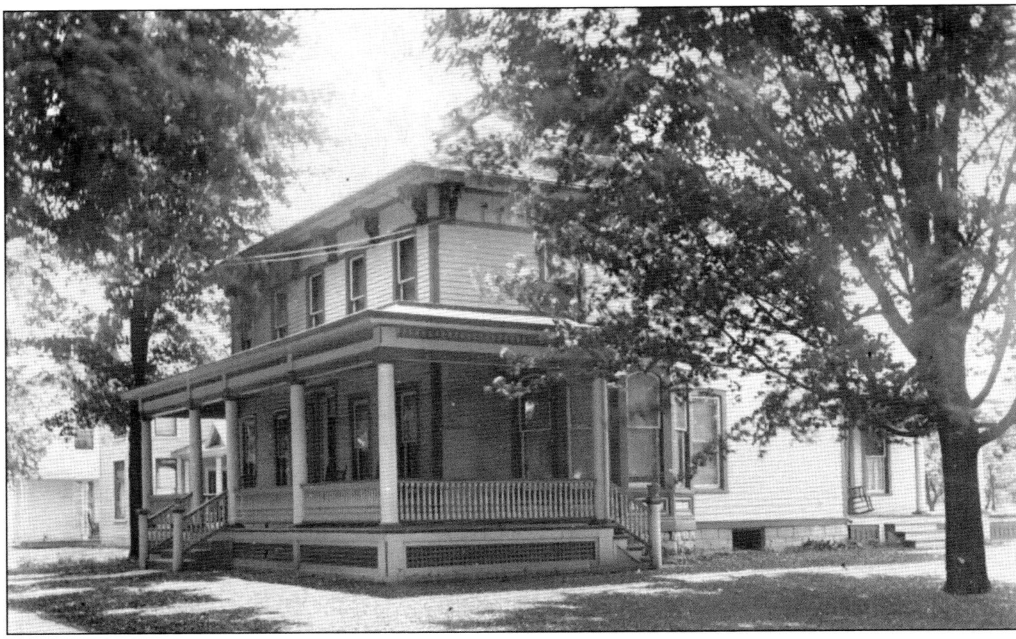

The David Wilson home, located at 240 Riley Street, has been electrified—the sign of a successful merchant. Note the wooden Italianate features and the expansive porch. Wilson had a drugstore on Park Place. Later, his son Seeley, who was born in the home, became a partner with Cliff Meyer in Wilson and Meyer Hardware on Riley Street. The Wilson home remains today.

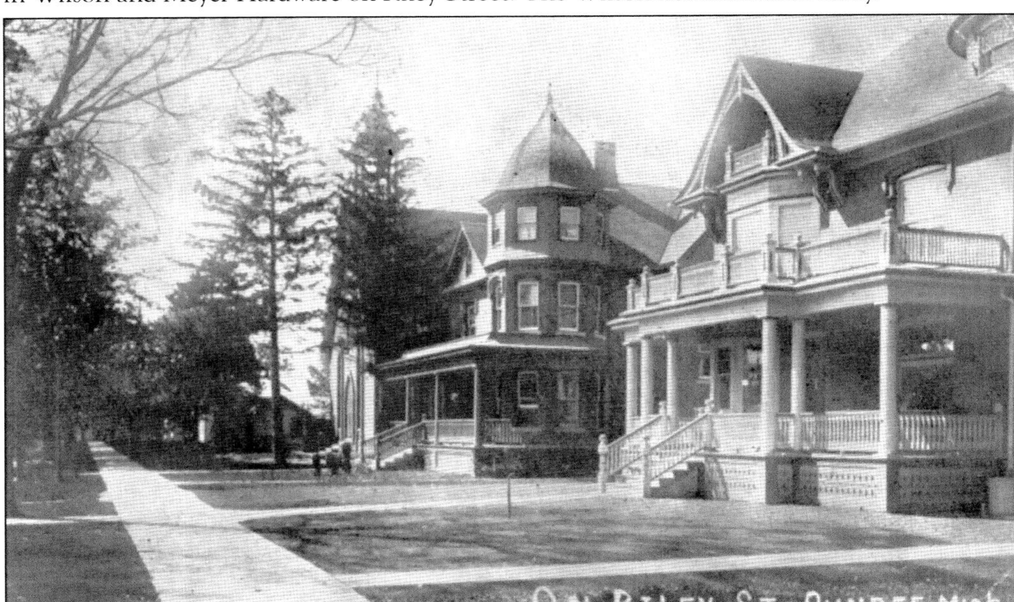

Riley Street was lined with many lovely late Victorian homes. It was a very pleasant streetscape, and all the buildings in this photograph still exist. The home in the foreground is at 292 Riley Street. In 1905, George Knowles built this brick Queen Anne–style home for Dr. John B. Haynes, who had an office on the triangle. Knowles also built the neighboring Queen Anne. Beyond them is the Methodist church.

Two

SAMPLING EARLY BUSINESSES

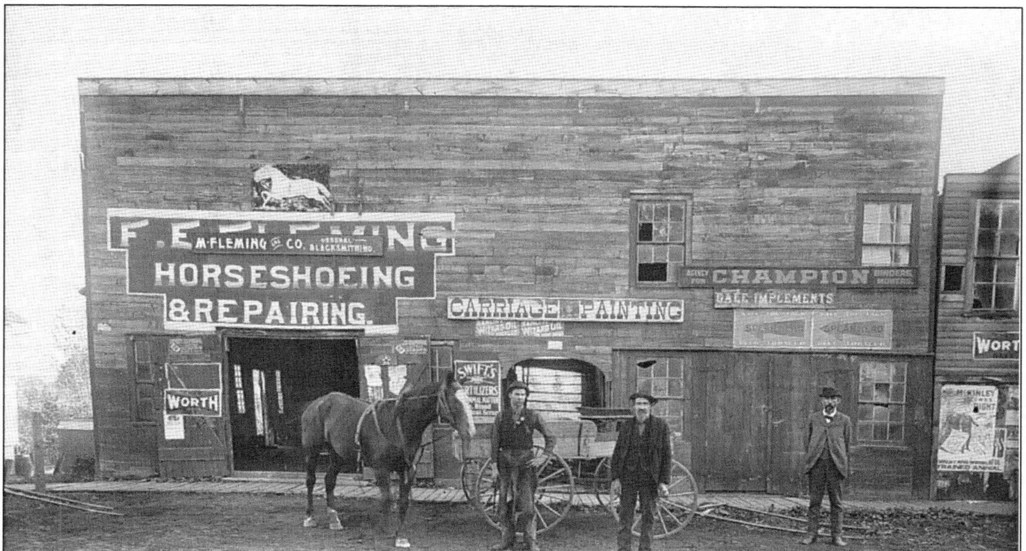

Fred Fleming (left) stands in front of his Fleming Horseshoeing and Repairing, located at 180 Main Street, which he may have just sold to M. Fleming at the time of this picture. Besides blacksmithing, horseshoeing, and carriage painting, the shop displays many advertising signs, including Chew Worth Navy, Swift's Fertilizers, Wizard Oil, Gale Implements, Champion Binders and Mowers, and a 1900 campaign poster stating, "McKinley Was Right."

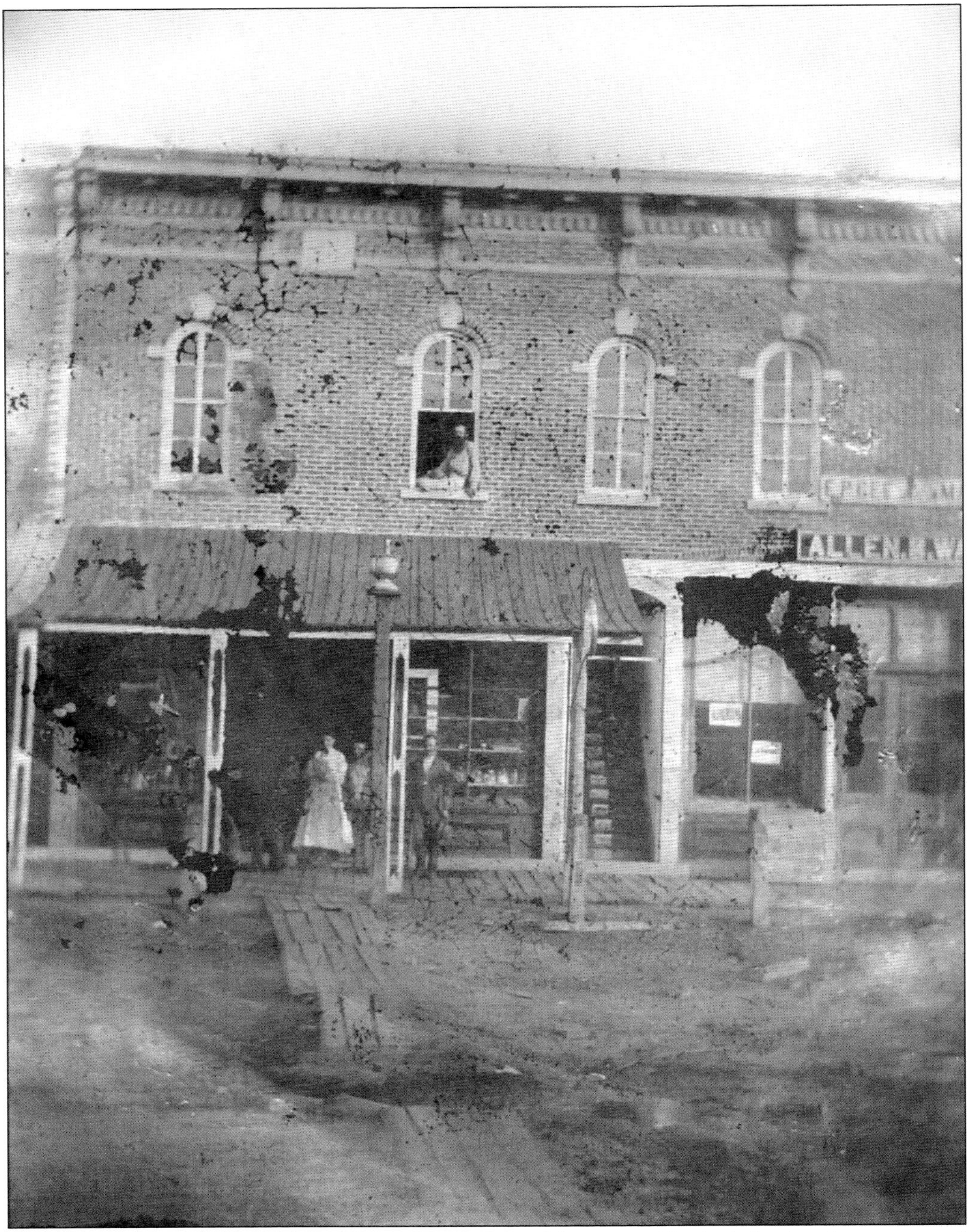

Dr. George W. Jackson's brick building is two store-widths across. To the left is his drugstore, and his office is probably above it. Maybe Dr. Jackson is the bearded gentleman seated in the window. To the lower right is an unidentified business, and the Masonic Lodge is on the second floor. The building is at 107–115 Riley Street. The Masonic date stone with Masonic symbols, near the top of the building, is 5869, the equivalent of 1869. A pole with mortar and pestle advertises the pharmacy. At the time of this tintype image, Dundee contained 500 citizens, plank sidewalks, and muddy streets, and horses could be tied to the wooden hitching posts.

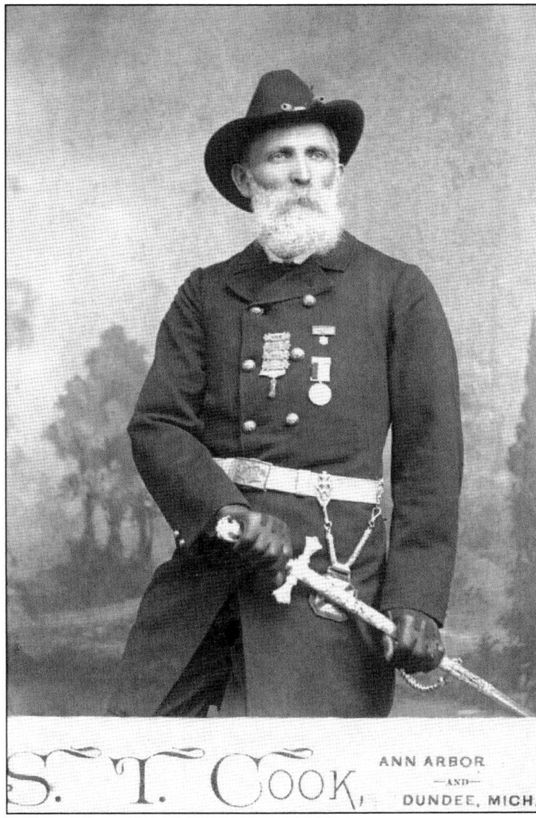

Dr. Jackson is shown wearing his Grand Army of the Republic uniform and medals, a reminder of his service in the Union army during the Civil War. He enlisted as a private and mustered out as a surgeon. He grew up on a farm near Dundee and earned his medical degree from the University of Michigan in 1867.

Dr. George W. Jackson advertised in *Hostetter's Illustrated United States Almanac of 1896*. Local editions were sold to advertisers, who in turn sold them to their customers. Medical knowledge was crude in those days, so drugstores sold liquor "for medicinal purposes." Dr. Jackson also offered "stomach bitters," along with books, stationery, and even wallpaper.

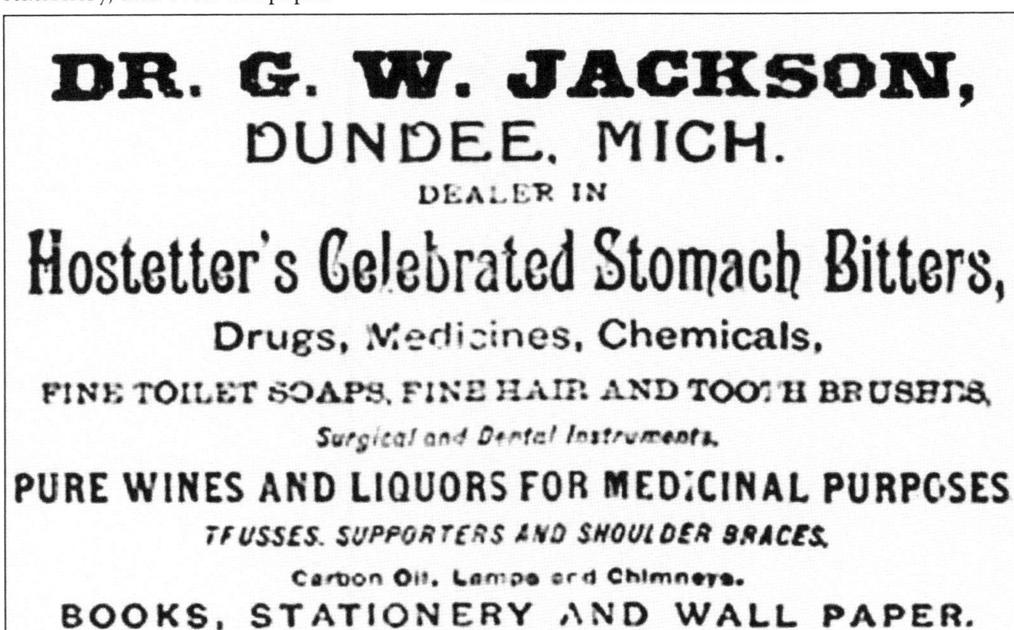

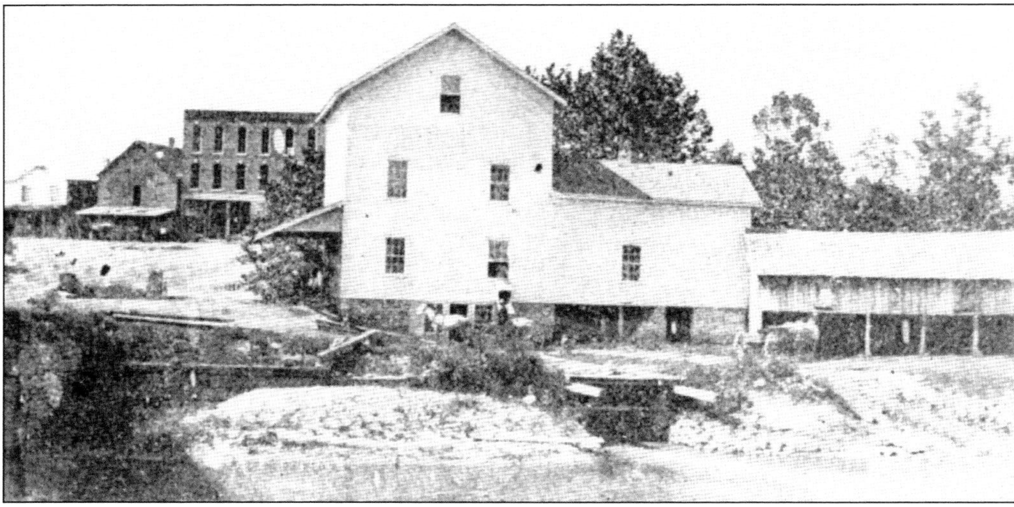

A wood sawmill or paper mill is seen on the north side of the River Raisin in the early 1870s. Behind it, the Johnson Block is visible at 110 Main Street. To the left of the brick Johnson Block, note the wood storefront, which was the source of the Christmas Eve fire in 1875.

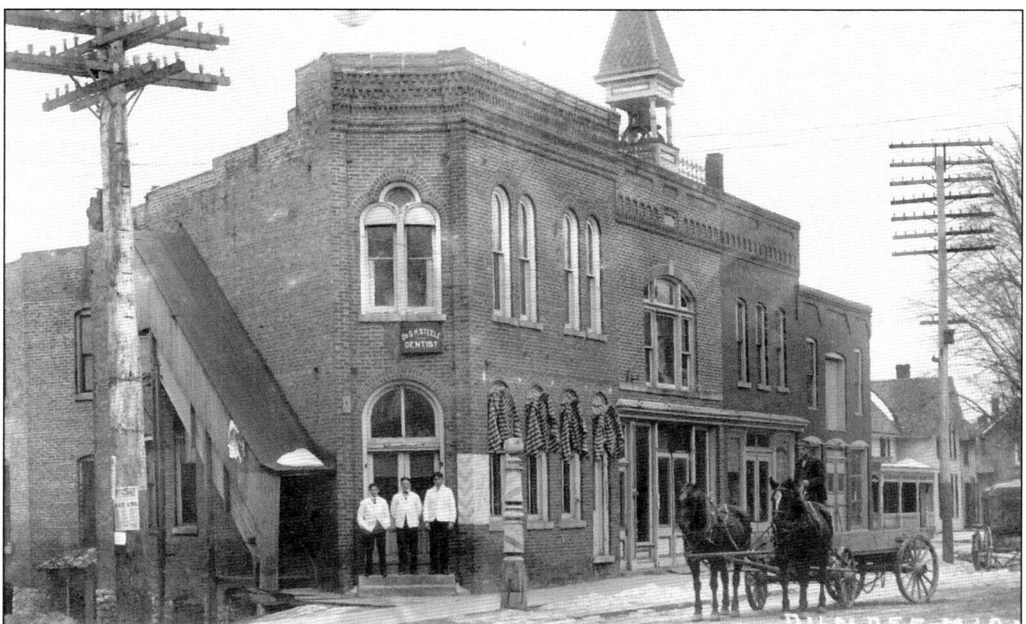

The building in the foreground was located on the south side of Riley Street and the alley. At the time of this picture, the building housed a barbershop, with the barbers posing, and a dentist on the second floor. Previously, it was a restaurant. Later, Basp Shoe Repair shop was located here. The eastern part of this commercial block was torn down in the 1960s.

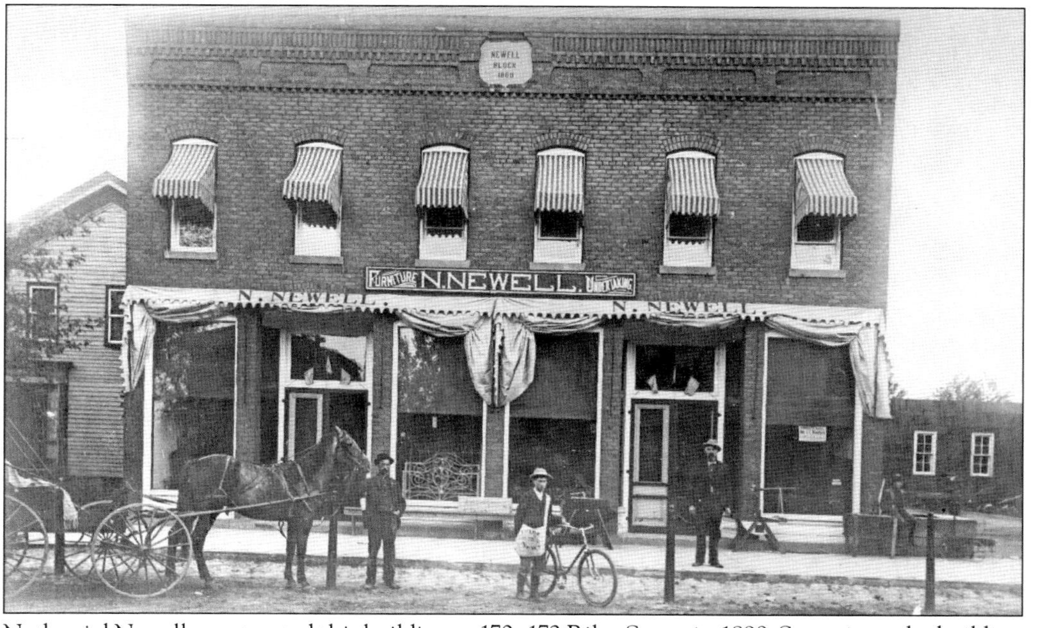

Nathanial Newell constructed this building at 170–172 Riley Street in 1899. Sometimes the building housed two businesses, sometimes only one. Newell specialized in furniture and undertaking, a combination that was popular until the 1940s. A paperboy stands in front with his *Toledo News* bag. The building later was home to a car dealership and still stands.

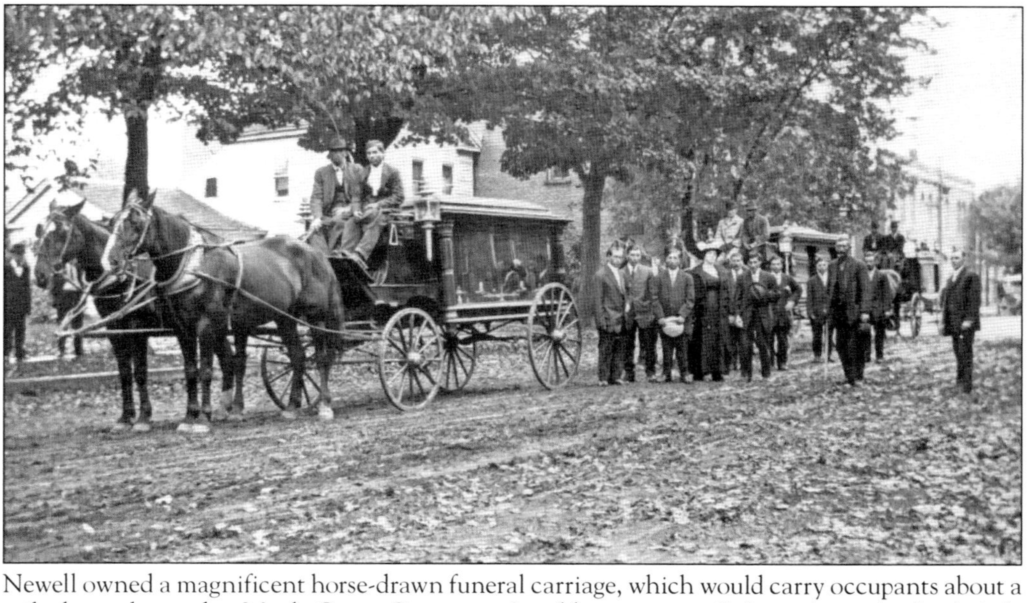

Newell owned a magnificent horse-drawn funeral carriage, which would carry occupants about a mile down the road to Maple Grove Cemetery. An older cemetery, Oakwood, involved a slightly longer trip to Summerfield Road at Lloyd Road. This funeral may have involved more than one deceased person, as there are three funeral carriages.

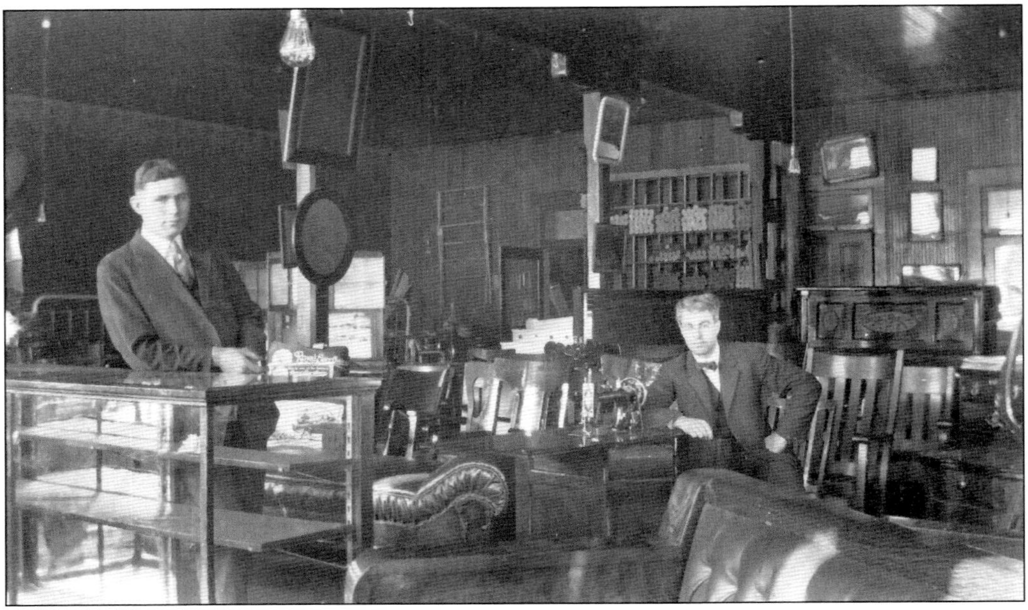

Hemenway Furniture Store was in the Newell Block on Riley Street. Fred Hemenway was the son-in-law of Nathaniel Newell and worked with him for a time. Hemenway opened this store in 1913. A featured item was the Royal Easy Chair. Everything to furnish the home could be found here, including wallpaper rolls on the back wall.

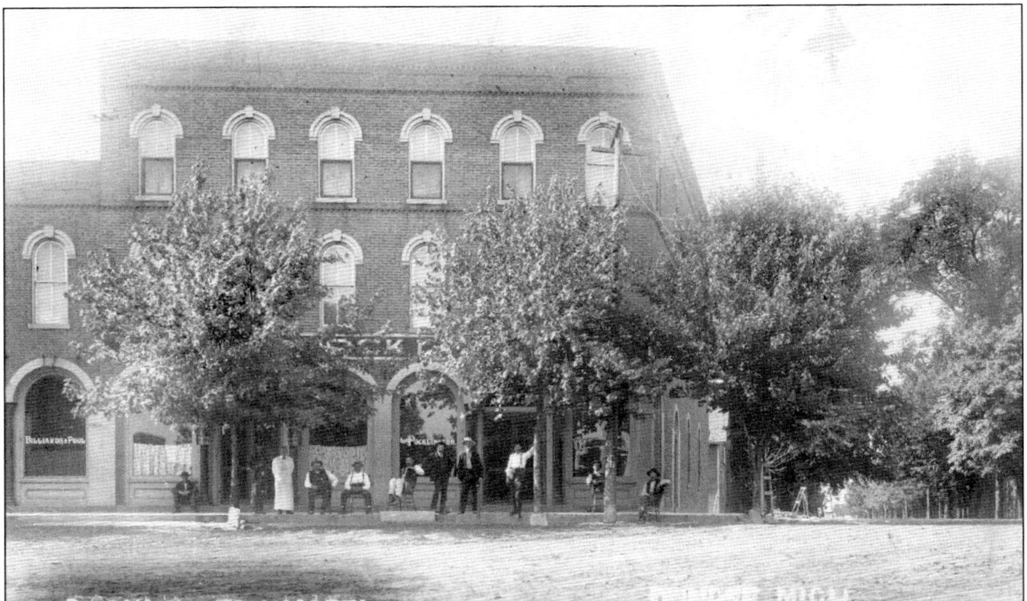

The old Johnson Block became the Hotel Pocklington around the turn of the century. This photograph must have been taken just before the streets were paved in 1908. Hotels were used by traveling salesmen and by people traveling by train. In an adjunct to the hotel, there is a sign on the window advertising billiards and pool. Men are enjoying the shade of the trees on a sunny day.

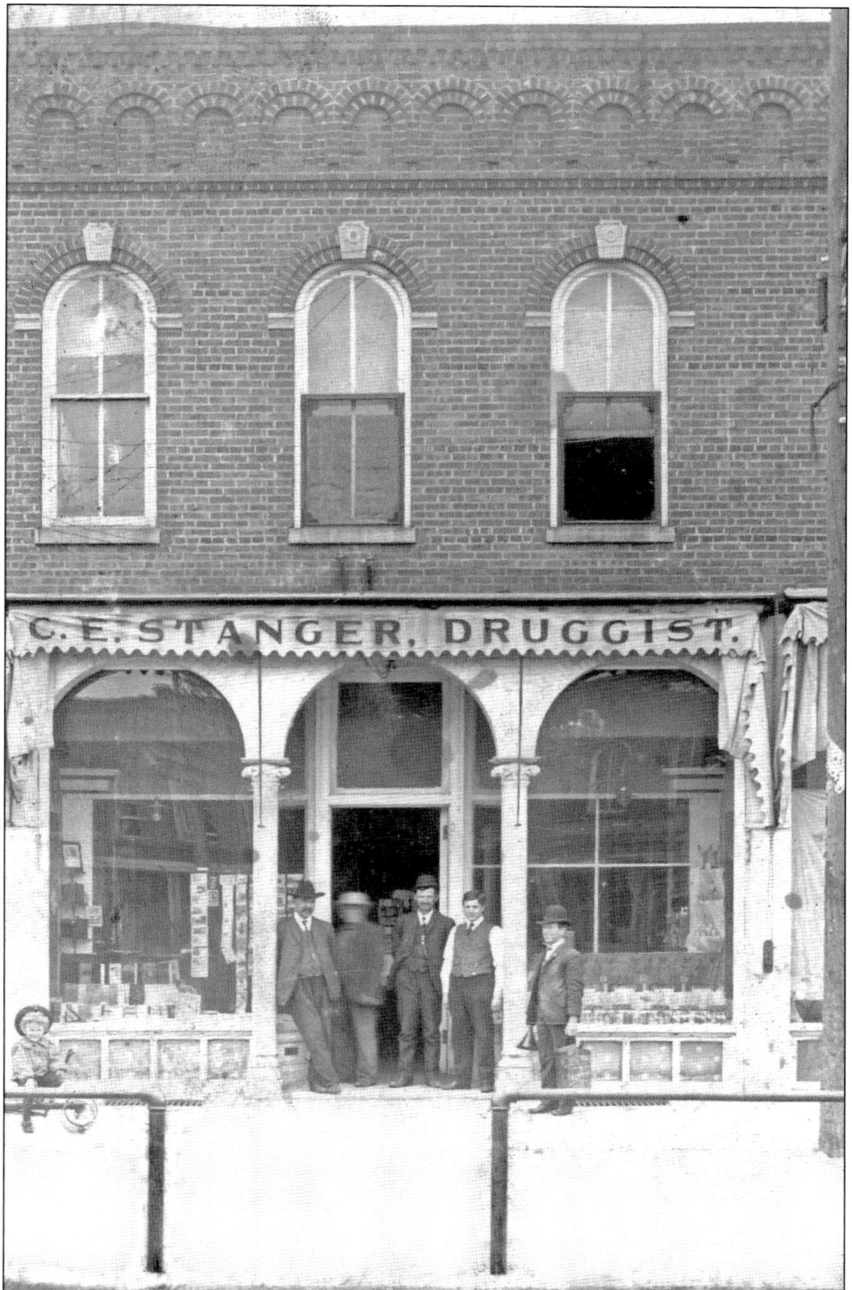

Charles E. Stanger is one of the men standing in front of Stanger's Drugs at 112 Tecumseh Street around 1910. The gentleman on the right is probably H.J. Meyer, owner of a grocery store for 40 years. The little guy on the left riding a handcar is his son Cliff, who would operate a hardware store for some 50 years. This building shows the typical commercial Italianate architecture with the rounded window trims and rounded arches. Stanger's Drugs was a longtime feature of Dundee's downtown and eventually opened a store in Ann Arbor. Stanger commissioned and sold postcards, a valuable source of local history.

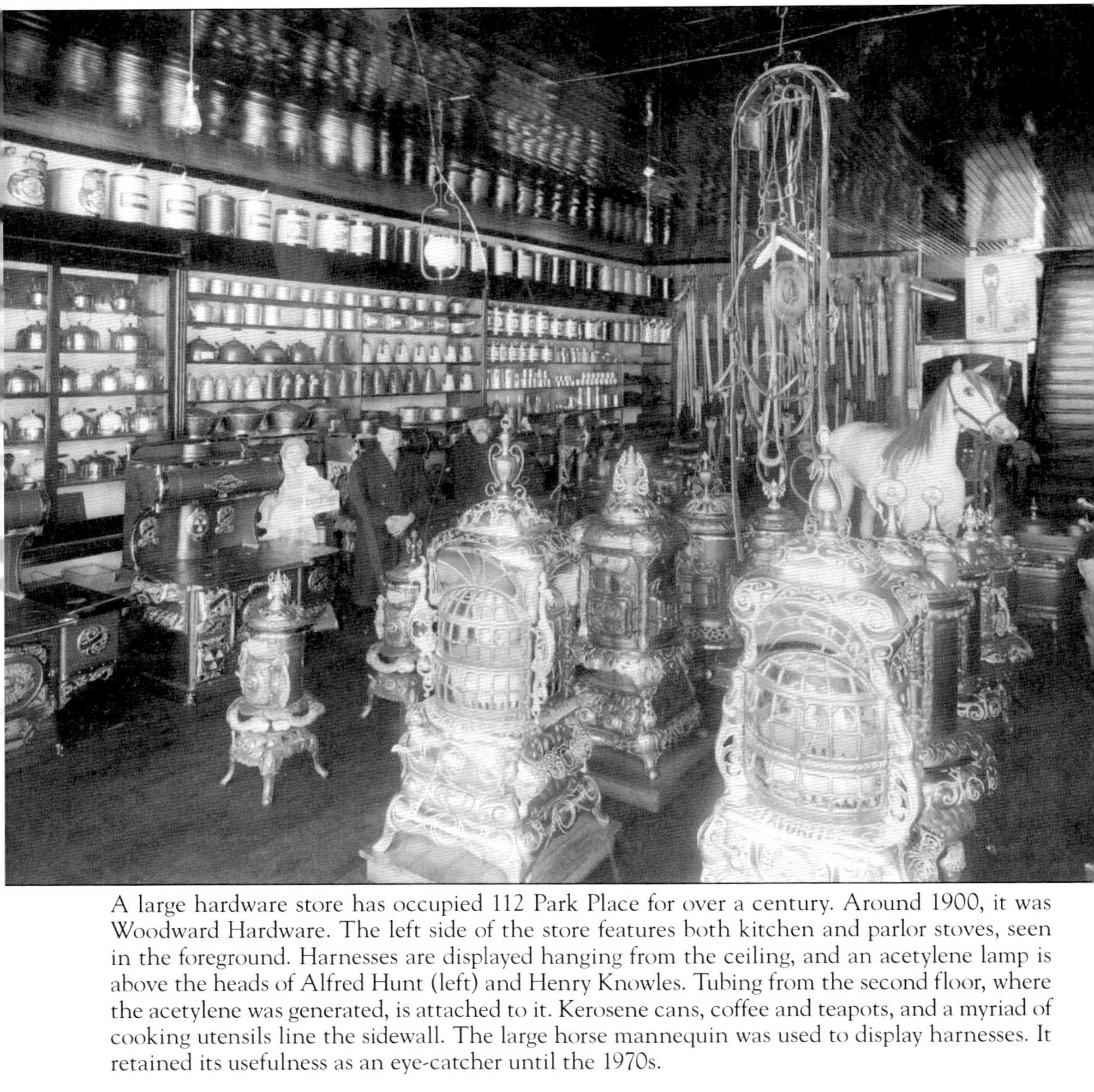

A large hardware store has occupied 112 Park Place for over a century. Around 1900, it was Woodward Hardware. The left side of the store features both kitchen and parlor stoves, seen in the foreground. Harnesses are displayed hanging from the ceiling, and an acetylene lamp is above the heads of Alfred Hunt (left) and Henry Knowles. Tubing from the second floor, where the acetylene was generated, is attached to it. Kerosene cans, coffee and teapots, and a myriad of cooking utensils line the sidewall. The large horse mannequin was used to display harnesses. It retained its usefulness as an eye-catcher until the 1970s.

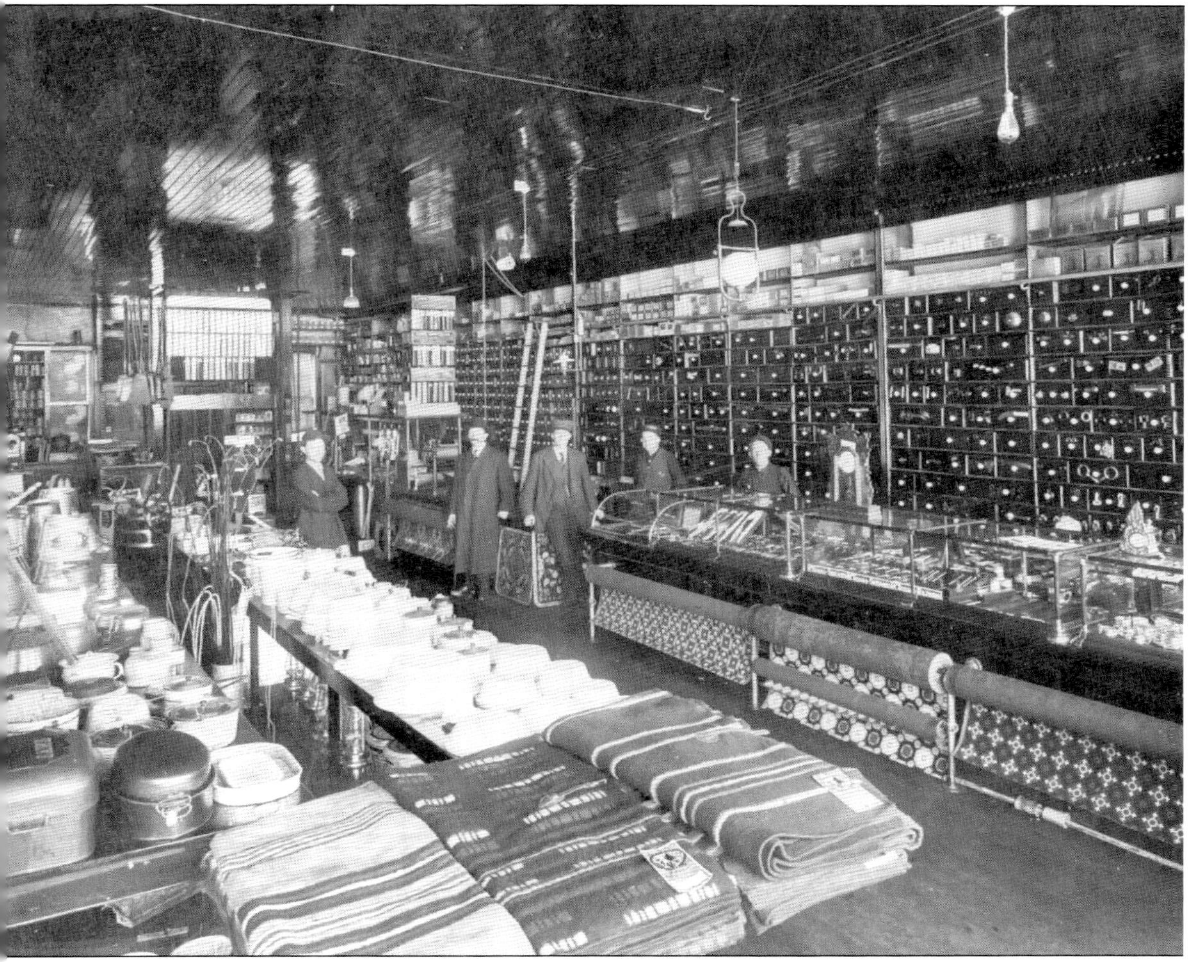

The right side of Woodward Hardware shows linoleum or oilcloth displayed in rolls on the right. Drawers of hardware, with their white knobs, line the right wall. Various types of lighting systems are shown, a matching acetylene lamp, bare electric bulbs, and probably kerosene lamps. Rugs or horse blankets, products of Mackinac Mills, are folded neatly on tables along with dishes, pans, and other household items. In the glass cases on the right are scissors, shears, razors, and cutlery. Lanterns are for sale under the crockery, and brooms are hanging on the back wall. Standing in the back from left to right are Bert Larry, Fred Mills, O.H. Woodward, Mike Drew, and Leo Schaffer.

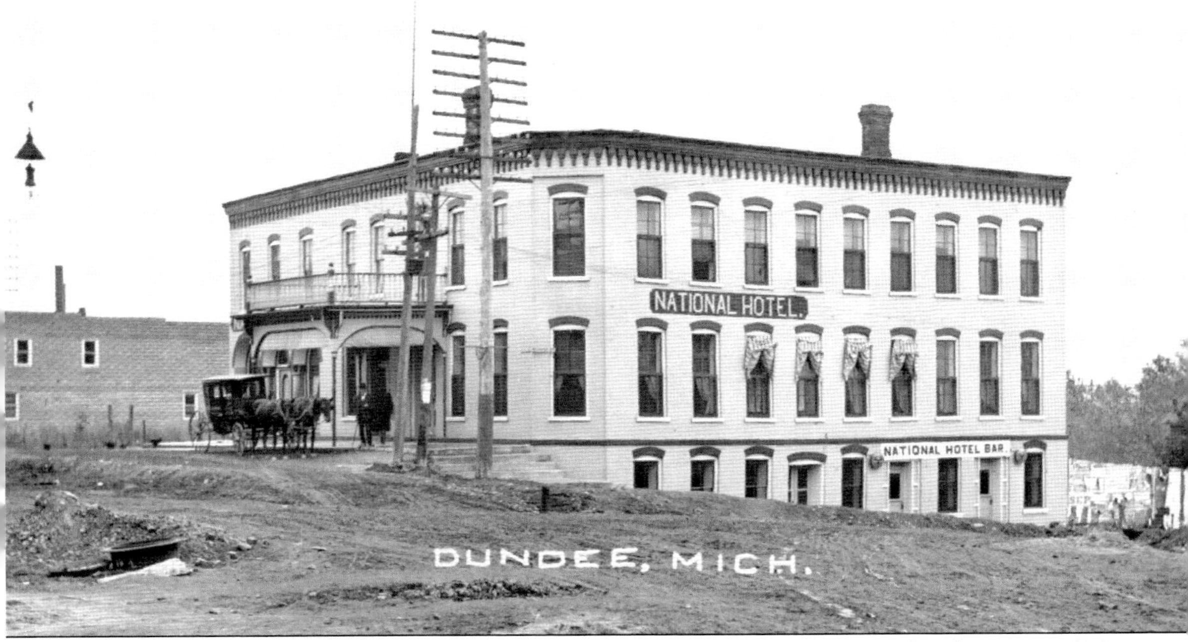

The National Hotel was Dundee's main hotel for many years and was located at the corner of Main and Monroe Streets. Pictured around 1907, it appears that street and sewer work are being done on the intersection. A carriage pulled by horses is stopped at the entrance. Railroad passengers arriving at Union Station normally traveled in this kind of vehicle to the hotel downtown. Besides hotel rooms, the National offered businessmen rooms to display samples of their merchandise. Doctors from as far away as Detroit rented space once or twice a week. The hotel bar was located in the lower level.

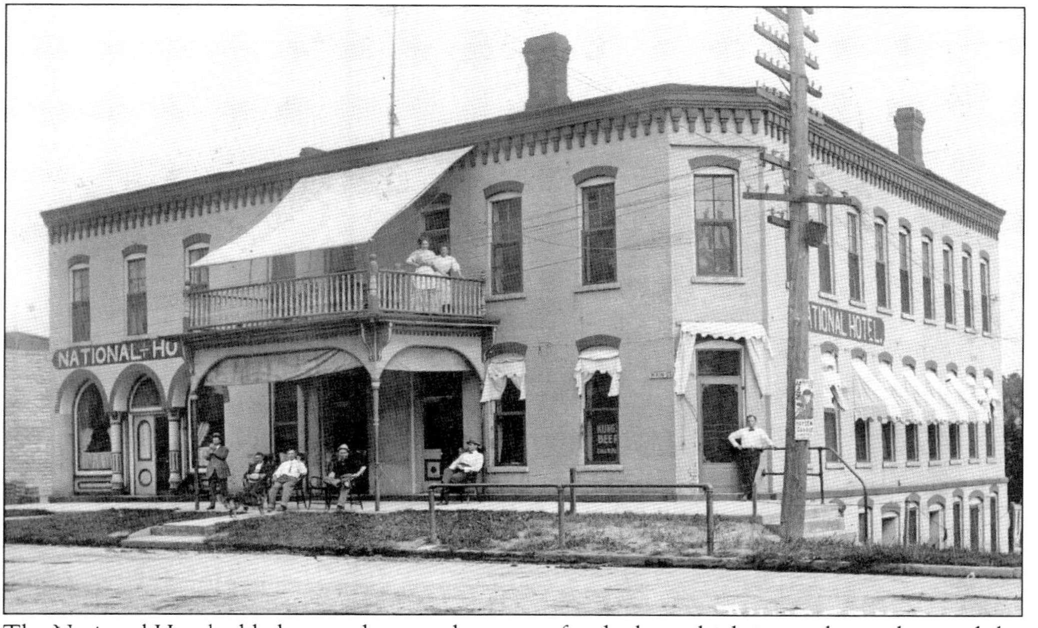

The National Hotel added a new door on the corner for the bar, which is now located toward the front. Maids appear on the canopied porch. A story is told that a teacher, new to town, left her door open at the hotel on a Sunday afternoon and entertained a gentleman at tea. A maid spied her and informed the board of education, and by midnight the teacher had to leave town.

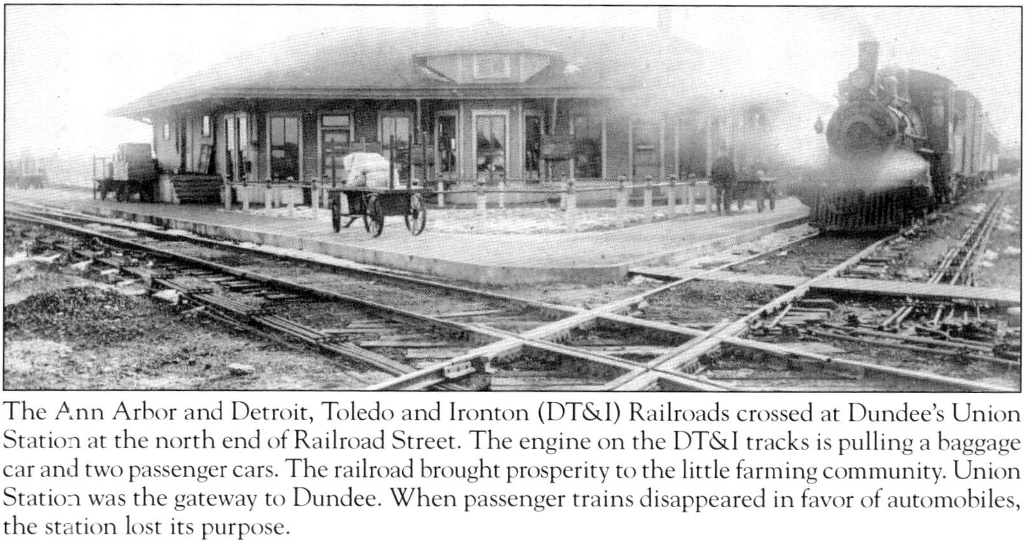

The Ann Arbor and Detroit, Toledo and Ironton (DT&I) Railroads crossed at Dundee's Union Station at the north end of Railroad Street. The engine on the DT&I tracks is pulling a baggage car and two passenger cars. The railroad brought prosperity to the little farming community. Union Station was the gateway to Dundee. When passenger trains disappeared in favor of automobiles, the station lost its purpose.

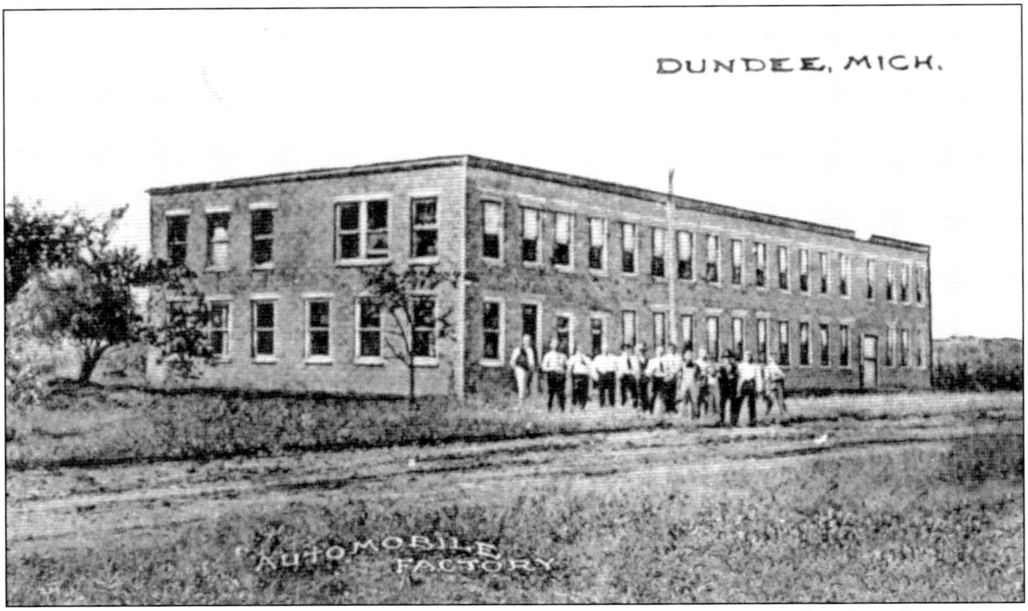

The Pope Car Company set up a manufacturing plant in 1905 on the west side of Ypsilanti Street, shown here. Later, the DeVilbiss Plier Company moved in. In 1917, the Nu Way Stretch Suspender factory occupied the building. Later yet, the Monroe County Road Commission stored equipment there. A school parking lot is all that remains today.

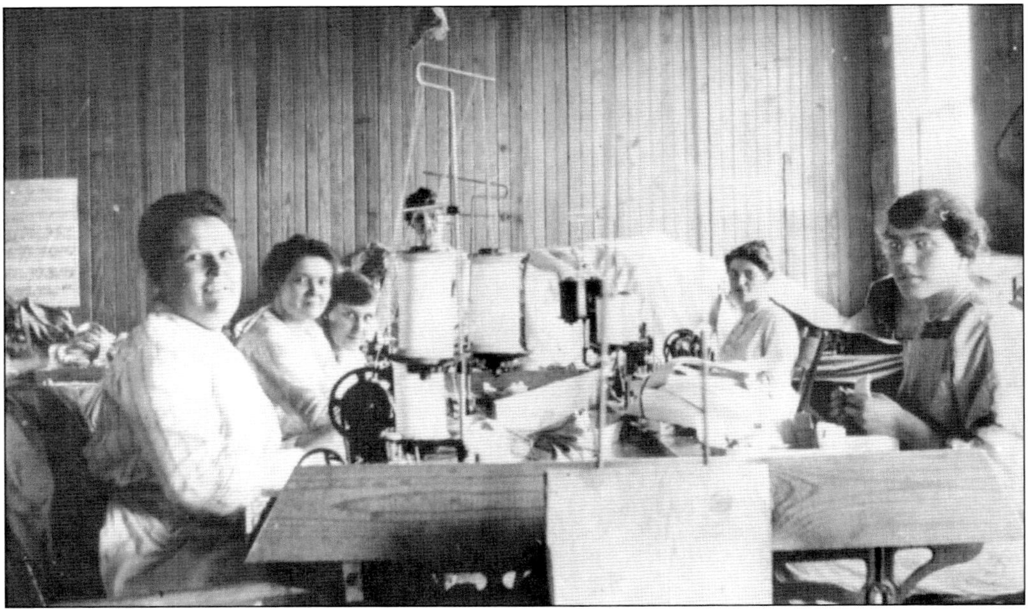

The Nu Way Stretch Suspender factory took over the pliers factory in 1917, offering employment to women in the area. Thread in giant bobbins fed the sewing machines. O.E. Mott, a local department store owner and mayor, started the firm. Sewing was honorable work for women at that time and one of the few jobs open to them before World War II.

The Slayton butcher shop is seen displaying fresh meat by hanging it in the open, which was a common practice in the world before refrigeration. The butcher in the white apron on the left is Dave Martin; the butcher in the doorway is owner John Slayton, with his son Eugene and his dog. The Slayton Meat Market was located on Tecumseh Street around the corner from Park Place. The building burned in 1994.

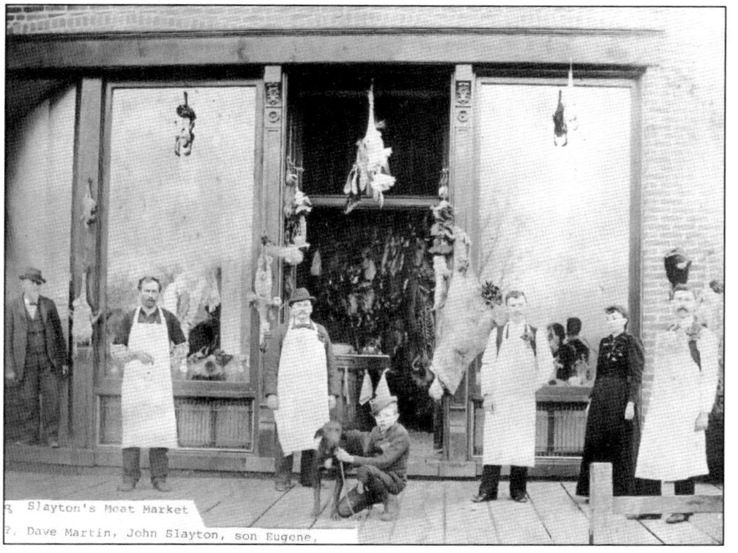

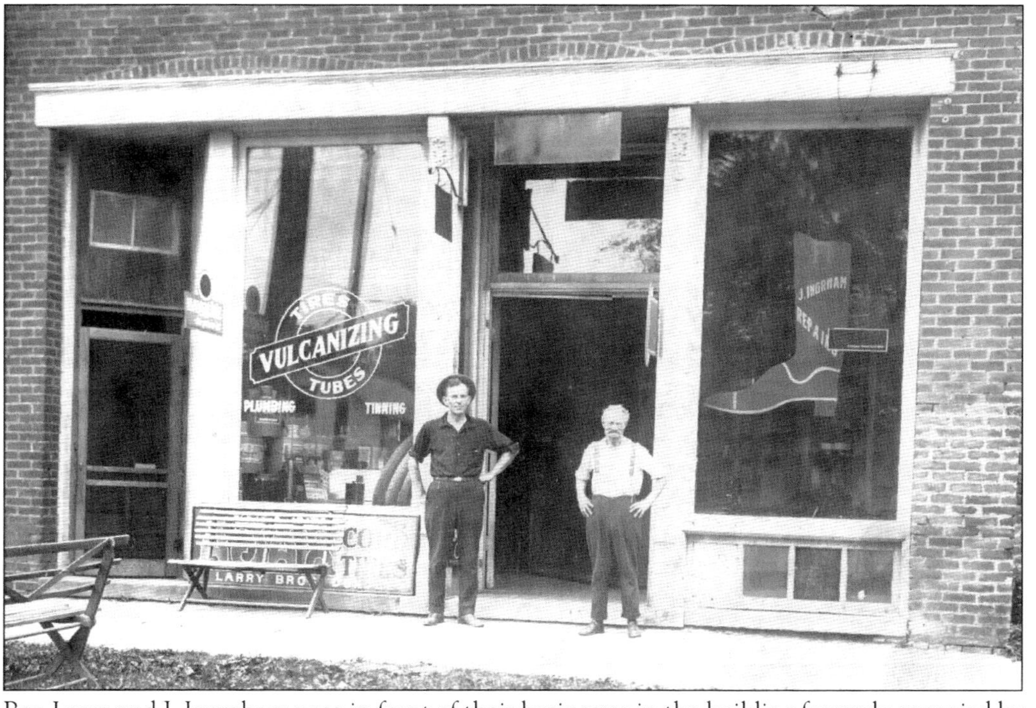

Ben Larry and J. Ingraham pose in front of their businesses in the building formerly occupied by Slayton's Meat Market at 167 Tecumseh Street. Larry did plumbing, tinsmithing, and vulcanizing inner tubes. His brother Floyd, a plumber, was the other half of Larry Bros. noted behind the bench. Ingraham had a shoe repair shop. These businesses were important in a self-sustaining small town.

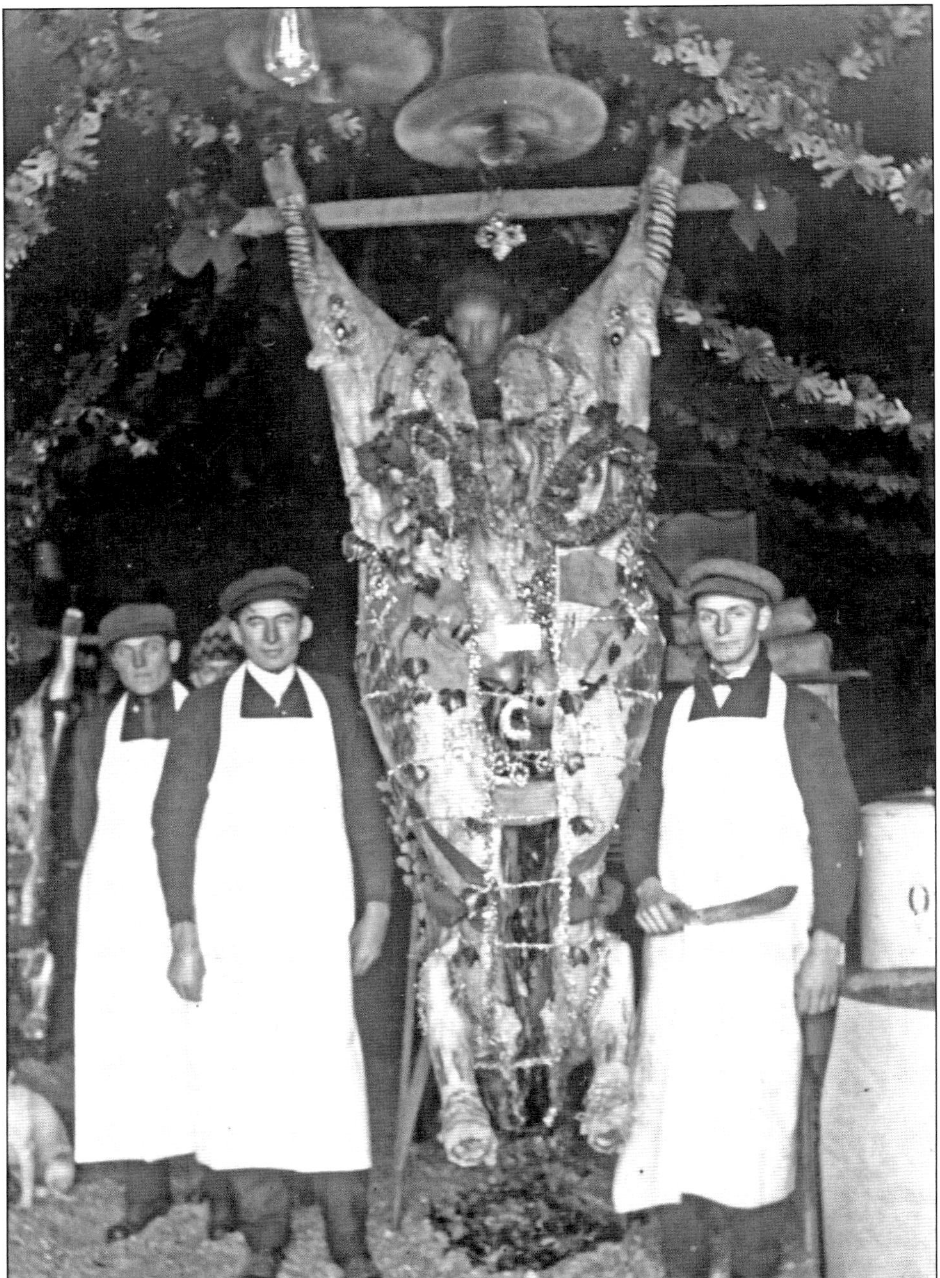

Heinie Borgert's meat market employees look to have gotten into the Christmas spirit, decorating a steer with holiday wreaths and hanging garlands and bells. Around 1913, Borgert used this particular postcard for advertising, sending it to R.B. Davis, the former gristmill owner. Heinie is on the far left; next to him is his brother William. The meat market probably was located in the same building as undertaker F.D. Moser at this time. It has been said that when Borgert went home for lunch, he would shake the blood-tinged sawdust from the floor out of his pants cuff as he crossed the street.

A very colorful citizen was James Cassidy, as can be seen by his distinctive mustache. He was a veteran of the Civil War, and he also served a term as Dundee postmaster. Originally a shoemaker, Cassidy opened a barbershop in 1871 in the National Hotel. He opened a second shop and filled it with relics and stuffed animals. A local citizen declared, "It was quite a sight."

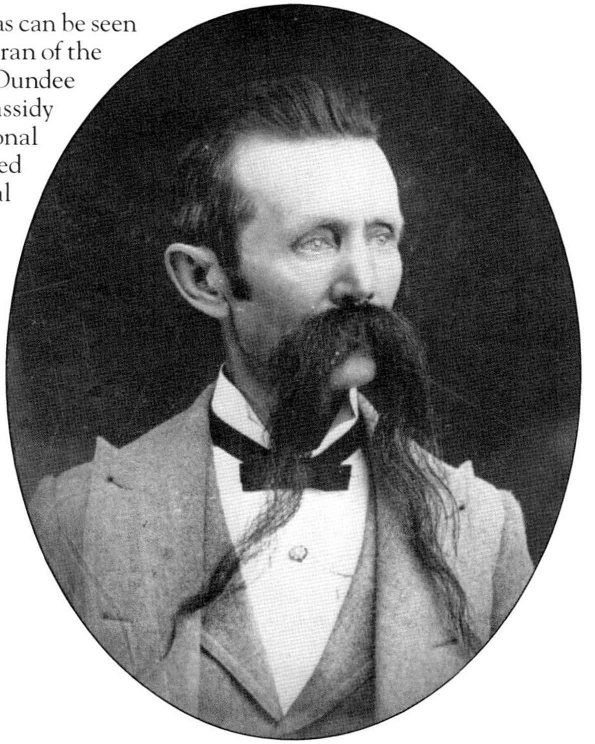

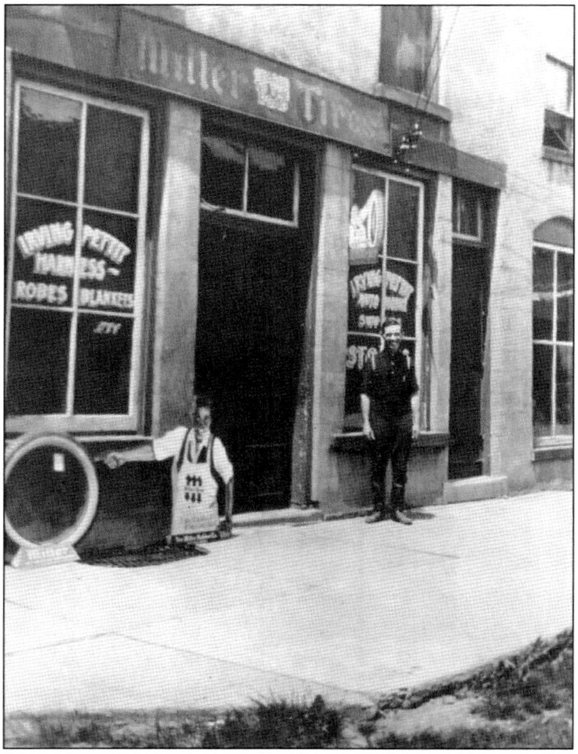

Irving Petitt bridged two eras. Around 1915, he was selling tires to auto owners and harnesses to the horse-drawn transportation crowd. His shop was on Monroe Street on the hill near the bridge. Irving succeeded his father, Cyrus, who moved to Dundee in 1869 and purchased the harness shop at the same location.

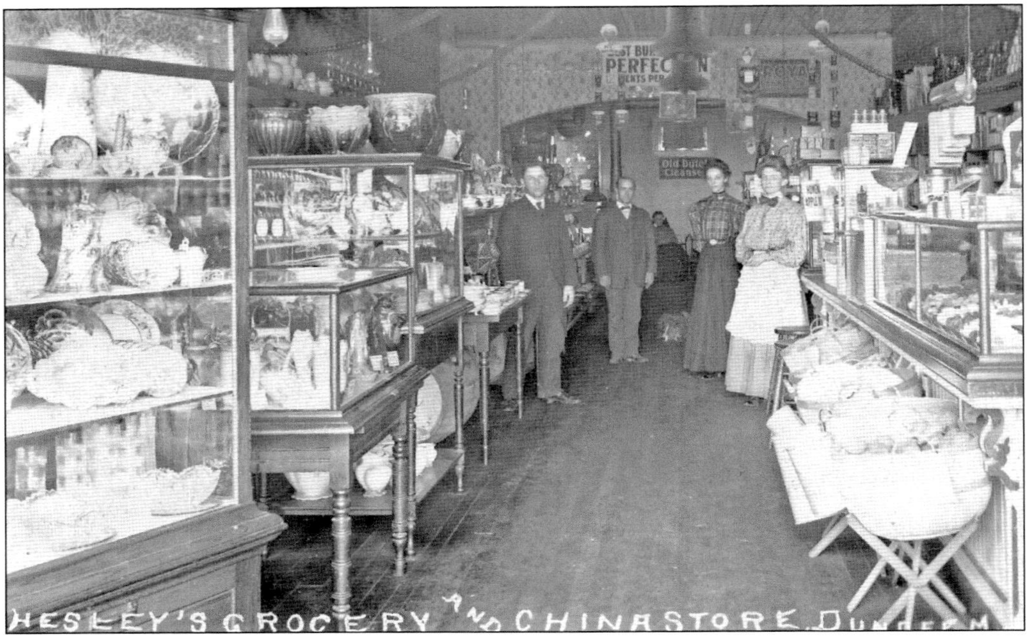

Hesley's Grocery and China was located at 135 Riley Street. The interior shows the many showcases used to house the china. Large *jardinières* (flower vases) stand atop a case, and groceries are on the right. To take this photograph, everyone had to hold a pose for some time. Looking closely, in the very rear, the dog appears two-headed because he moved.

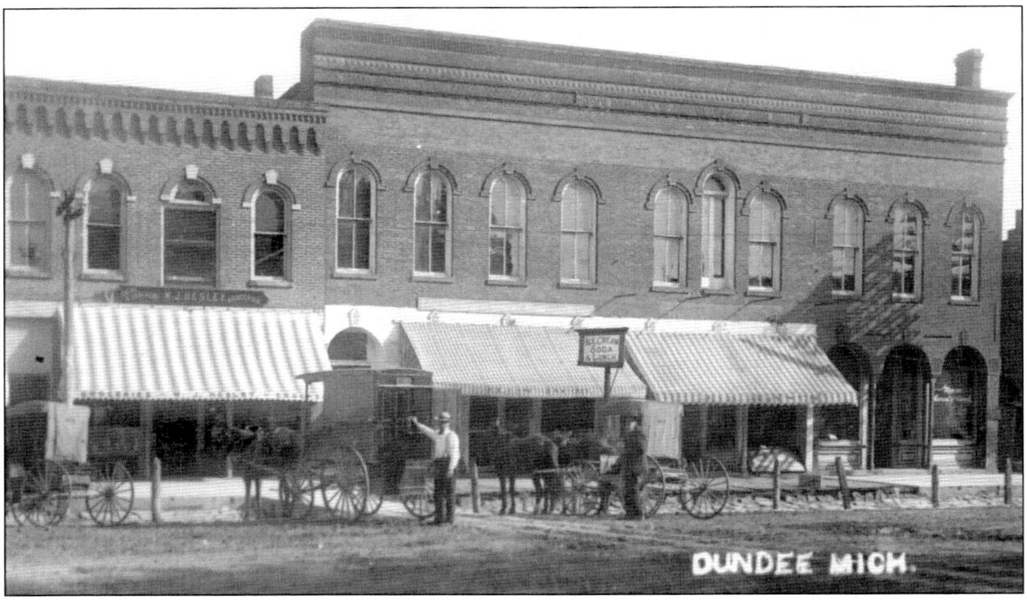

Hesley's delivery wagon is in the center with the driver opening the door. On the reverse side of this postcard that was not mailed, written in 1907, a lady from nearby Azalia explains to her cousins that Hesley's is the store where she trades, where she works during the Christmas rush, and that the Hesley delivery wagon and driver are featured on the front of the card.

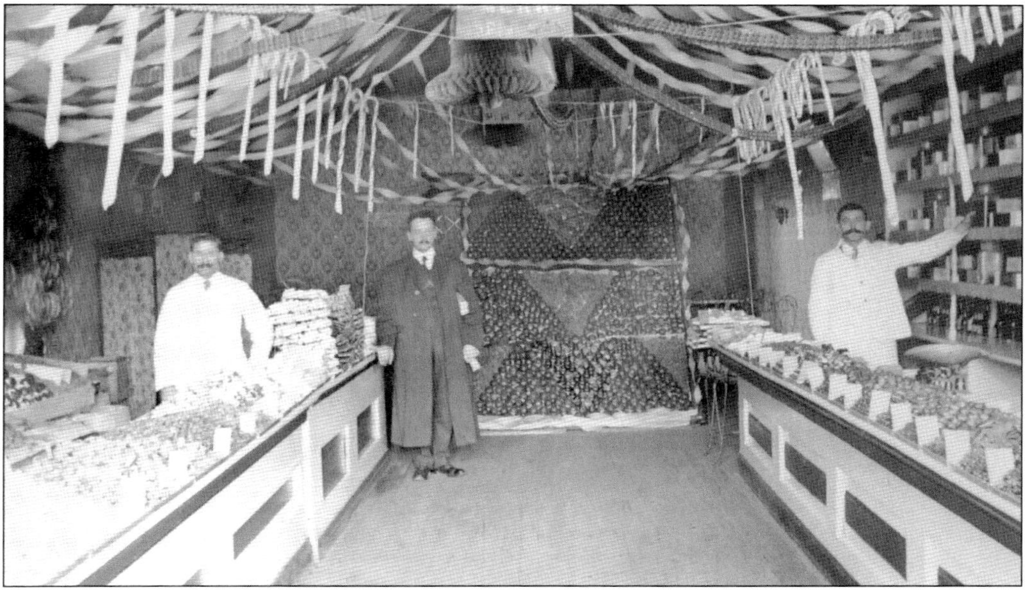

The Dundee Candy Kitchen, at 111 Riley Street, was a popular confectionery. It is decorated in typical early-1900s Christmas fashion. The confectionery was started in the 1880s and was purchased in 1921 by Greek immigrant Spero Mitchola, who renamed it the Ideal Sweet Shop. Mitchola, a village favorite, eventually changed his shop into a restaurant, remaining in business for 60 years.

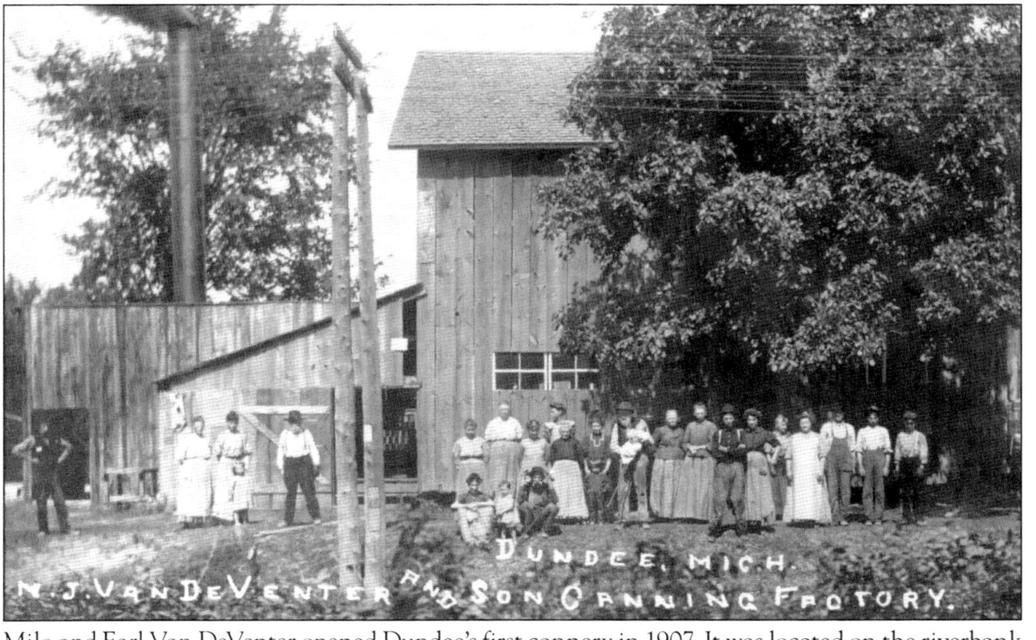

Milo and Earl Van DeVenter opened Dundee's first cannery in 1907. It was located on the riverbank at 225 Monroe Street across from the family home. Tomatoes were brought to the cannery by farmers and peeled by women. The majority of those pictured are women peelers who were paid by the pail. During World War II, German prisoners of war worked in the cannery. The last cannery closed in 1958.

M. Hershfield's Sons....

DEPARTMENT STORE

The Leading Store of Monroe County.

Dry Goods, Carpets, Cloaks, Men's, Boys and Children's Clothing, Hats, Ladies' and Men's Fine Shoes, Furnishings, Trunks, Traveling Bags, Staple and Fancy Groceries. . . .

Our entire fall stocks will be complete by Sept. 15. Special sales in every department during the Fair. Don't fail to guess on the tape in our window—you may be one of the lucky guessers and secure one of the following prizes :

Finest Black Dress in our store. Choice of any pair Kid Gloves, Calico Dress, Chenille Spread, $10 00 Suit, $3 00 pr. Shoes, $1 50 Hat, or choice of any Tie.

Contest closes Saturday, Oct. 1st.

M. HERSHFIELD'S SONS, Dundee

Hershfield's Sons Department Store was at 102 and 108 Tecumseh Street. It appears that the owners had a flair for advertising proclaiming that theirs was "the Leading Store of Monroe County." It is also taking advantage of Dundee's Fair, held in September, to encourage business by holding a guessing contest. One of the prizes was a $10 suit. A department store was at this address for many years.

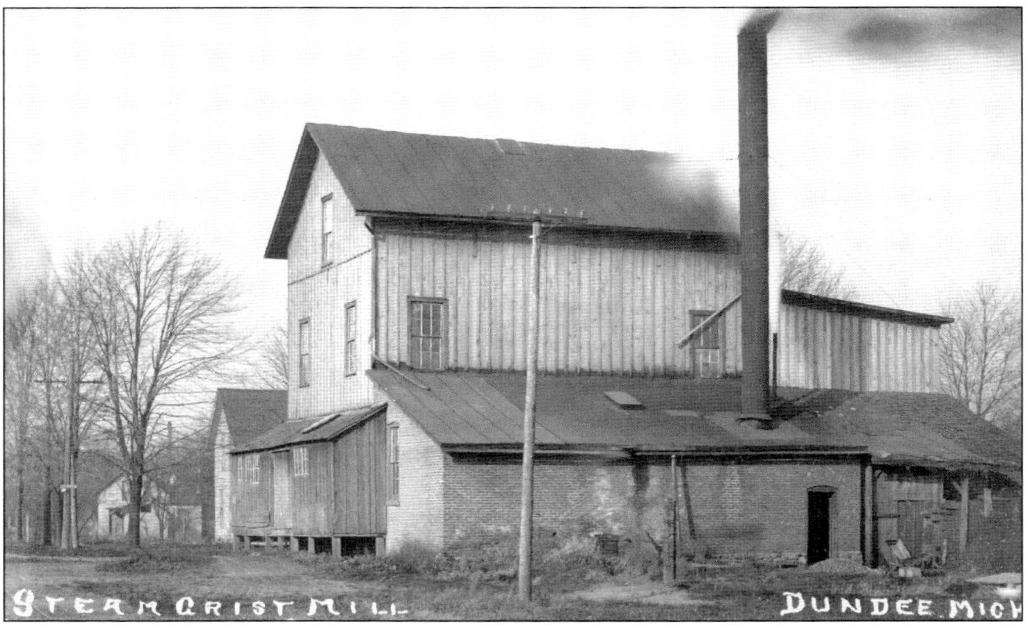

This steam mill, at the corner of Franklin and Washington Streets, is shown in 1876. Called the Watling Mill after its original owners, it produced flour and later made cereal for the Five Colonels Food Company. During World War I, a quota was placed on wheat, and subsequently fall buckwheat became the most profitable run. John Schmidt purchased the mill in 1926. It ground feed until it burned down in the 1950s.

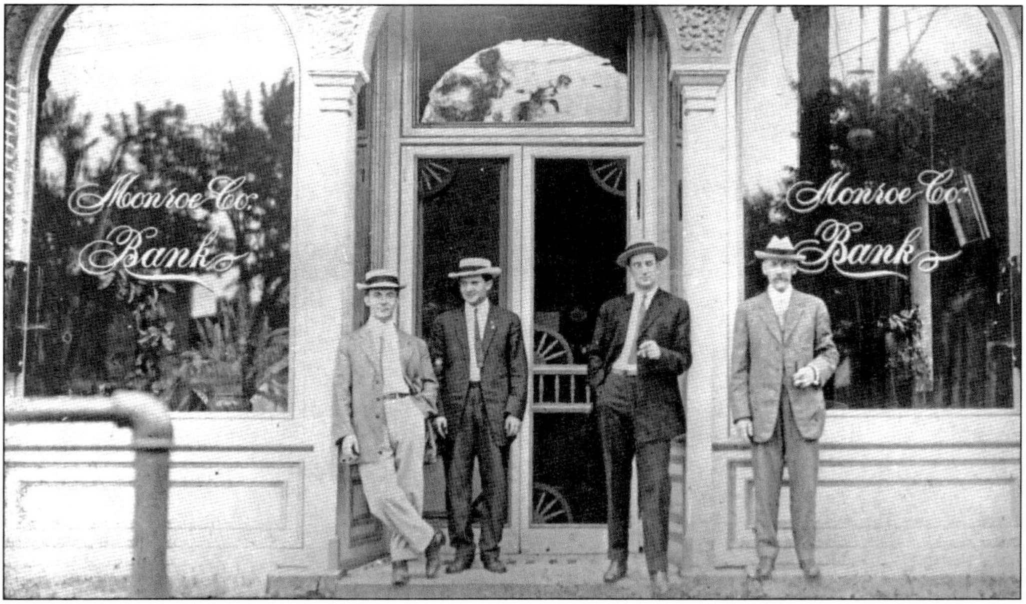

The Monroe County Bank was located for many years at 145 Riley Street. Four men are seen posing in front of their bank around 1915. They are identified as, from left to right, William F. Haas, attorney; William Corbin, businessman; Levi Williams or Perry Keehn, businessmen; and William Clute, who was the cashier from 1911 to 1915. In 1916, the bank advertised that one could open a savings account and earn three percent.

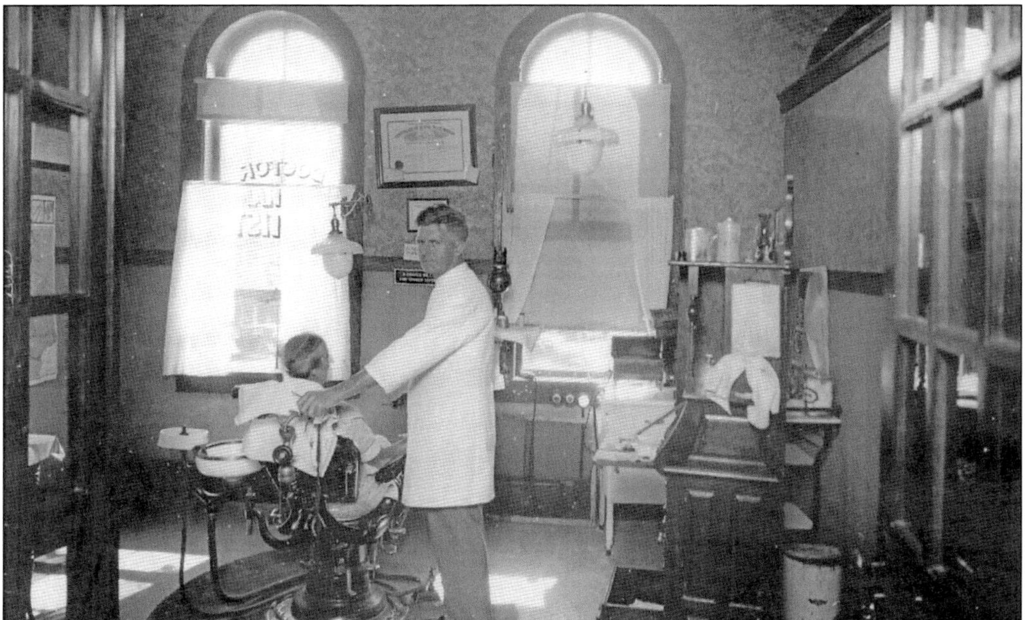

Dr. Frank Benham was Dundee's only dentist for nearly 50 years. He is shown with an elderly female patient in his office above the Monroe County Bank. He became a director of the bank and also served 35 years on the school board. A sign on his back wall states a charge will be made for broken appointments. (Courtesy of Randi Kominek.)

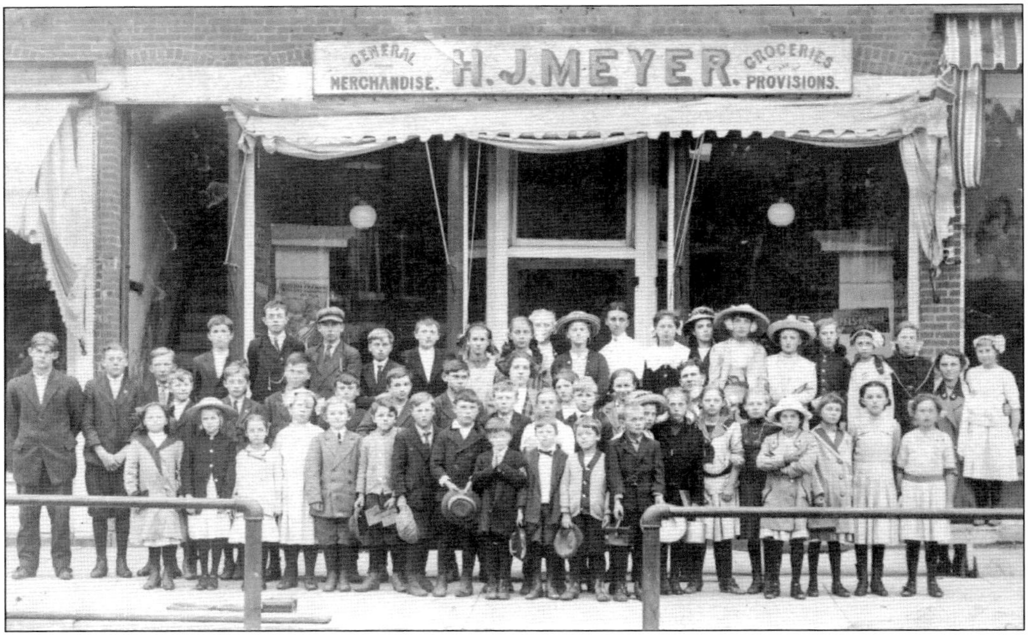

Henry J. Meyer had his grocery store in at least two locations. A group of students, probably from the Lutheran school, poses in front of his store at 120 Tecumseh Street. Meyer's son Cliff, born in 1903, is the little boy in short pants, fifth from the left, in the front row. Meyer, a short man, is standing amongst the children on the right side.

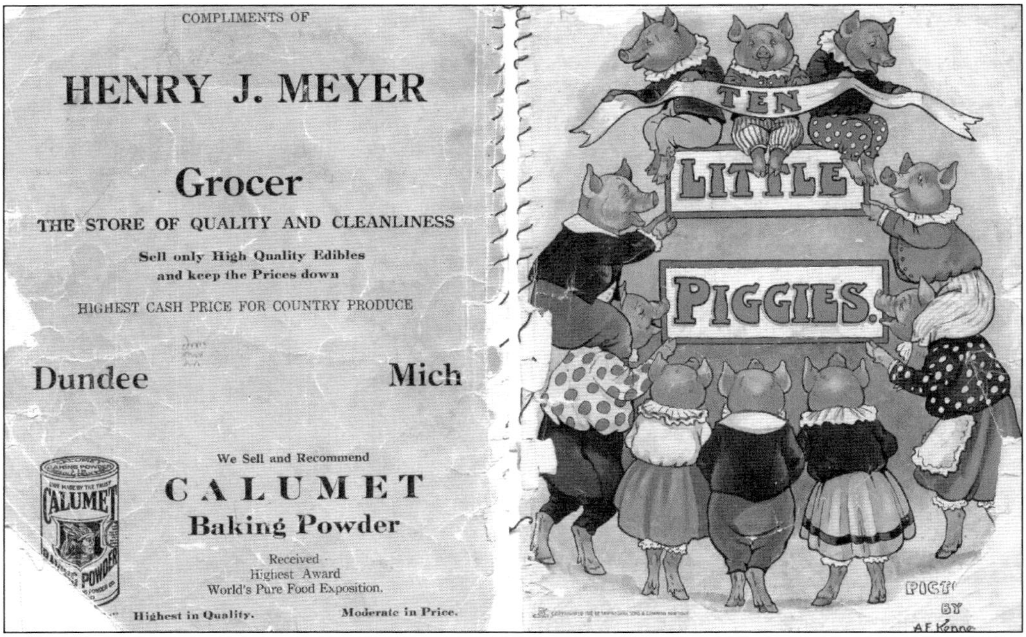

When Henry Meyer was located at 102 Park Place, he distributed this little booklet, with a full-color cover, as a promotional piece; his ad was on the back cover. The popular Calumet Baking Powder is still available. The beloved children's story, in this version, began with well-dressed pigs, fresh from the market, frolicking on the front cover.

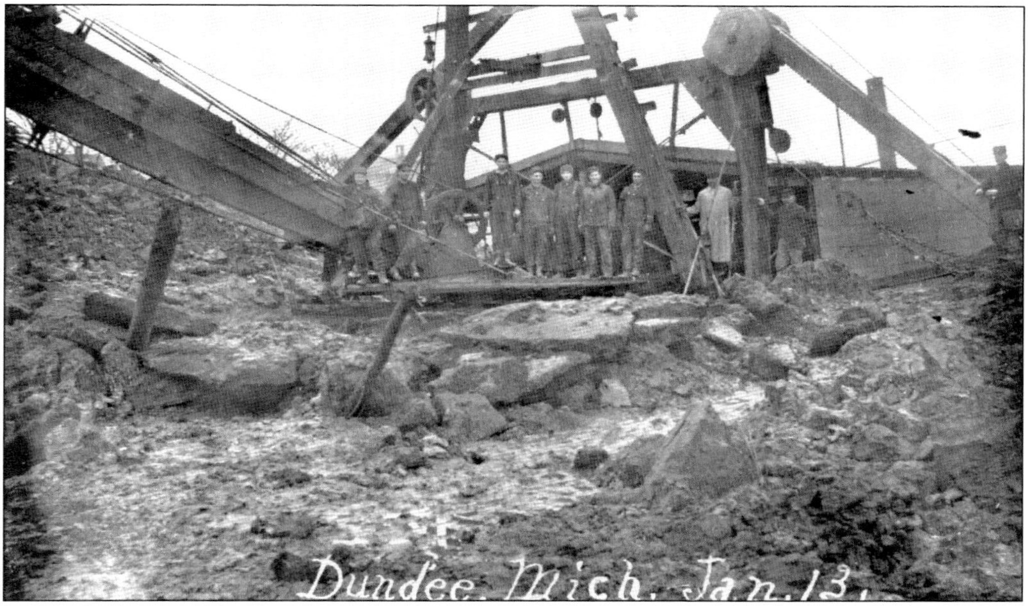

R.E. Bullock operated a stone quarry at 2486 Bunce Road, about two miles east of Dundee. Extracting stone in the early 1900s was the quarry's main economic activity, although attempts were made in the 1880s to find gas and oil. The resulting open quarry is now used as a swimming park.

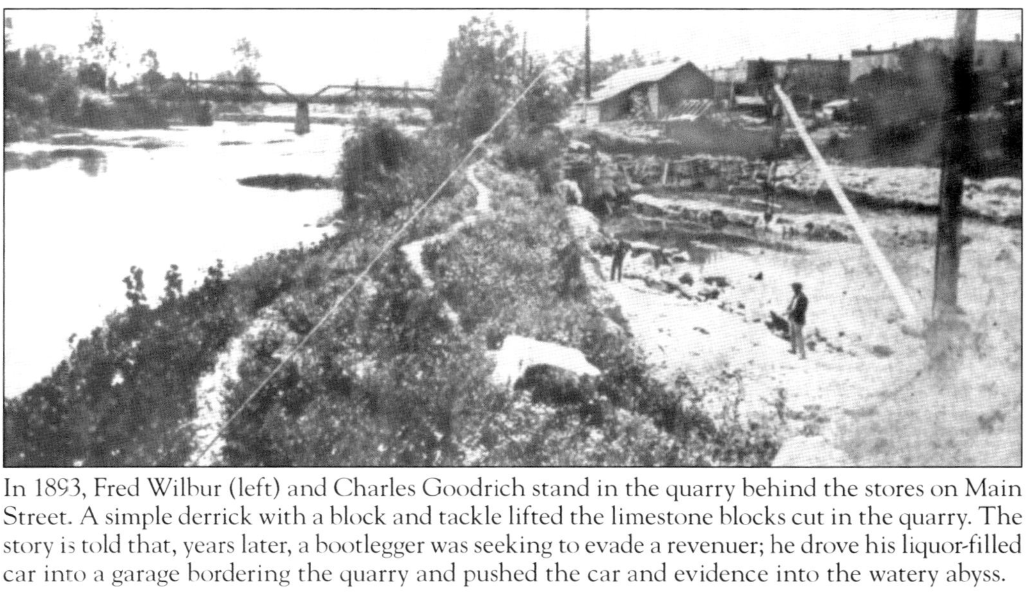

In 1893, Fred Wilbur (left) and Charles Goodrich stand in the quarry behind the stores on Main Street. A simple derrick with a block and tackle lifted the limestone blocks cut in the quarry. The story is told that, years later, a bootlegger was seeking to evade a revenuer; he drove his liquor-filled car into a garage bordering the quarry and pushed the car and evidence into the watery abyss.

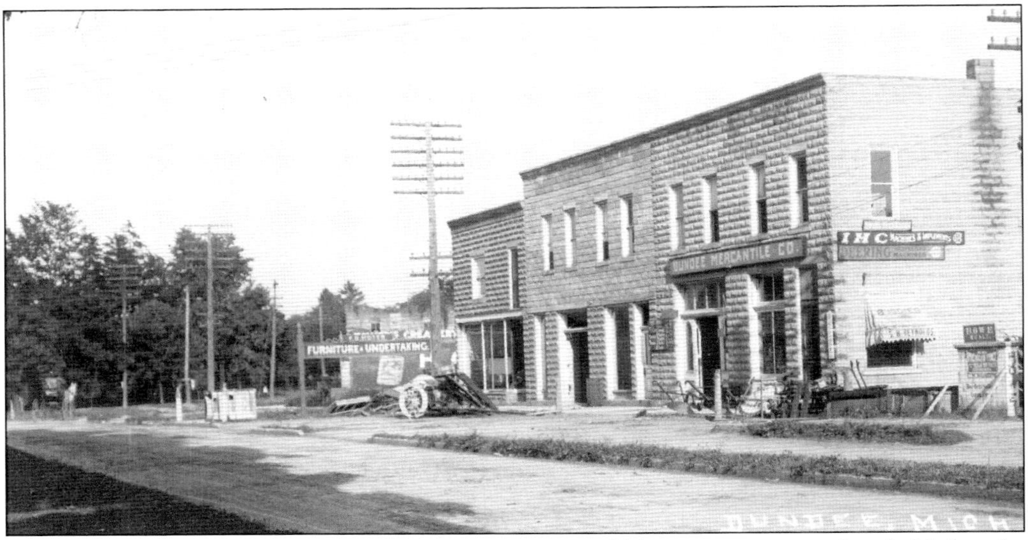

The Dundee Mercantile Company, at 152 Main Street, sold farm equipment and probably bought farmers' produce. The sign to the left of the door lists prices for crops. There are signs for Deering Harvesters, IHC Machines and Implements, and Swift's fertilizer. The April 27, 1923, *Dundee Reporter* indicated the council allowed the mercantile to put the Howe scale outside its building. It was placed in the vacant lot to the right.

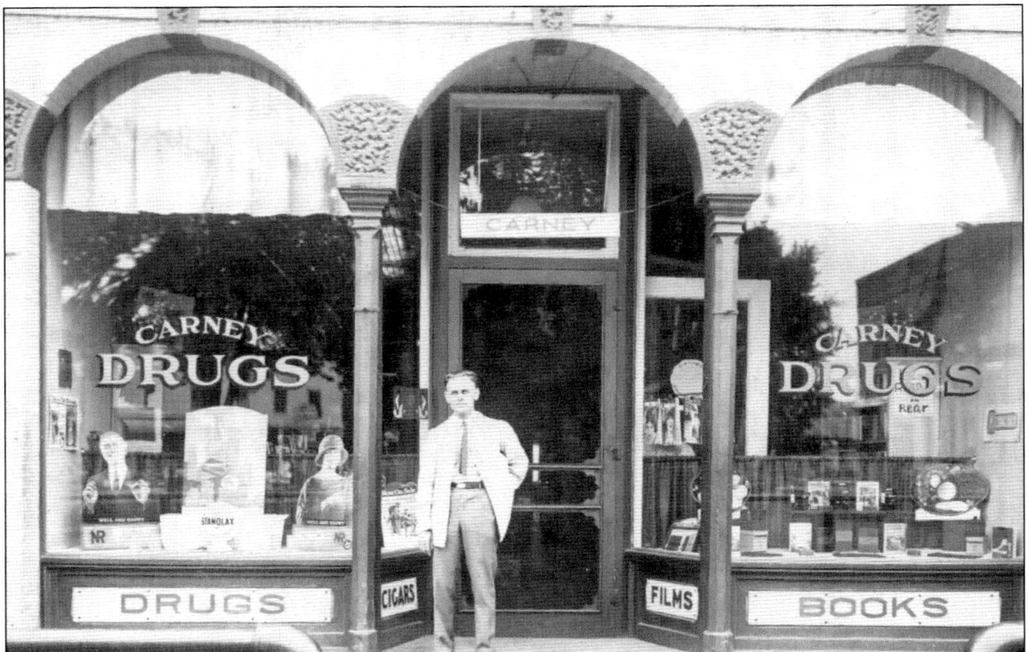

Longtime druggist Fay Carney poses here in 1924 in front of the store he ran with his wife, Delia, at 143 Riley Street. The November 17, 1922, of the *Dundee Reporter* commented that Carney spent the week in Sandusky, Michigan, taking a special short course in pharmacy. He later moved his business to 115 Riley Street, where his store served as a Short Way Bus Station and Western Union office.

Three

DUNDEE ENTERTAINMENTS

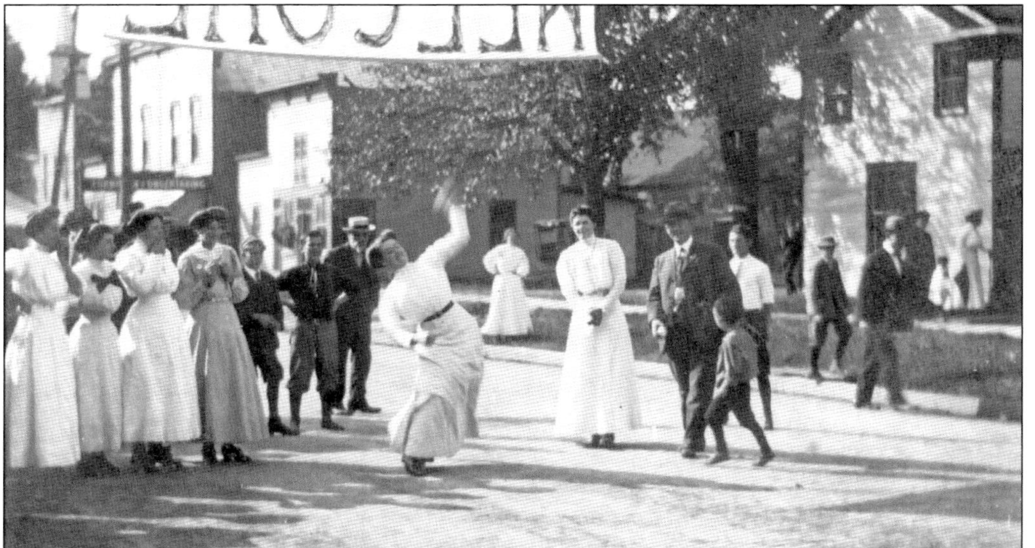

This ladies' ball-throwing contest was held in the early 1900s on Tecumseh Street near Barnum Street. An enthusiastic audience watches as a lefty does her best. The young lady is so intent on winning that she has hitched up her skirt to help her throw. Dundee enjoyed many public forms of entertainment.

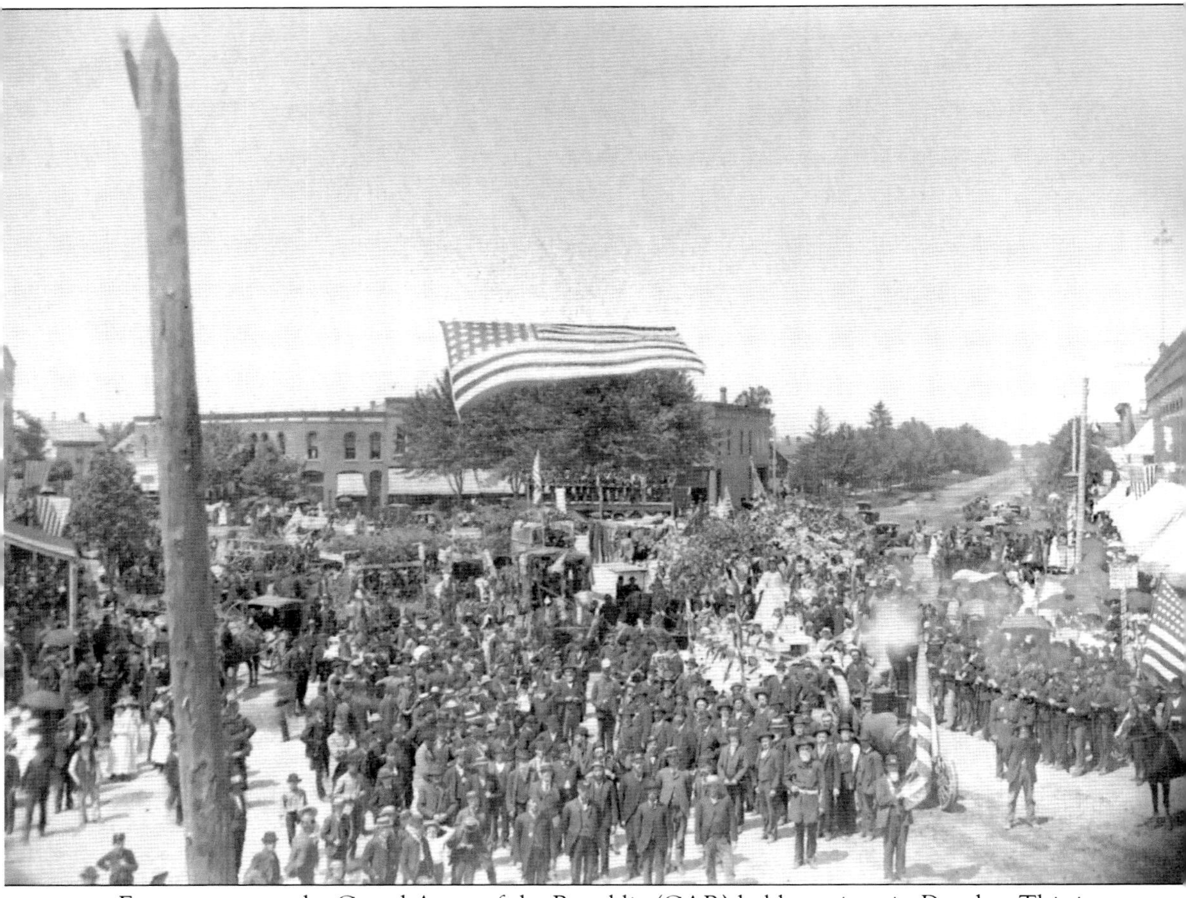

For many years, the Grand Army of the Republic (GAR) held reunions in Dundee. This is one of the early ones based on the fact that there are telegraph lines and no electric lines, indicating it is before 1894. The fact that there are flags with both 38 and 42 stars would date the gathering to around 1890. The Civil War veterans are front and center, and there is a contingent of current soldiers on the right. Note the steam from the traction engine pulling the young ladies in a wagon. A huge flag is suspended over the intersection of Riley and Tecumseh Streets, and a temporary reviewing stand has been constructed on the triangle.

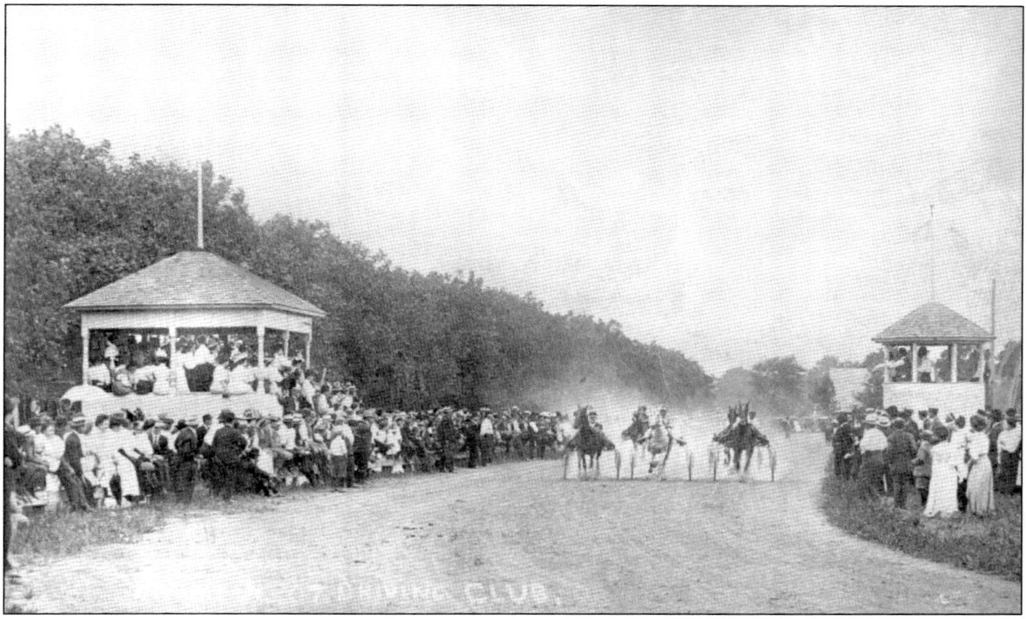

The Prairie Depot Driving Club sponsored trotting races at the Dundee Fairgrounds. The Dundee Agricultural Association sponsored the Dundee Fair for about 17 years, beginning in 1891. The fair was the forerunner of the Monroe County Fair and issued a 60-odd-page program. The track was visible from the air until the senior citizen's complex on Rawson Street obliterated the southern half and the manufactured housing subdivision covered the rest.

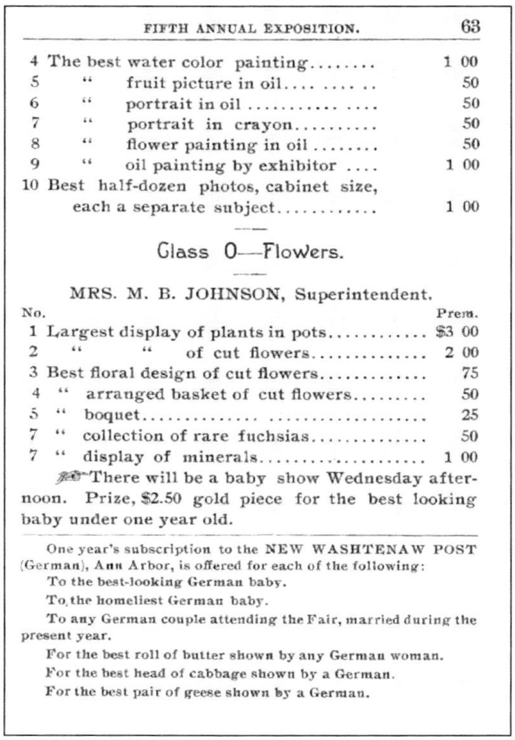

FIFTH ANNUAL EXPOSITION. 63

4	The best water color painting........	1 00
5	" fruit picture in oil....	50
6	" portrait in oil	50
7	" portrait in crayon..........	50
8	" flower painting in oil	50
9	" oil painting by exhibitor	1 00
10	Best half-dozen photos, cabinet size, each a separate subject............	1 00

Class O—Flowers.

MRS. M. B. JOHNSON, Superintendent.

No.		Prem.
1	Largest display of plants in pots............	$3 00
2	" " of cut flowers..............	2 00
3	Best floral design of cut flowers.............	75
4	" arranged basket of cut flowers.........	50
5	" boquet..............	25
7	" collection of rare fuchsias..............	50
7	" display of minerals....................	1 00

There will be a baby show Wednesday afternoon. Prize, $2.50 gold piece for the best looking baby under one year old.

One year's subscription to the NEW WASHTENAW POST (German), Ann Arbor, is offered for each of the following:

To the best-looking German baby.

To the homeliest German baby.

To any German couple attending the Fair, married during the present year.

For the best roll of butter shown by any German woman.

For the best head of cabbage shown by a German.

For the best pair of geese shown by a German.

The annual Dundee Fair lasted four days. This is part of a page from the 1895 premium book. In addition to listing the various classes for competition—horseracing to chickens to flower arranging—and the prizes being offered, the book contained advertisements and special contests. This contest focused on German pride. Many residents identified strongly with their German heritage. This was 22 years before America entered World War I.

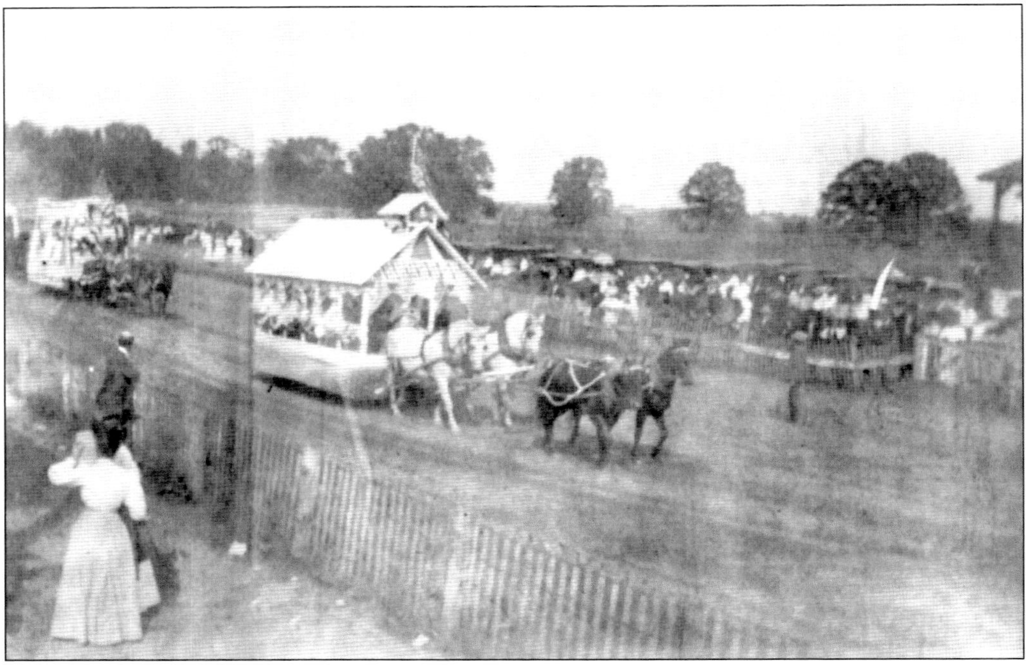

Here is a parade at the Dundee Fairgrounds. It is a clear day in 1904, and men and women watch from the sidelines. The first float, resembling a country school, is so heavy that it requires two teams of horses to pull it. The second float also needs extra horsepower.

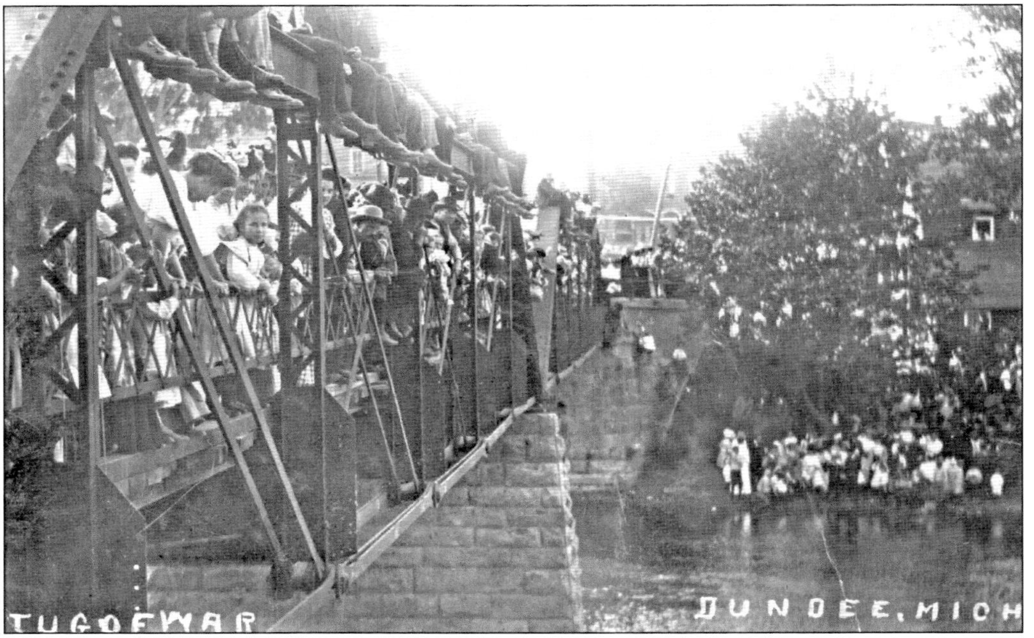

In addition to a fair, Dundee also hosted an annual carnival downtown. This rare c. 1908 photograph shows the Monroe Street Bridge packed with eager spectators of all ages. They are watching the tug-of-war staged across the River Raisin. Sitting on the girder seems to be reserved for males, as a female might expose more than an ankle.

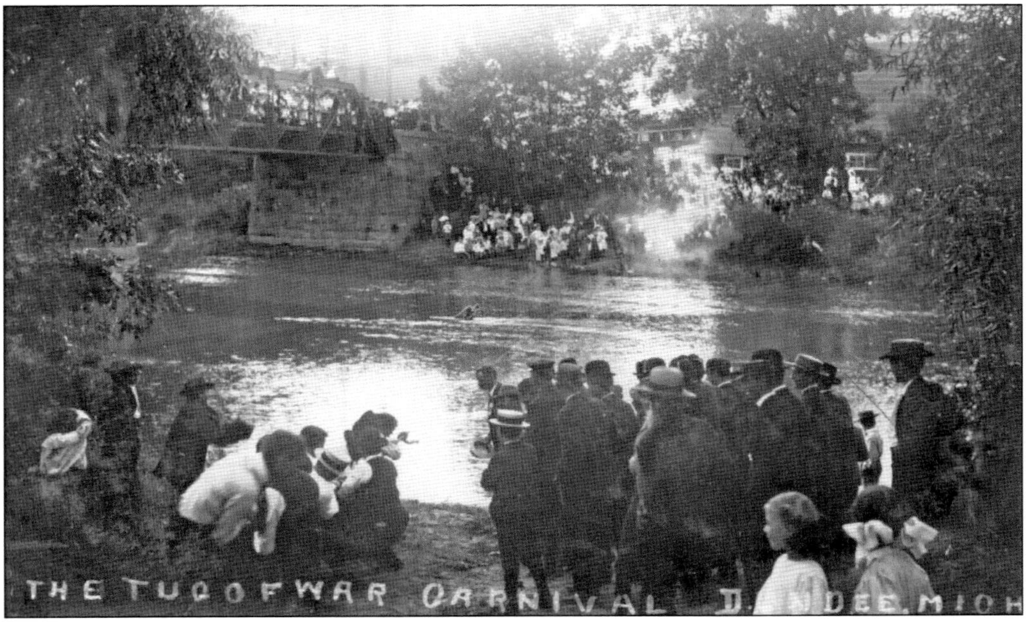

A group of spectators gathers on the south bank of the River Raisin. The tug-of-war has just begun, with both sides pulling. The excitement builds when one side finds itself being pulled into the water, as it will have to decide whether to give up and let go before getting soaked.

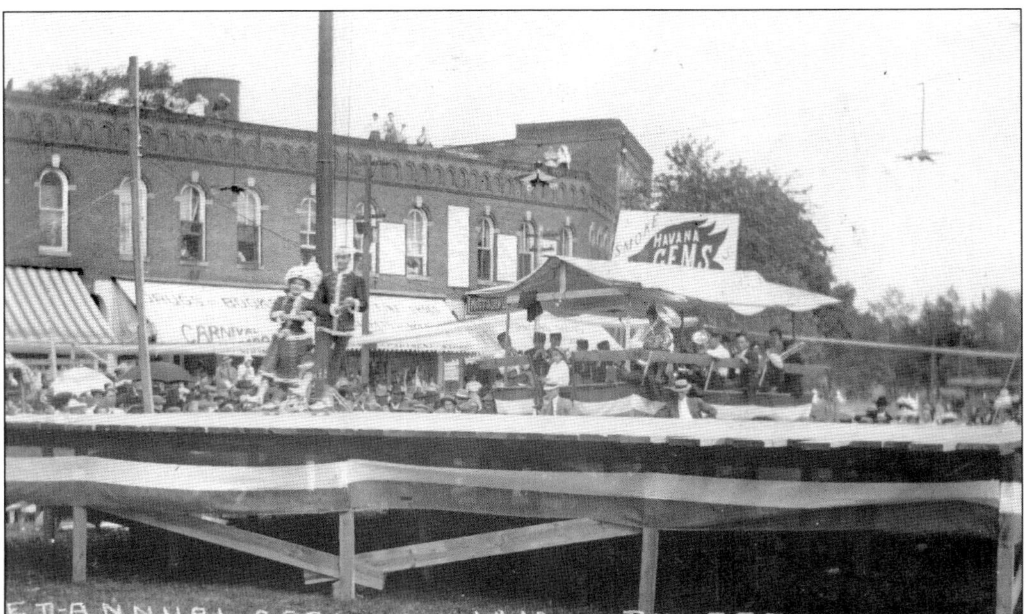

The 1910 Dundee Carnival featured performers roller-skating on a raised platform on the triangle. A roller-skating rink at 127 Barnum Street and one on the third floor of the building in the background catered to this popular sport. At a separate stand, the band was providing music. A "Havana Gems" banner advertised the handiwork of a local cigar manufacturer.

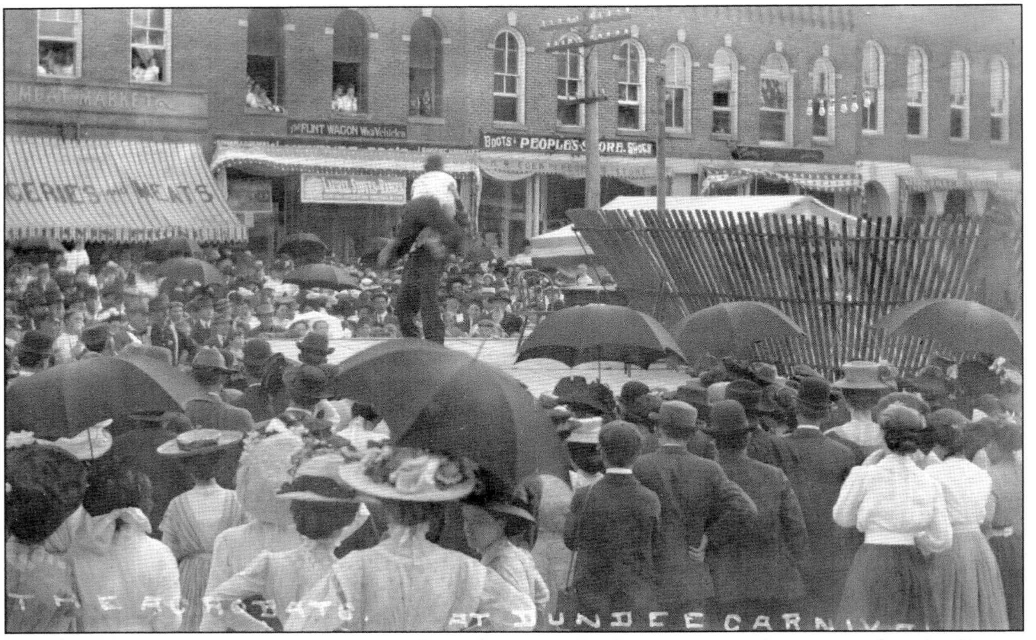

Acrobats are seen entertaining a crowd on the triangle. Some women have raised umbrellas to protect themselves from the sun while watching the show. The hats displayed here are more modest, attesting to the transition in fashion that is taking place in Dundee. Carnivals gave citizens something to look forward to when the whole town would gather to watch or compete.

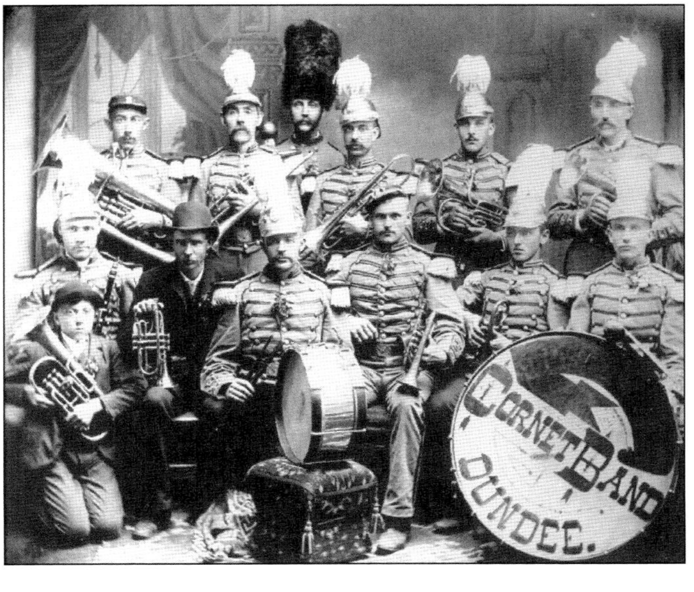

The Dundee Cornet Band was probably formed before 1900. Its oldest member, Charles Grimitz, was born in 1837. Another member, Fred Fleming, was the organizer of the William French Band in Dundee. The Dundee Cornet Band members included, from left to right, (front left) George Drake; (first row) Art Gee, Fred Fleming, Will McNeal, Fred Edwards, Chet Casey, and Olin Sparks; (second row) Henry Grimitz, Charles Grimitz, Steve Rawson, Dell Trowbridge, George Mills, and Phil Scranton.

The Electric Theatre was in the IOOF Building, located at 168 Riley Street. This was the era of silent movies, and the theater's popularity is confirmed by an item from the February 24, 1911, issue of the *Dundee Reporter*, "*His Trust, and His Trust Fulfilled* had standing room only for several performances at the Electric Theatre." In its waning years, Claribel Rod played the accompanying piano.

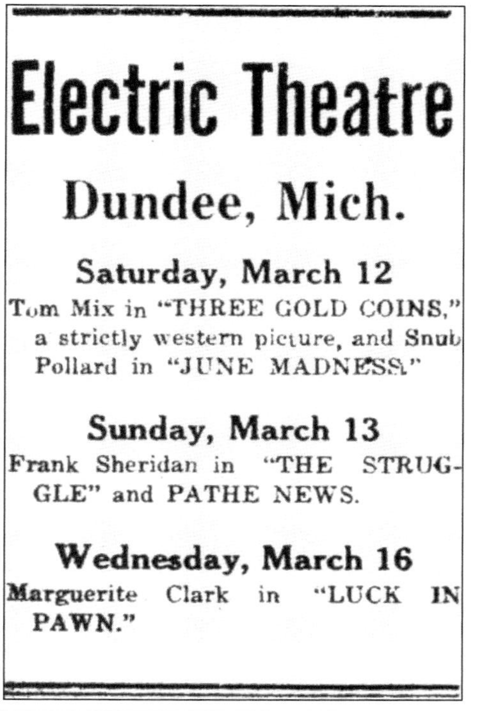

Electric Theatre

Dundee, Mich.

Saturday, March 12

Tom Mix in "THREE GOLD COINS," a strictly western picture, and Snub Pollard in "JUNE MADNESS."

Sunday, March 13

Frank Sheridan in "THE STRUGGLE" and PATHE NEWS.

Wednesday, March 16

Marguerite Clark in "LUCK IN PAWN."

Dundee had a mandolin club, as is documented in this undated photograph. The gentleman on the left is probably Seeley Wilson. Wilson was a member of the Dundee Band, organized in 1908, and a member of the Dundee Crescent Orchestra in 1915. He and an unidentified mandolin player appear in a photographer's studio surrounded by string and percussion instruments.

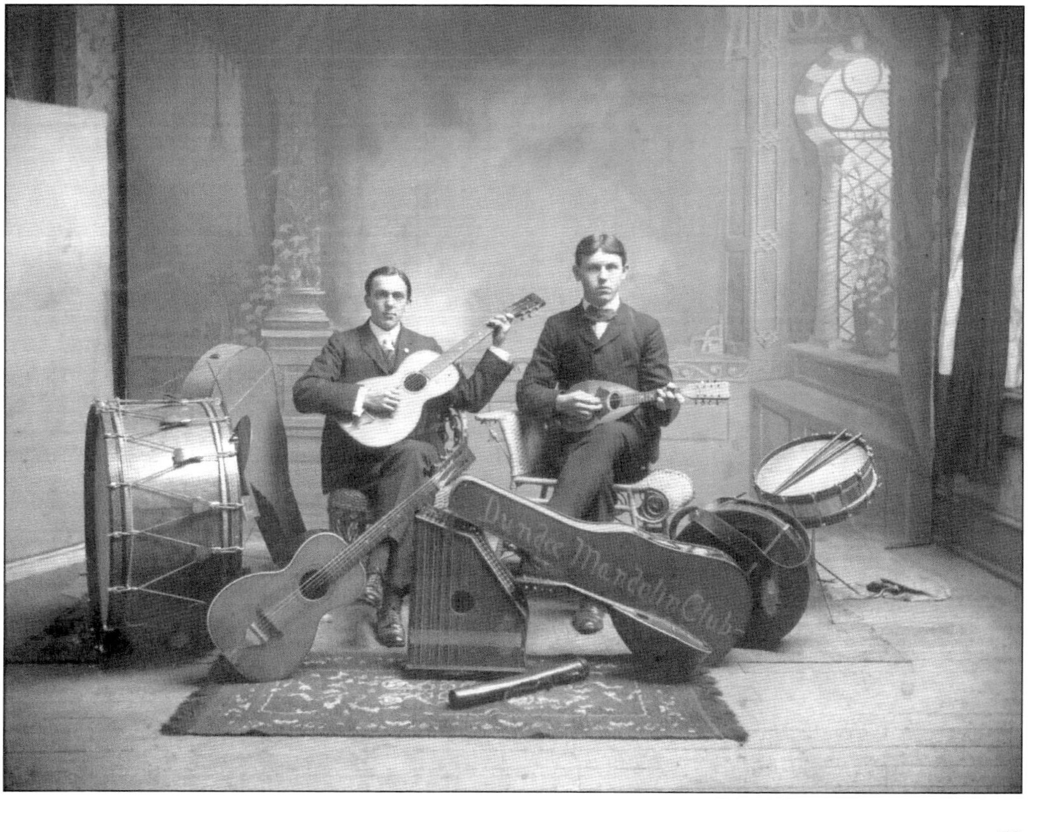

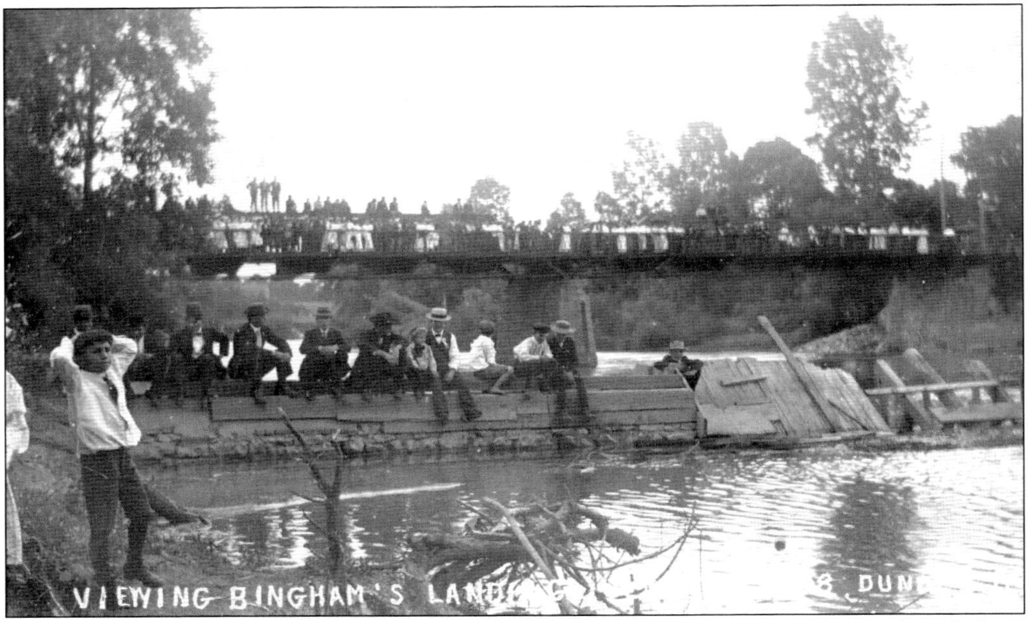

Another diversion was watching tightrope walking. In 1908, a large crowd has gathered along the bank of the River Raisin, some standing on the girders of the bridge. A smaller group perches on the partially defunct dam. The people are waiting to see a high-wire artist named Bingham walk on a tightrope (not pictured), which has been strung above the river from the mill to a tree on the north side.

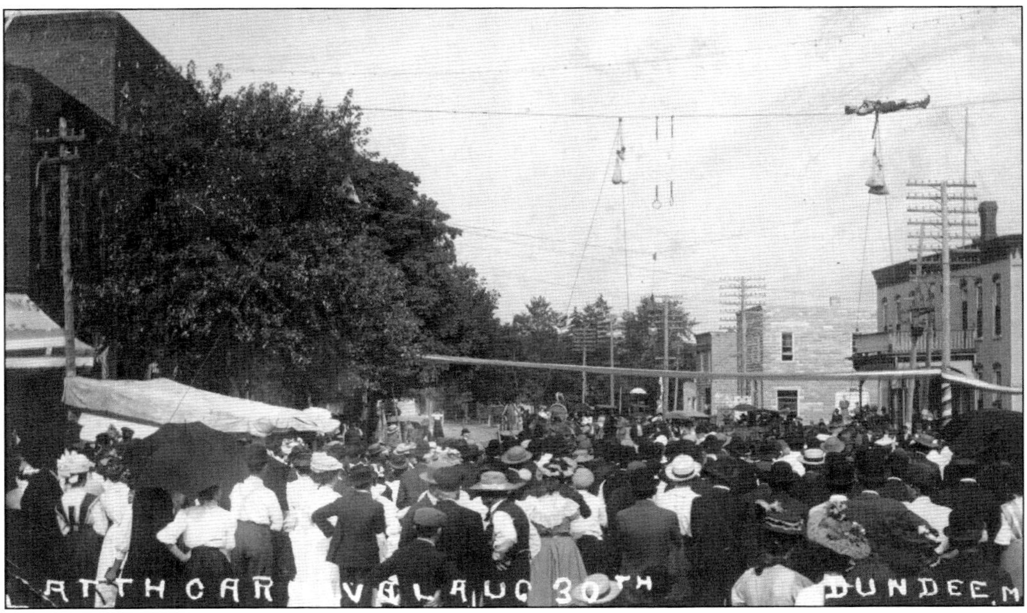

This is another high-wire act from the same time period. A wire strung from the Hotel Pocklington (left) crosses Main Street to the first brick building on Riley Street. Rings are visible hanging from the wire, which has been stabilized with guy-wires and bags of sand. In the image, the artist is lying on the wire on the right. In the background, a rope of bunting stretches across Main Street.

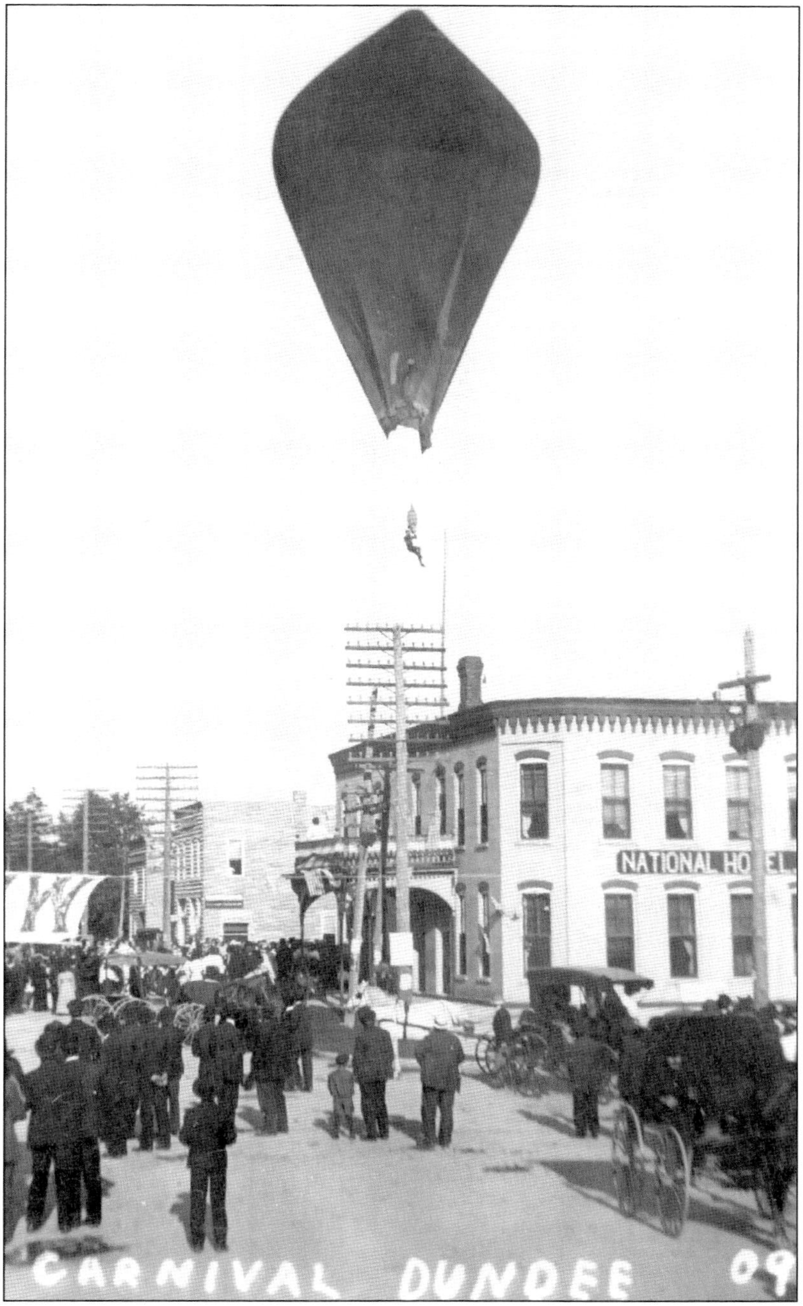

An acrobat provides another way to get himself into the air where he can perform; his balloon rises beyond the National Hotel. The acrobat has to be careful because it is a long way down without a net. The balloon is probably tethered and will come down when the hot air cools. A large banner, facing east, stretches across Main Street welcoming people to the 1909 carnival. Main Street was a principal entrance into town, especially for those arriving by train. The block building in the distance, the Mercantile, sports a Pacific Express sign. Pacific Express was the freight carrier of its time.

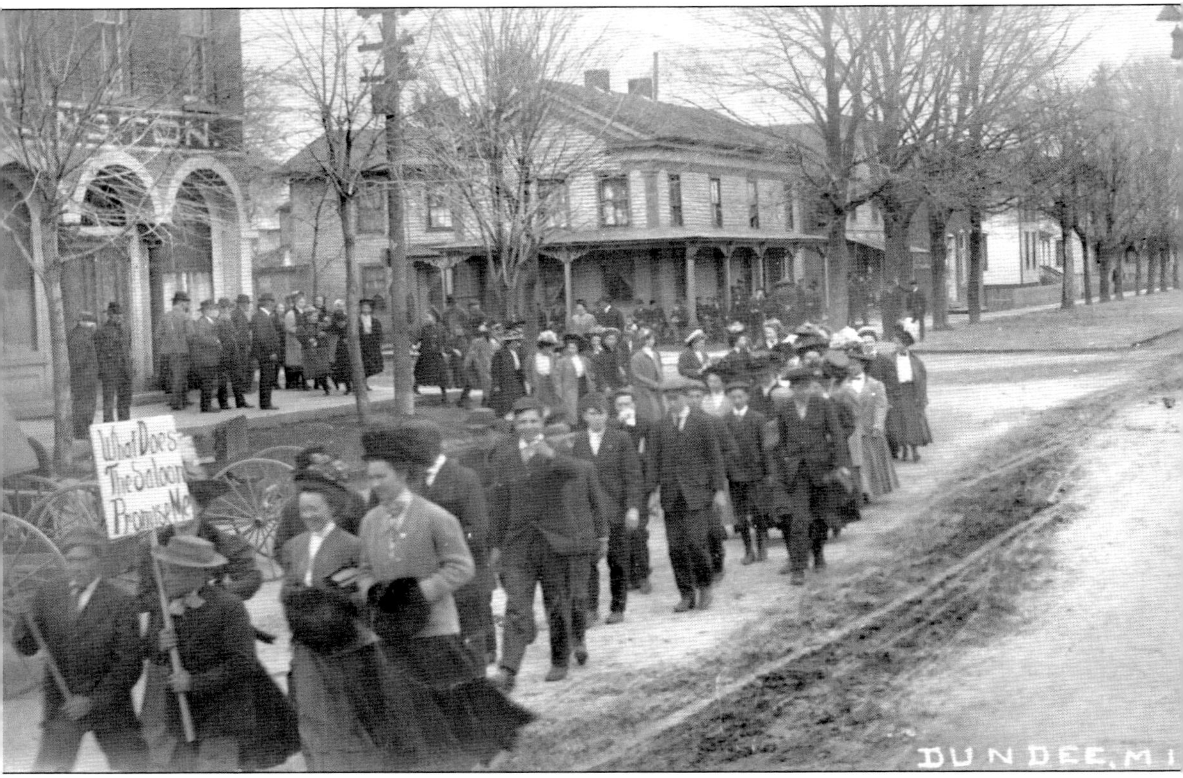

This temperance parade, around 1909, shows marchers coming down Ypsilanti Street and turning on to Main Street. Onlookers may have just exited the Hotel Pocklington's dining room, which serves alcohol. The sign reads, "What Does the Saloon Promise Me?" The *Dundee Reporter* of April 1, 1910, stated that the Michigan Anti-saloon League would appear at both the Congregational and Methodist churches and carried a list of local Prohibition candidates: Dennis Van Vleet ran for supervisor, William Coleman for clerk, and Clark N. Miller for treasurer; candidates for other positions included Willis Allman, Albert Miller, Perry Miller, Lamont Bragg, William Leach, Delmar Pelton, Earnest Spaulding, and Frank Leit. Not all agreed with the movement. When nearby counties went dry, some Dundeeites hoped to entice their thirsty neighbors.

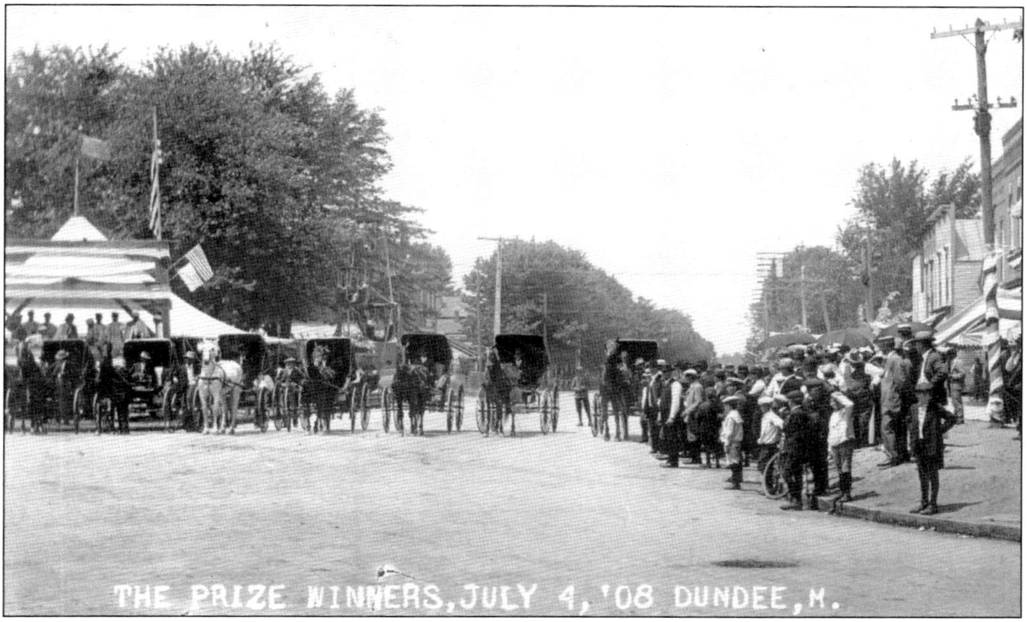

Horse-and-buggy judging took place during carnival times. Here, the horse-and-buggy prizewinners in the July 4, 1908, competitions line up across Tecumseh Street. The temporary reviewing stand can be seen on the left as well as a barely visible Ferris wheel to the right of it. The modest flagpole would be replaced in two years with a real skyscraper.

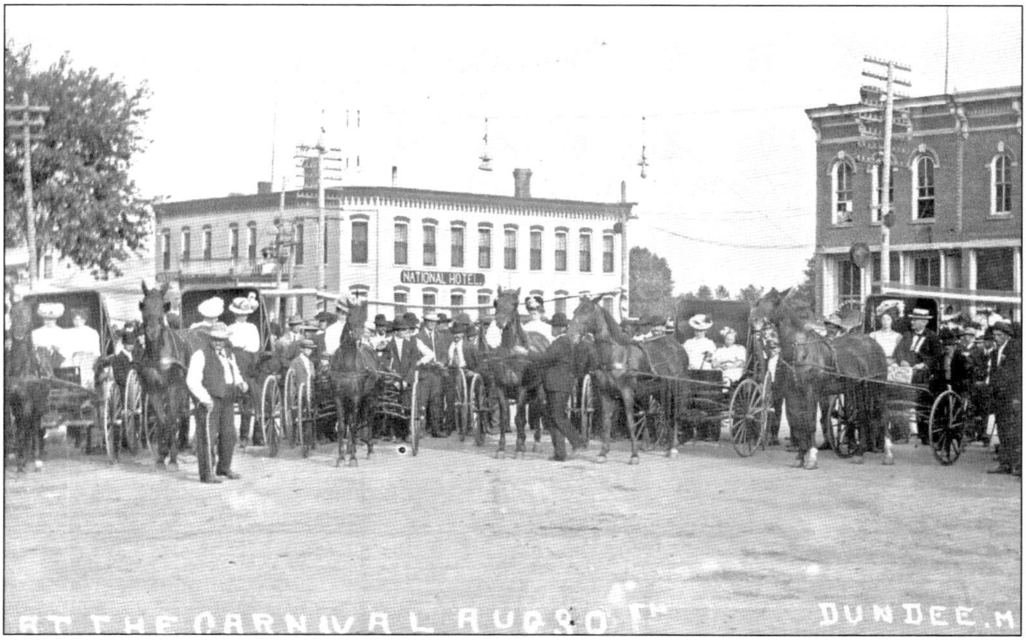

Posing looking west is a line of horse-drawn buggies driven by women, who are participating in the carnival. To the right, the first brick building displays a circular sign advertising beer and wine. It appears that this midtown intersection has been paved, removing the need for a water wagon to hold down dust.

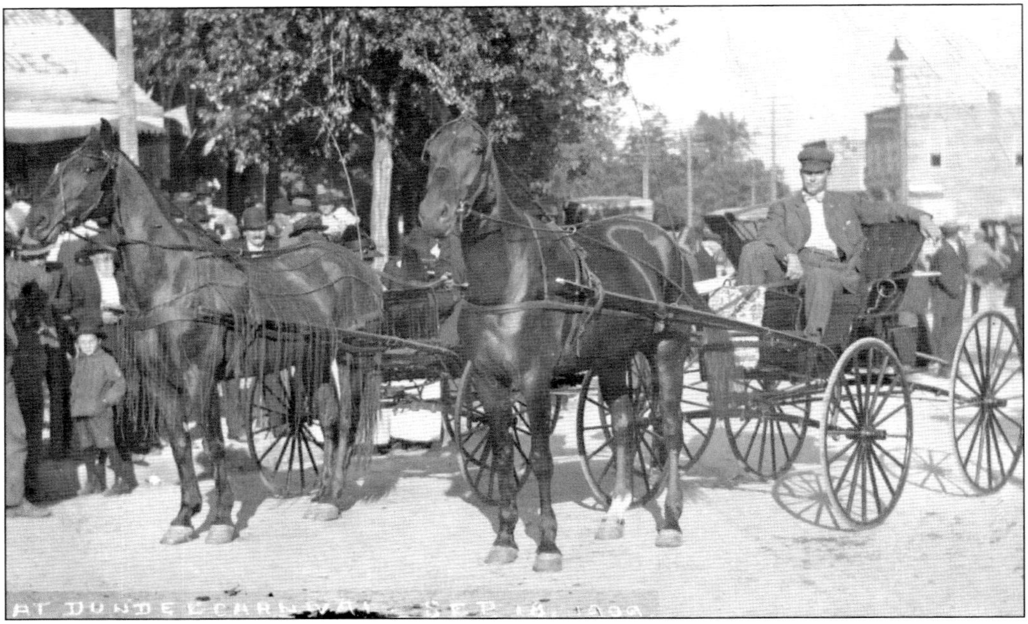

Here, one of the participants in the Dundee Carnival on September 18, 1909, is Thurlow Ellis driving two horses, one of which is Lady Ellis. He strikes a debonair pose while the horses suspiciously eye the camera. Ellis had driven in from his farm on Michigan Highway 50 west of town, taking a break from his busy life as a farmer. His horse and buggy are definitely high class.

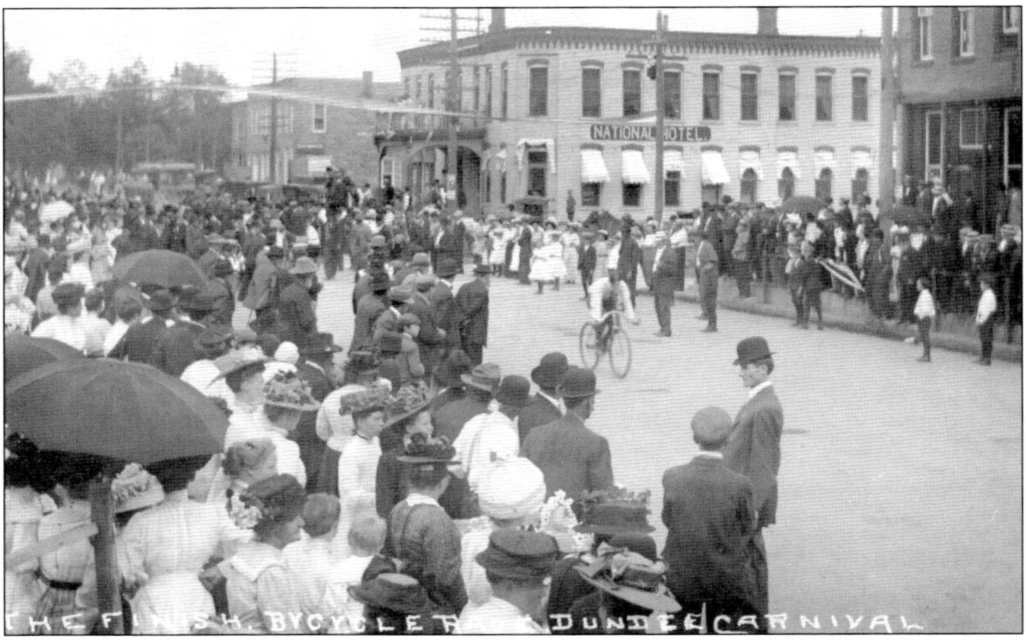

Horses were not the only racers. Bicyclists took part in the 1908 Dundee Carnival. A throng watches the race as a bicyclist (center) reaches the finish line. Several small groups are chatting among themselves while they wait. Many of the ladies are wearing bonnets, individualized with displays of "flowers." Umbrellas appear here and there, apparently to ward off the sun.

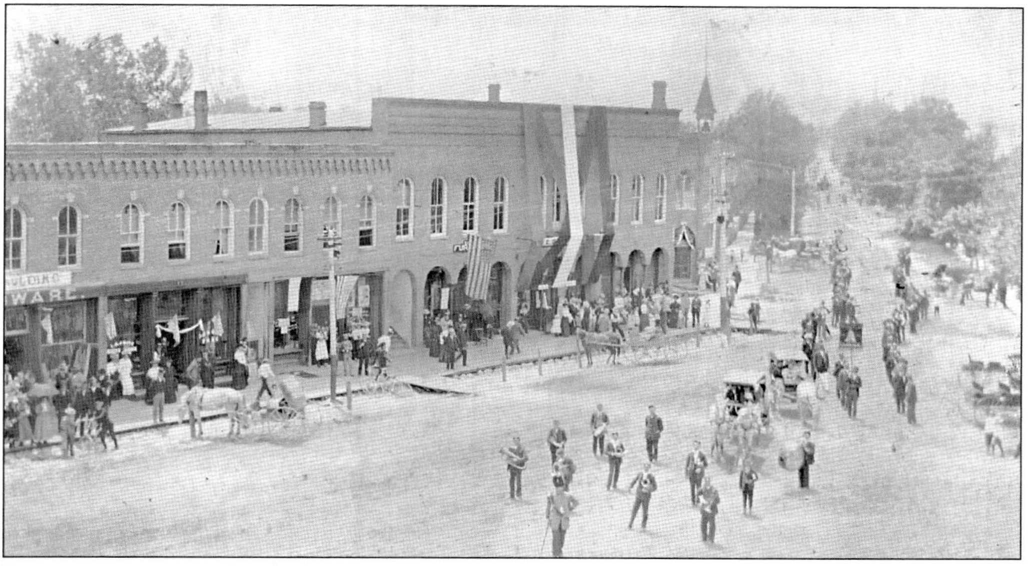

From time to time, individual organizations would stage parades. Around 1900, the Maccabees are seen marching down Riley Street. This was a fraternal insurance group with the men organized in tents and the women in hives. This scene shows electric poles, erected in 1894, painted white by council decree. The Dundee Bank shares a store with L.B. Smith, Boots and Shoes, and the horses are tied to wooden hitching posts.

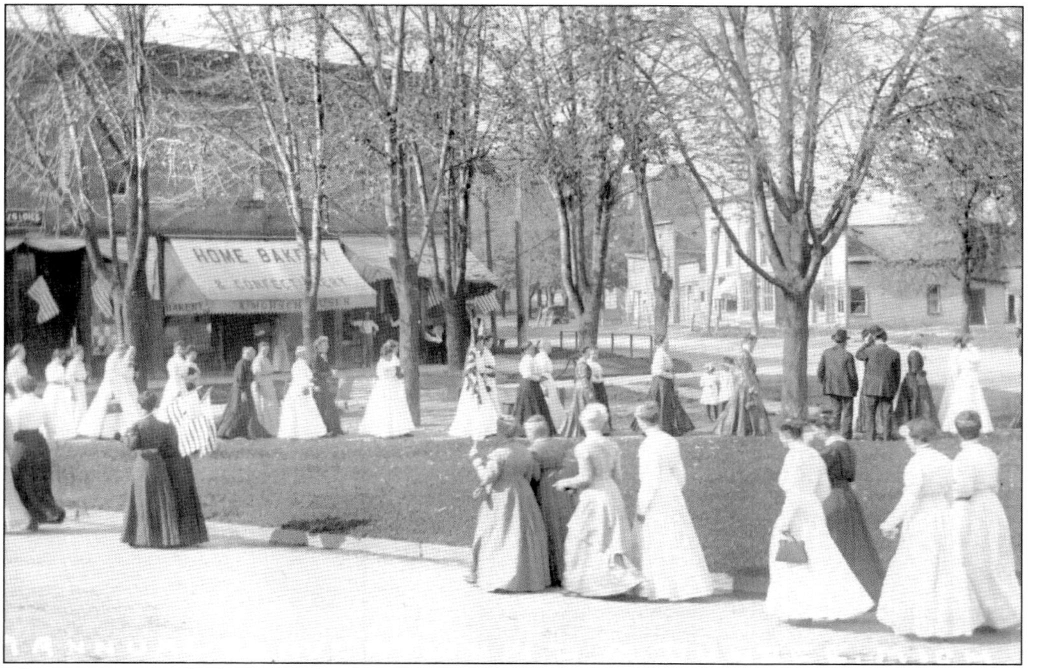

The Women's Relief Corps of Dundee marches around the triangle around 1911. It is corps No. 11, one of the first in Michigan when it was organized in 1884. Its mission was to offer assistance to Civil War veterans and their families. The group was quite active in Dundee into the 1950s and, unlike the Grand Army of the Republic, allowed succeeding generations to join.

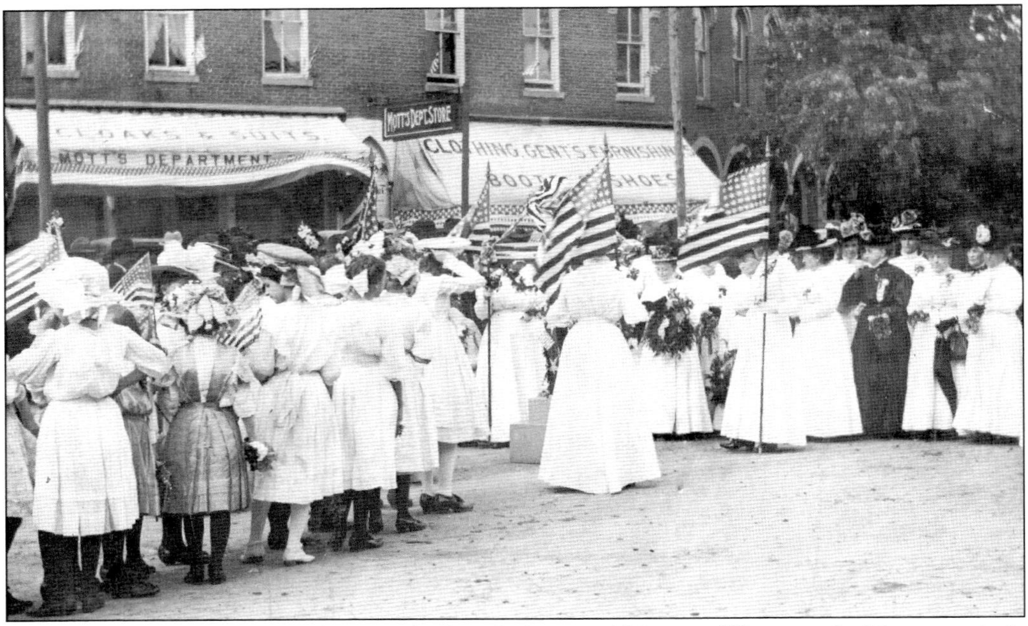

The Women's Relief Corps is forming for Dundee's annual Memorial Day parade. These patriotic women are organizing themselves in front of Mott's Department Store at 102 and 108 Riley Street. The younger girls are grouped to the left wearing slightly shorter white dresses than their older relatives. One of the ladies is carrying a wreath to be dropped from the bridge in honor of Civil War sailors.

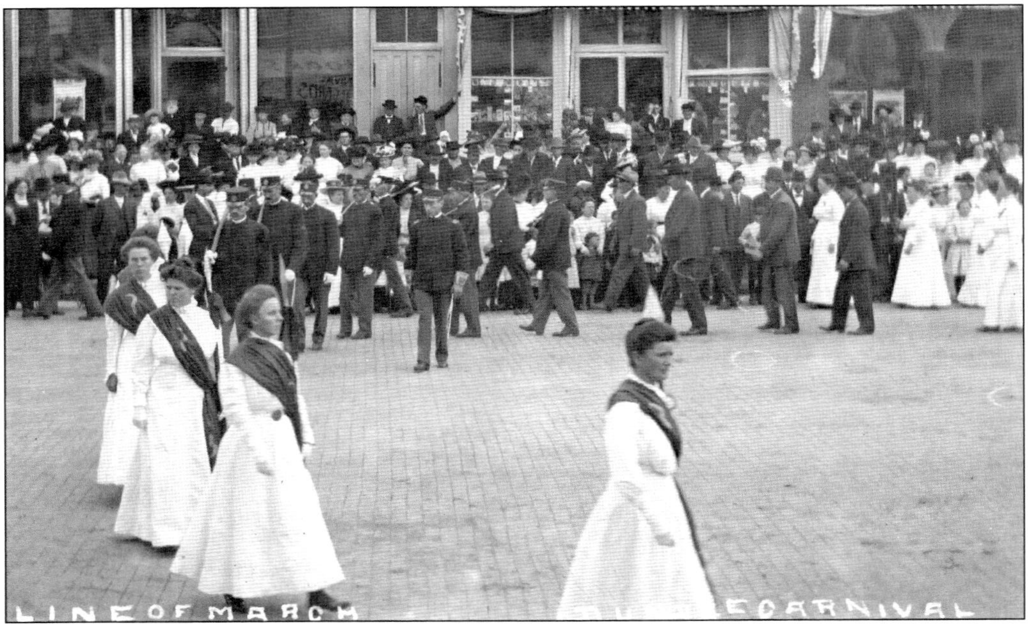

The Woodmen and their auxiliary, the Neighbors, are marching in front of the Dundee Candy Kitchen doing a drill in competition with other groups. The women are shown wearing distinctive sashes featuring scythes. The bricks on the newly paved street can be clearly seen. Among the posters in the store window is one advertising matinee trotting races at the fairgrounds.

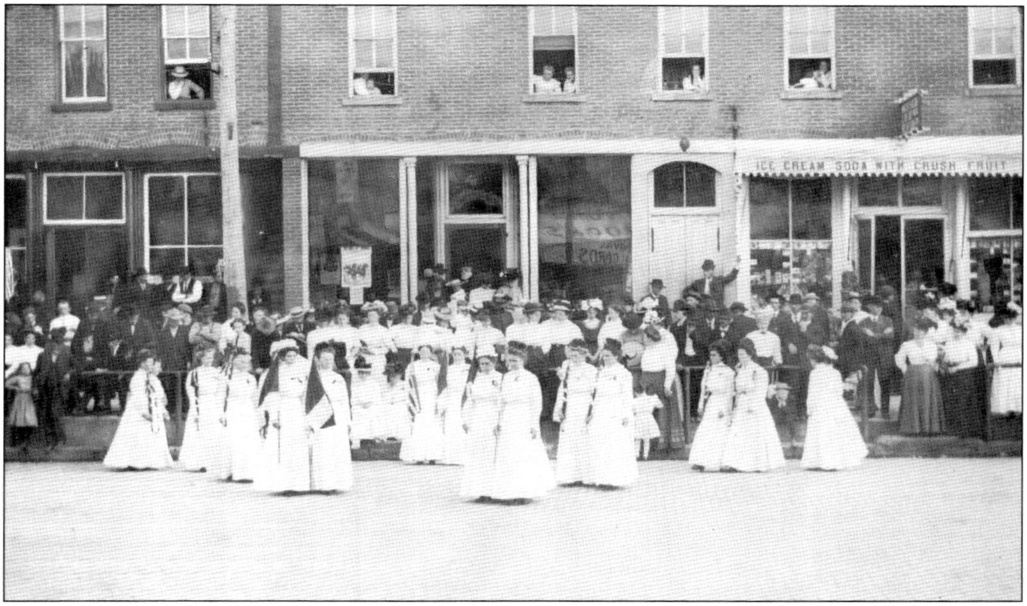

The Lady Maccabees won first prize for a drill at the Dundee Carnival around 1910. They are seen performing intricate formations on Riley Street in front of the reviewing stand, which is on the triangle. The women are carrying colored flags; most are wearing white bonnets, but a few wear black.

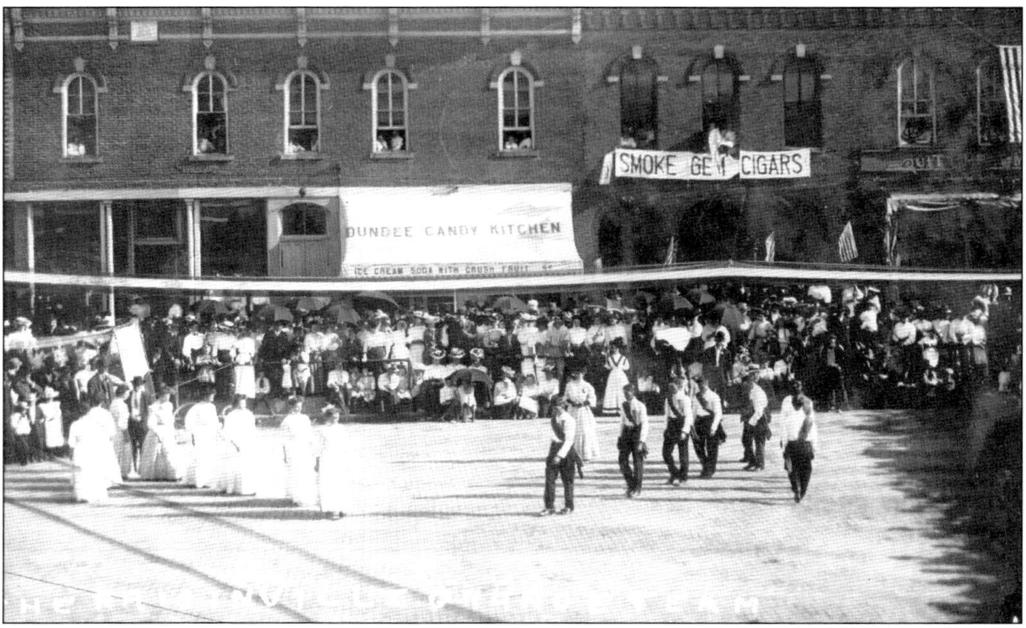

It is time for the Raisinville Grange Team to show its drill while competing at the carnival. The group is performing on Riley Street. A ribbon of decorative bunting is stretched behind the heads of the spectators. A cigar-manufacturing company is seen above them; two such stores were on the triangle. Here, the Gem Company is taking this opportunity to advertise. In many photographs, the Dundee Candy Kitchen awning appears.

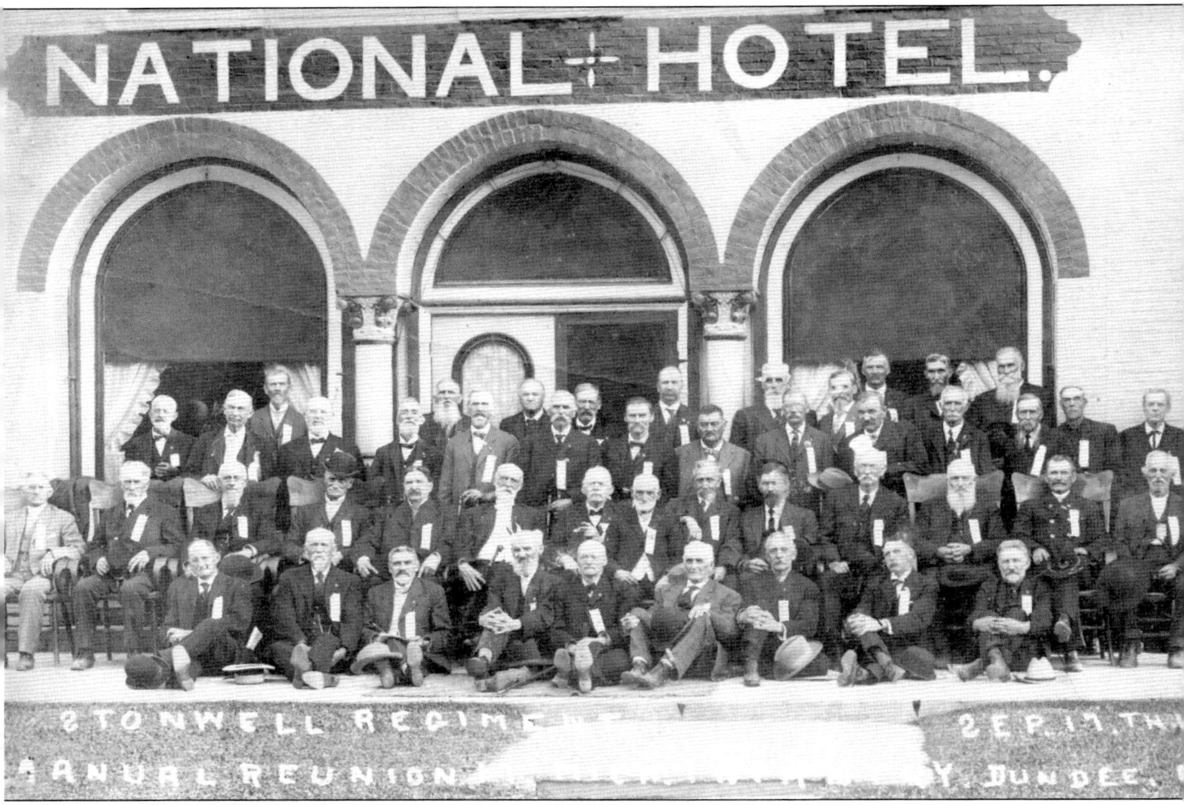

The date is September 17, 1908, and these grand gentlemen are posing in front of the National Hotel. This was the 27th reunion of the Stonewall Regiment of the Michigan 17th Infantry, which fought early in the Civil War. The regiment received its nickname from fighting at the Battle of South Mountain in western Maryland, where the Michigan boys drove the Confederates from behind a stone wall. At the time of the image, it was actually 43 years since the Civil War had ended. Note that on the photograph the "S" is printed backwards and "Stonewall" is misspelled. The lettering was done by hand on the negative.

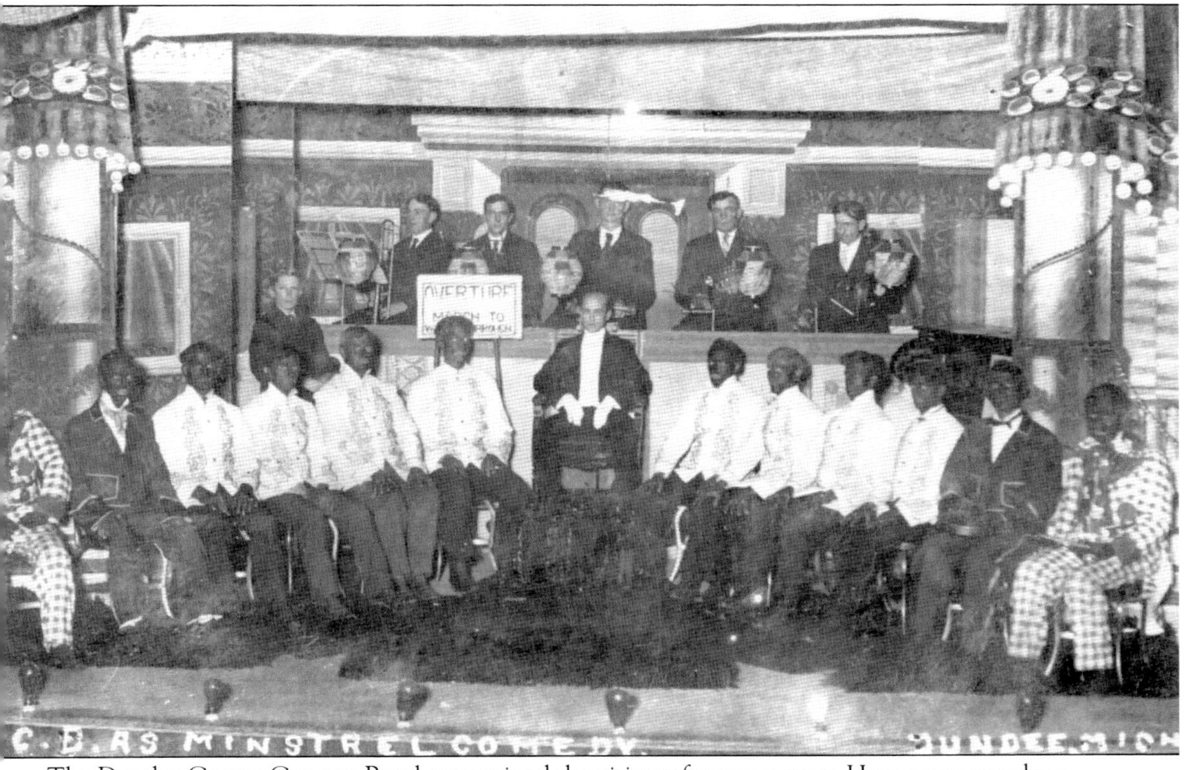

The Dundee Cornet Concert Band entertained the citizens for many years. Here, some members appear in blackface for a minstrel show. The trombonist's music sheet was published by Will Rossiter, who specialized in minstrels. This is a rare, undated photograph of the Dundee Opera House stage on Riley Street. The exact demise of the opera house is not known, but a notice in the *Dundee Reporter* of March 18, 1910, states that the Loyal Order of The Modern Maccabees "have served dinner each day for the Sir Knights, who were working in the old opera house, transforming it into one of the most convenient and spacious halls to be found in southern Michigan." Mimicking African Americans was considered acceptable entertainment at this time.

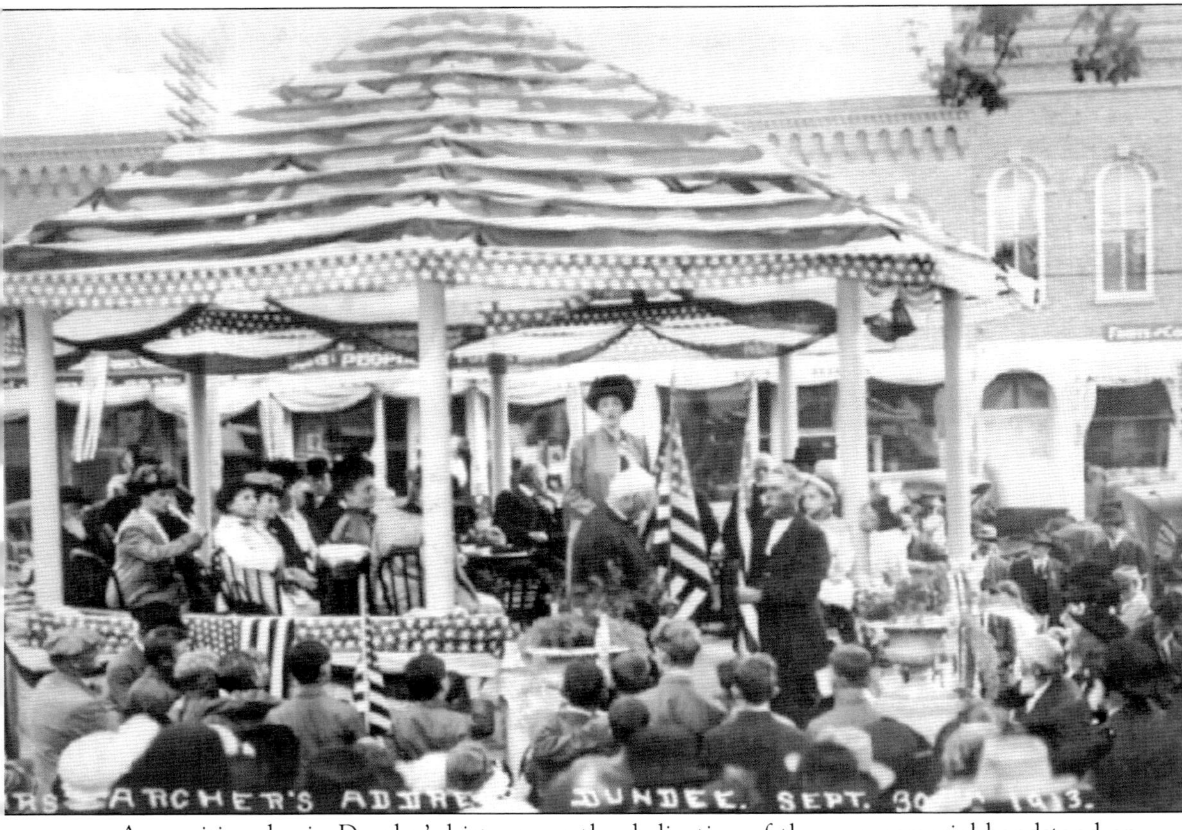

An exciting day in Dundee's history was the dedication of the war memorial bandstand on September 30, 1913. Martha Archer is seen here addressing the crowd. She was the sparkplug behind all the triangle memorials. Archer, the daughter of a Civil War veteran and the wife of a Spanish American War veteran, was a very patriotic lady with a devotion to her country's flag and its war veterans. She proposed and helped raise the funds for the following memorials: the Parrott gun, the very tall flagpole, and this bandstand. This culminating memorial contained engraved stones memorializing the veterans of the Civil and Spanish American Wars.

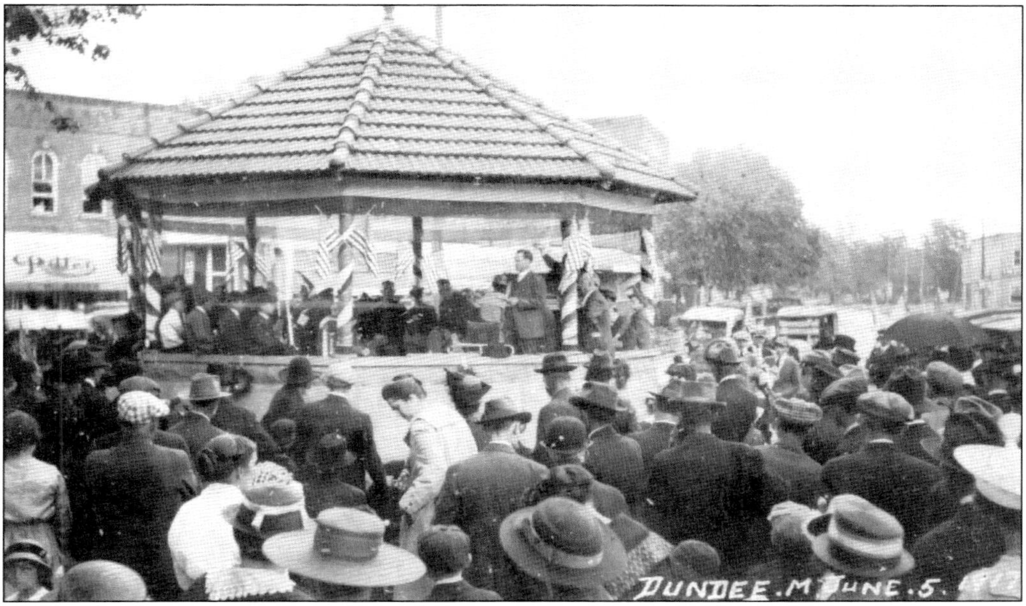

The bandstand is again the focus of a patriotic event. On June 5, 1917, two months after the United States entered World War I, Dundee held a parade. Mayor Ollie E. Mott is addressing the throng gathered at the gazebo. This was a time for the community to stand together to show its support for the troops.

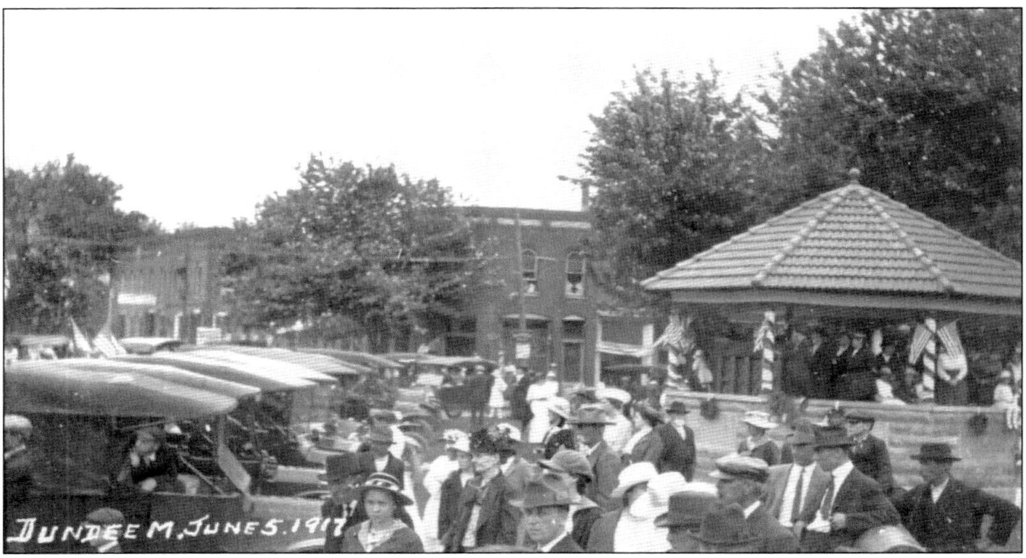

Times have changed, as seen on this June 5, 1917 image. Previously, horses and buggies lined Dundee's streets, but this day an impressive row of roadsters shows that the automobile has definitely caught on in Dundee. The milling crowd seems to suggest they are waiting for a parade to begin. The somberness of the faces reflects the seriousness of the war situation.

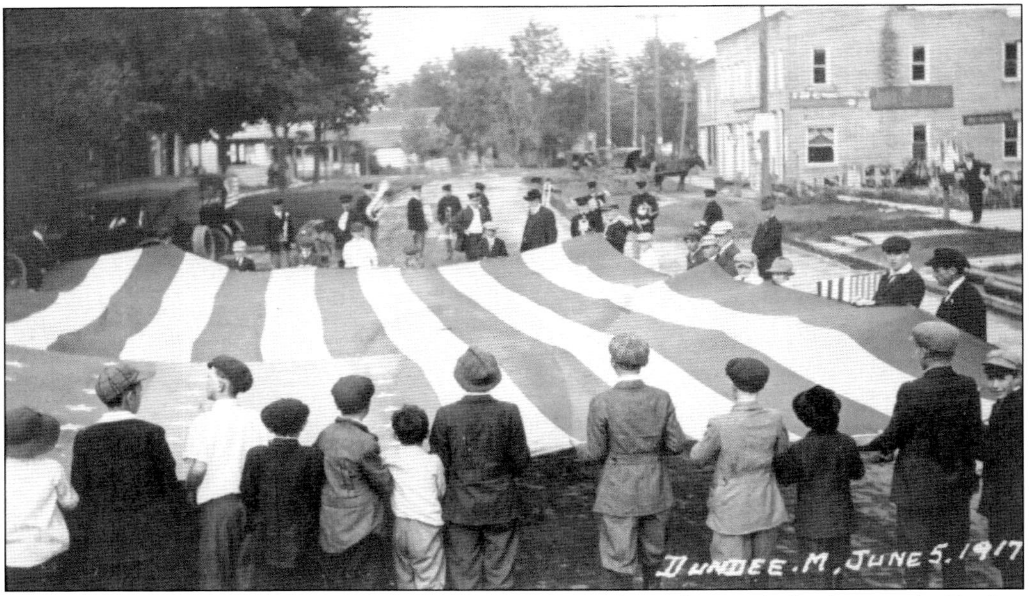

On June 5, 1917, a group of men and boys is seen getting a huge flag ready for the parade. Farther down Main Street, band members are assembling. A sign of the changing times, two cars are parked to the left, and two buggies are "parked" in front of the mercantile.

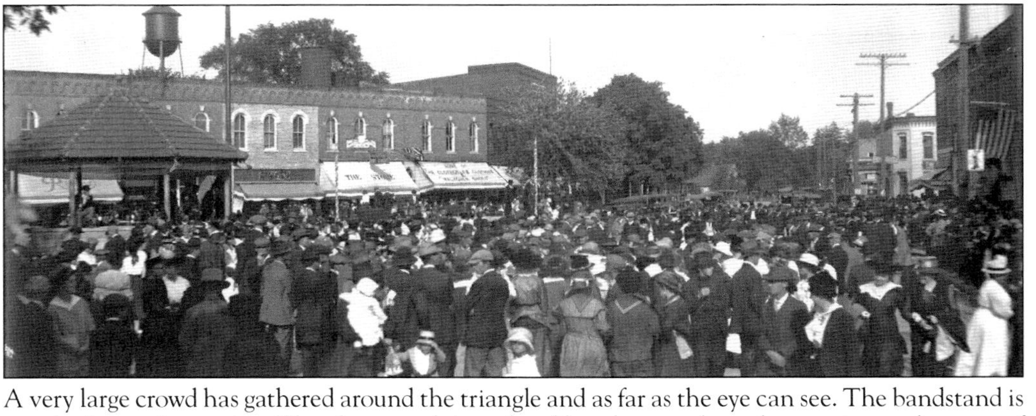

A very large crowd has gathered around the triangle and as far as the eye can see. The bandstand is not the focus of attention. The photograph is undated but the crowd may be reacting to the news of World War I victories as the end of the war approaches. (Photograph by Virgil Van DeVenter.)

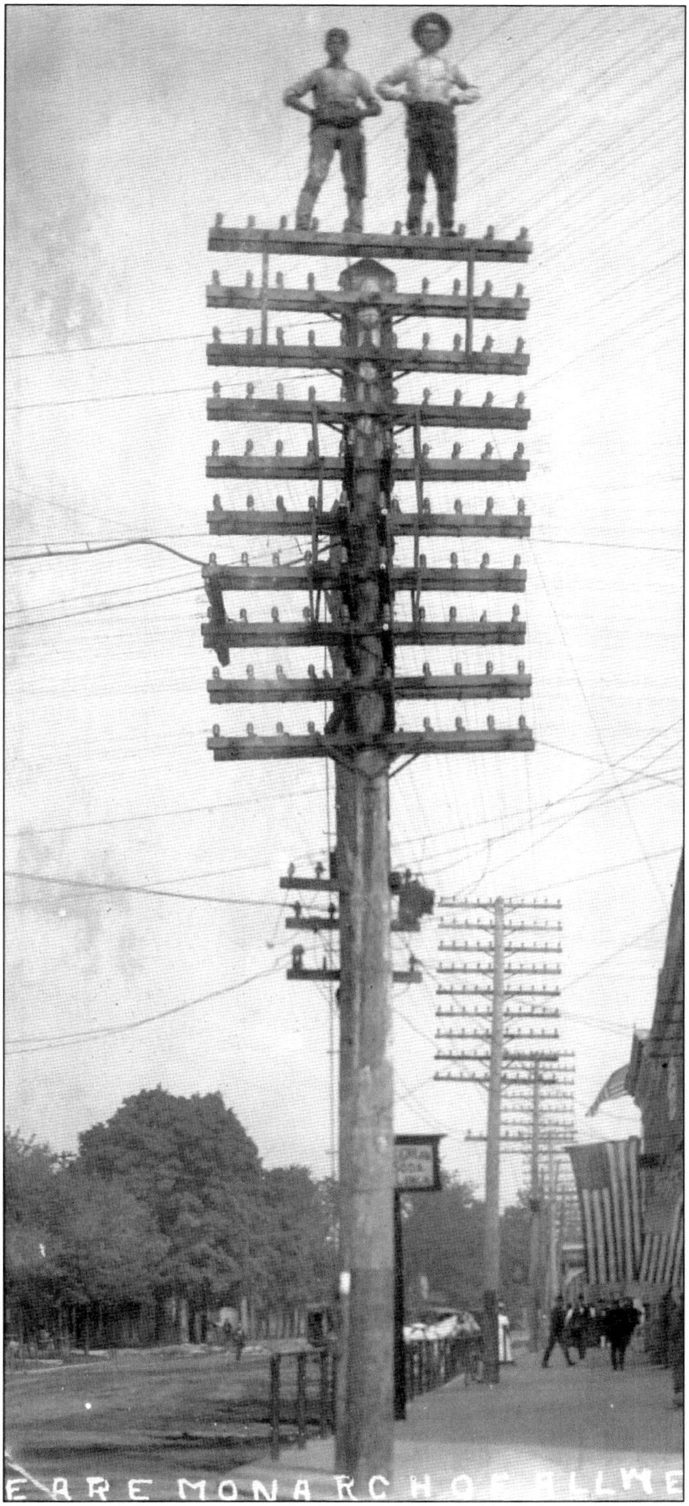

This could be called a form of entertainment—for only the most agile. In the early 1900s, two brave men have climbed up what was probably a telephone pole in front of the Monroe County Bank at 145 Riley Street. Both men got down safely. It is believed they were Fred Daly and Ham Munson. Written on the photograph is "we are monarch of all we survey," especially if the descent was uneventful. Daly worked as an electrician. The Dundee High School Ham Munson Trophy, given to each year's outstanding male athlete, is named in his honor. This was the era when the downtown had telephone poles with a multitude of crossbars even though many customers were on party lines.

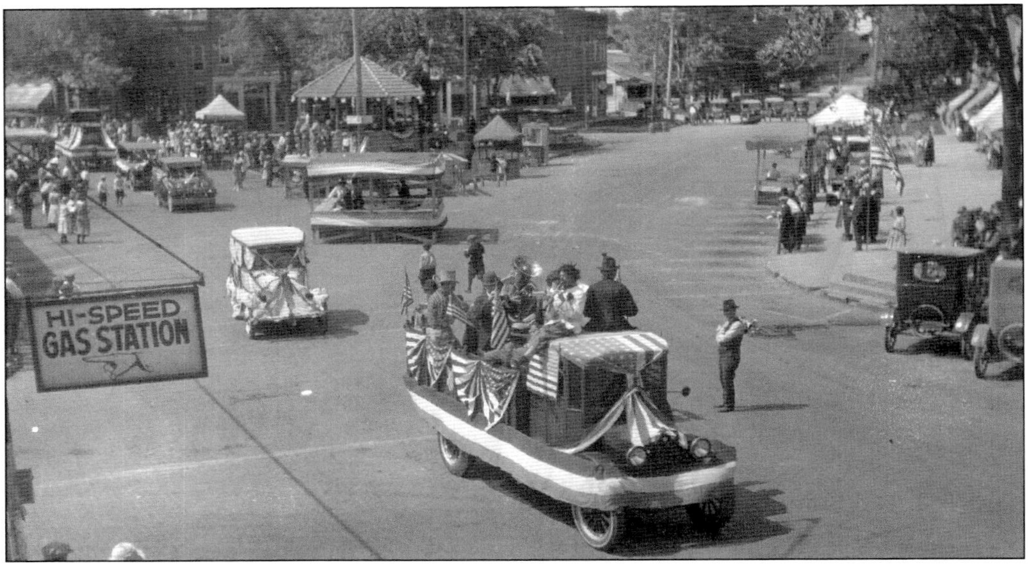

This parade took place September 4, 1924, as the town celebrated Labor Day. The line is marching west to east with a row of cars blocking traffic on Tecumseh Street. The bunting-draped float carries the popular Dundee Cornet Concert Band. The reviewing stand has been constructed at the point of the triangle. The sign for the Hi-Speed gas station, next to the National Hotel, peeks into view on the left.

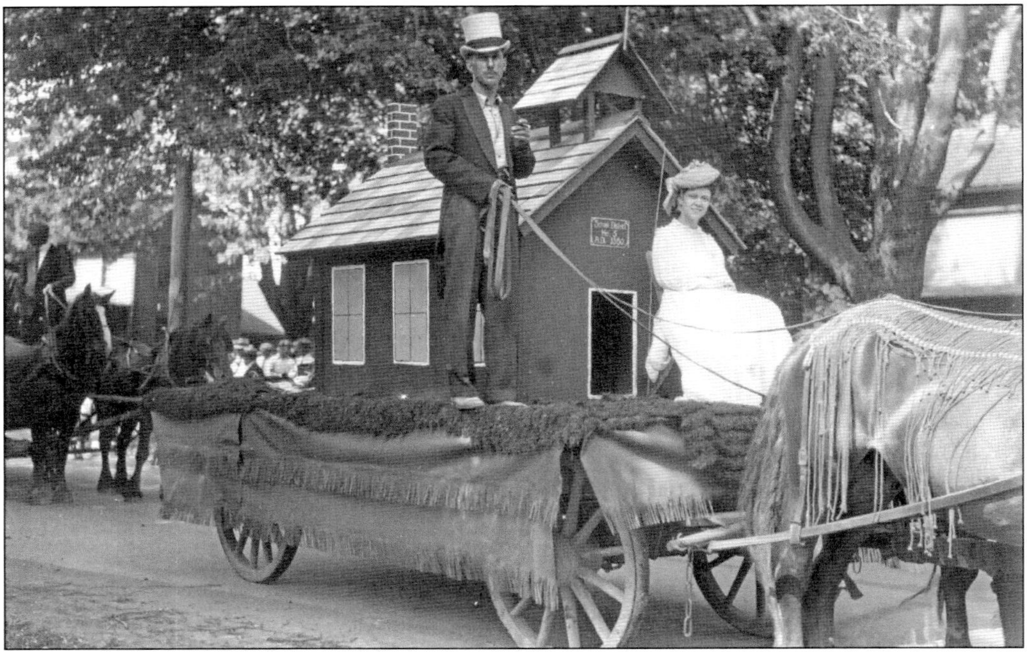

The town threw a dandy of a homecoming in 1929. It is possible that only the sesquicentennial rivaled it. Over 3,000 former residents returned to Dundee to celebrate for three days in September. The highlight of the activities was on Monday, September 2, with the old-time parade, which featured only animal-powered floats. In 1929, many of the one-room schools were still operating. This replica of an 1880s one-room school was a tribute to them.

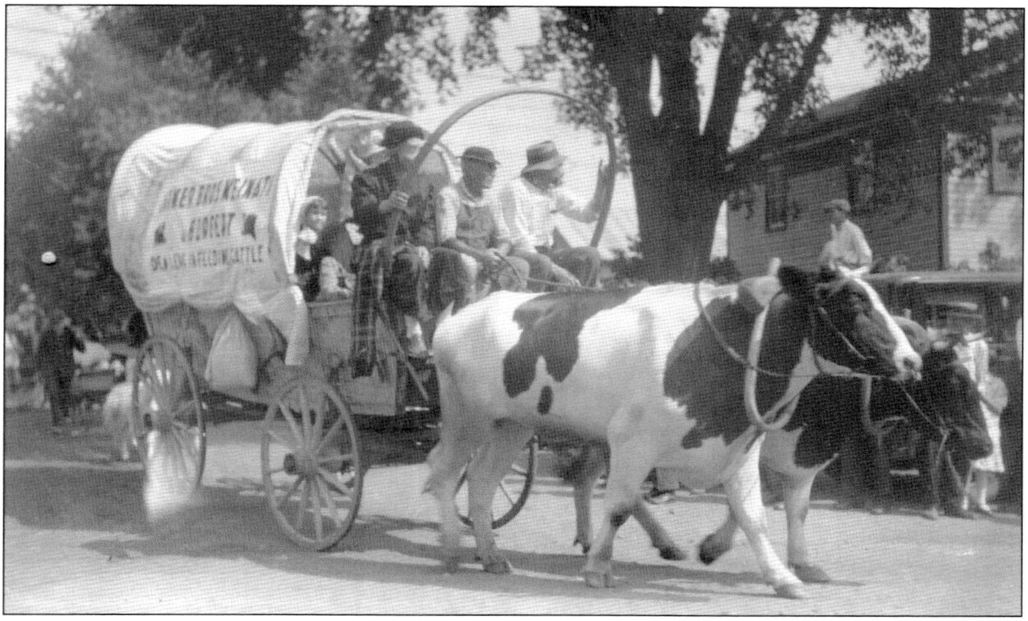

Karner Bros. and Keinath Elevator was on Main Street across the train tracks from Railroad Street. Its parade entry, a replica prairie schooner pulled by a team of oxen, won the $4 first prize. Although the wagon is more associated with travel across the prairie, some early settlers may have made their way to Dundee in this type of conveyance.

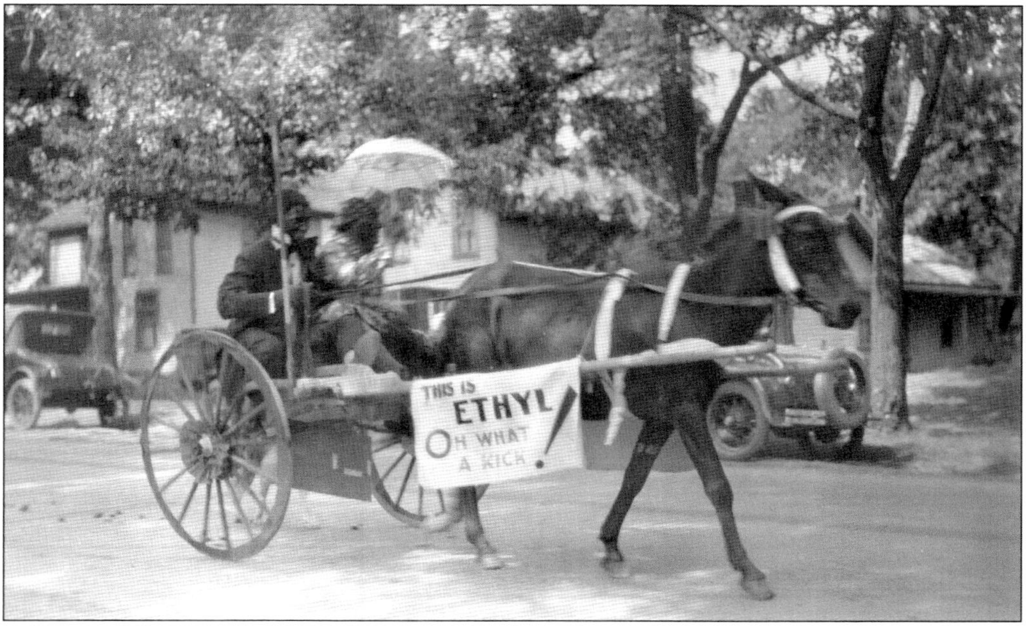

Leo Perry (left) and Stanley Collins are driving Ethyl. The mule wanted the "good old days" to continue. A new gasoline additive, tetraethyl lead, which promised to deliver a "kick," challenged her. Ethel wanted to remind everyone that she could actually kick as well. The gentlemen are in blackface. Citizens, apparently unaware or unconcerned that this might give offense, appeared in blackface in minstrels shows into the 1950s.

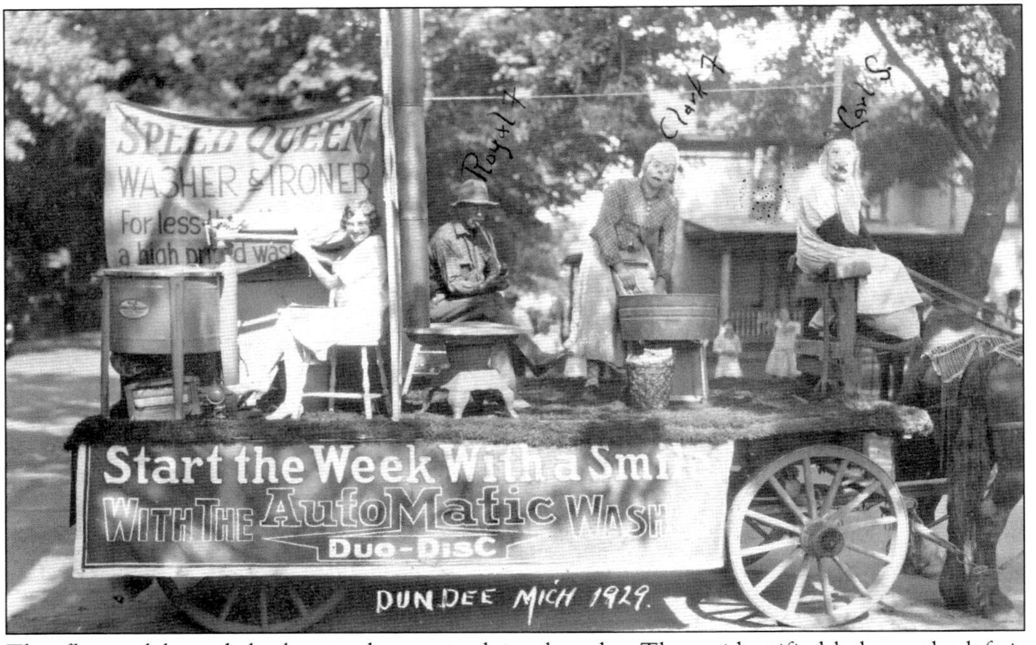

This float celebrated the latest advance in doing laundry. The unidentified lady on the left is enjoying her wringer washer and is oblivious to the antics of her male cohorts, one of whom, in drag, is willing to spoof doing the job the old-fashioned way. The gentlemen are Royal F(isher), Clark F(isher), and Carl S(chultz).

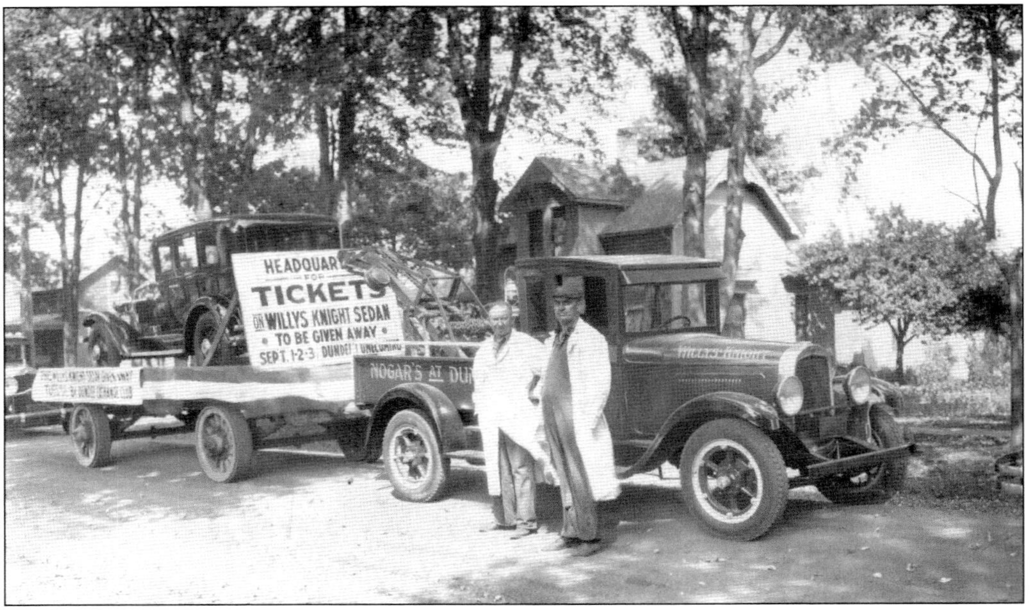

The culmination of three fun-filled, never-to-be-forgotten days was the drawing for the big prize, a $1,200 Willys-Knight sedan sponsored by the Dundee Exchange Club. The shiny new car is being displayed on a trailer behind the truck. Everyone held their breath while the winning number was drawn. The winner went home with a new car, and everyone else left with happy memories of their hometown. (Courtesy of Mary Jo Brossia.)

Four

Misfortunes of All Kinds

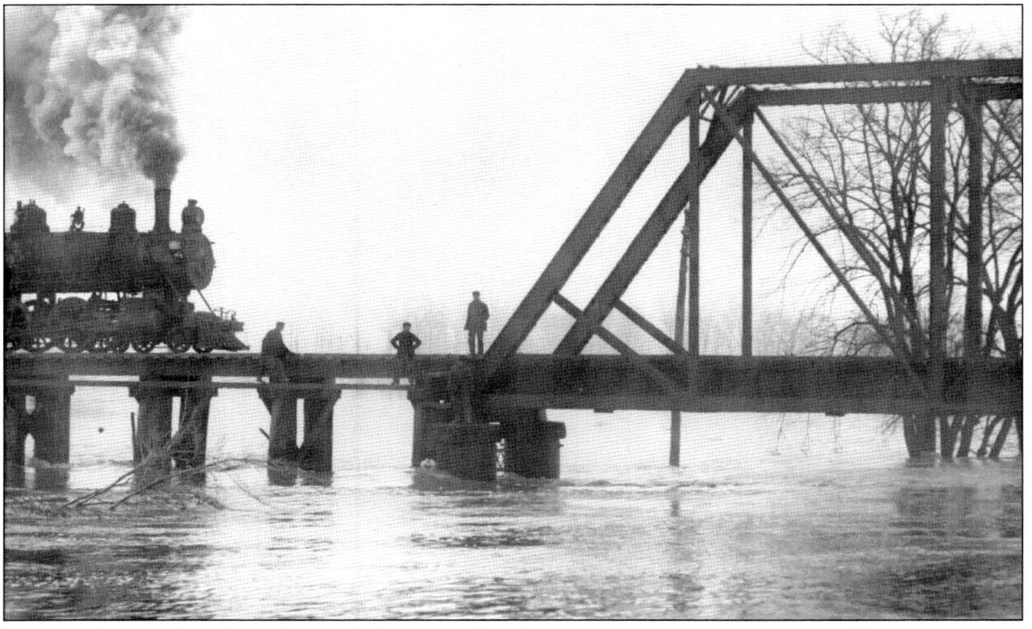

Dundee has endured its share of disasters: flooding, fire, wrecks, and storms. The continuing scourge is flooding from the River Raisin. The most serious event occurred in March 1908, with another in 1914. There have been notable floods in 1947, 1978, and 2009. In either 1908 or 1914, men are checking to see if the bridge will hold. An older steam engine—with a kerosene lantern at the front—waits to cross.

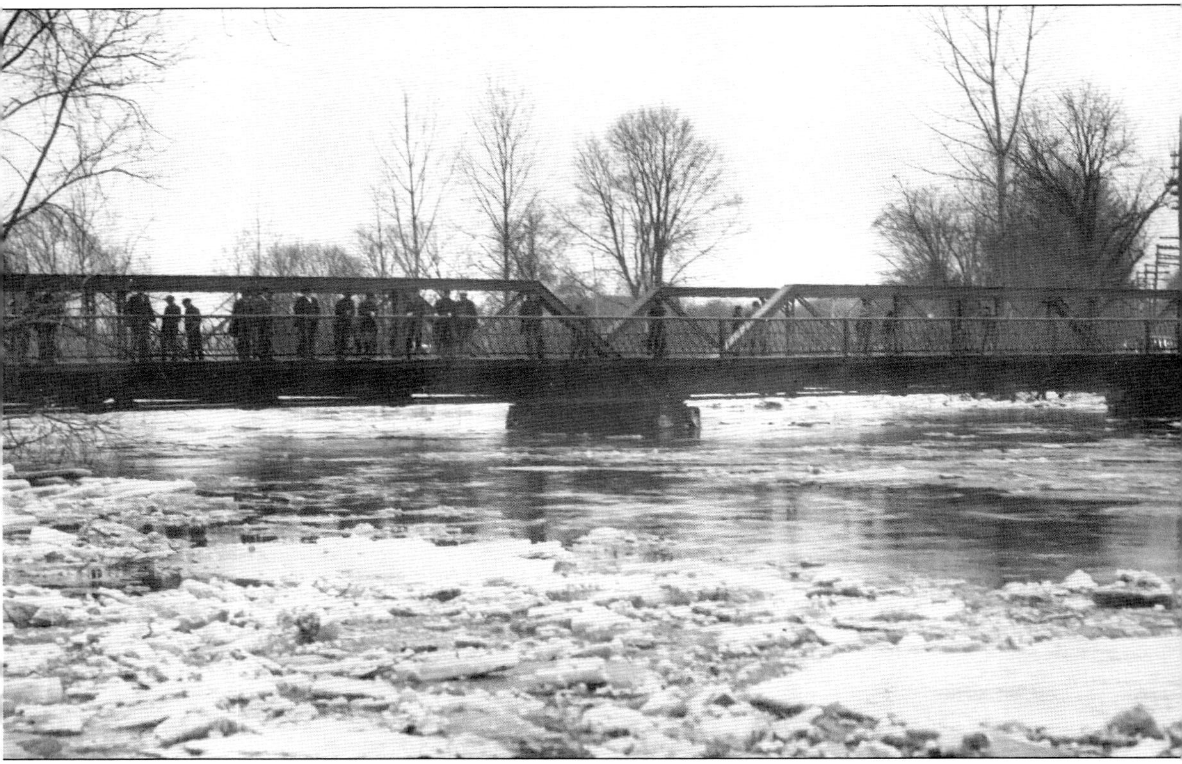

Men are assessing the condition of the Dundee Bridge in 1908. The March 13 *Dundee Reporter* noted, "Terror added to the situation when it was learned . . . that the bridge at Deerfield had given way. . . . Before night fall the water reached the iron girders of the [Dundee] bridge, and all the heavy blocks of ice, logs, and debris struck that iron structure with full force . . . officials set about to take all possible precaution. Two carloads of the heavy paving brick . . . were carried on the bridge and a force of workmen was kept busy all night caring for that property." The extra weight was to prevent the bridge from washing away. About midnight, the river was 15 feet above its normal level and 3 feet higher than the old "high water mark registered on the flouring mill forty years ago."

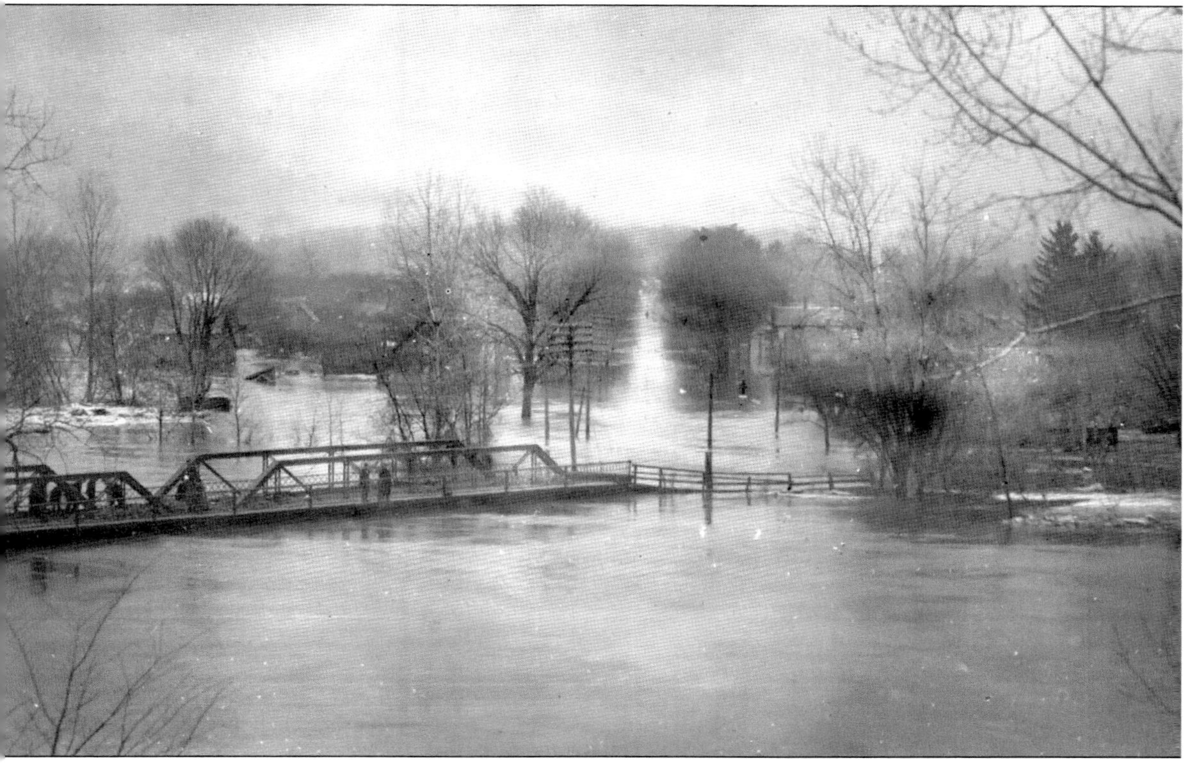

A heavy thunderstorm, an unusual amount of snow on the ground, ice, and a sudden thaw combined to create Dundee's worst flood. Great crowds visited the riverbanks all day Saturday and Sunday. "Despite the stinging chill of the damp air, people lingered for hours seemingly fascinated," the March 13, 1908, issue of the *Dundee Reporter* stated, "and loathe to leave the scene that was fast breaking all records of the past." This Sunday morning, March 8 photograph, looking east down Monroe Street, shows the River Raisin reaching almost to the flooring of the bridge. "A deluge," stated the *Dundee Reporter*, "good and plenty was come and had it not been for the bridge, no one would have known just where to locate the main channel of the river, as the current was everywhere strong and fierce."

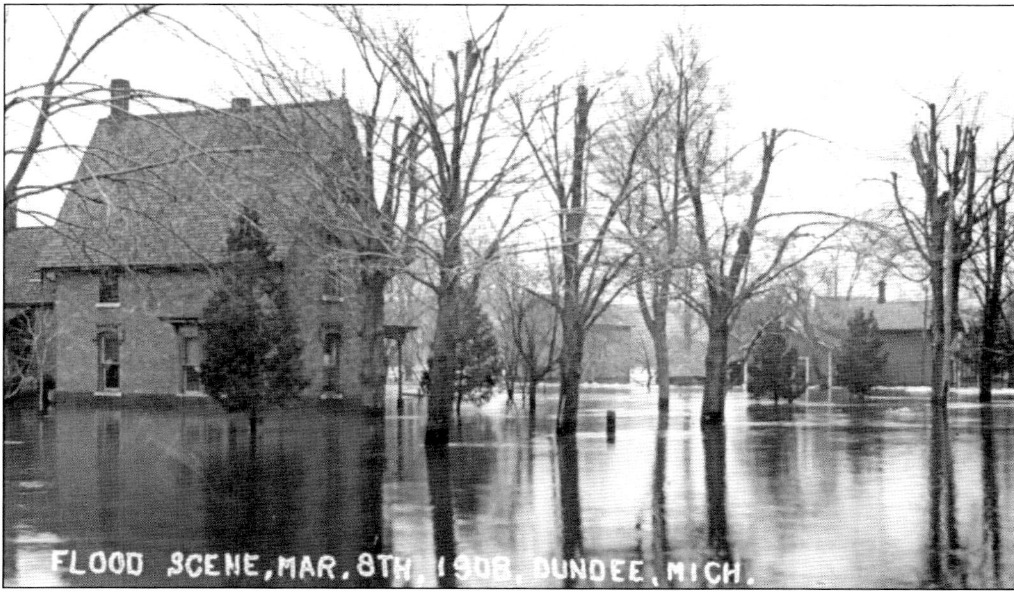

Toledo Street is seen here flooded in 1908. According to the March 13 *Dundee Reporter*, "The Ohio Dairy (located around the corner on Washington Street) was the first to feel the oncoming flood. . . . The men were marooned long before their work was done, but they made good their escape to terra firma by launching a milk vat and with the aid of a shovel, and some sticks, all reached the bridge in safety."

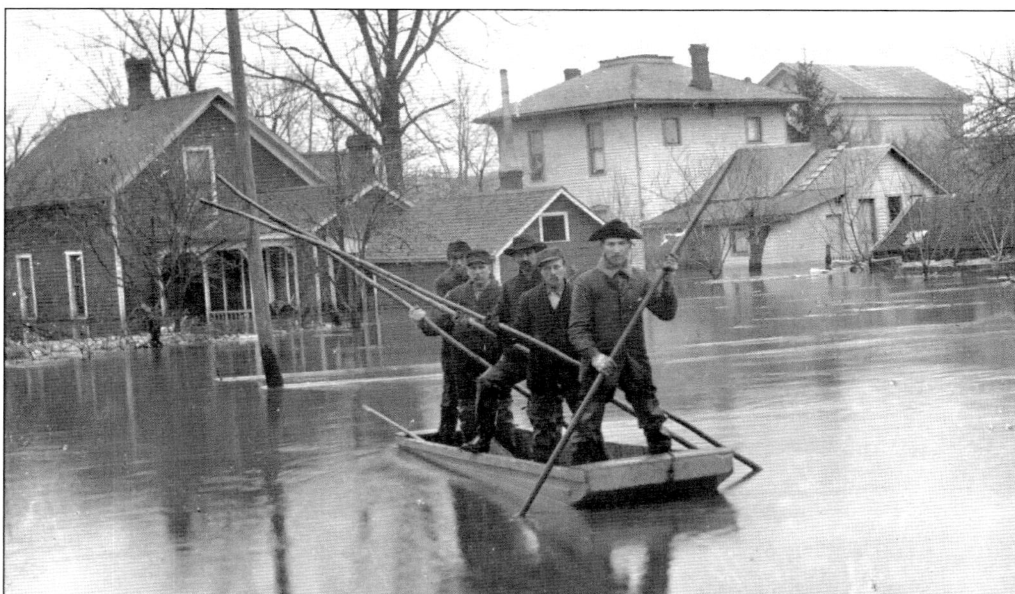

These men have commandeered a cement mixer to pole down Washington Street. During floods, five men called the "Band of Five" rowed through the stricken community offering assistance. The roof of the old mill is visible in the background. The Italianate home in the center still stands on Toledo Street.

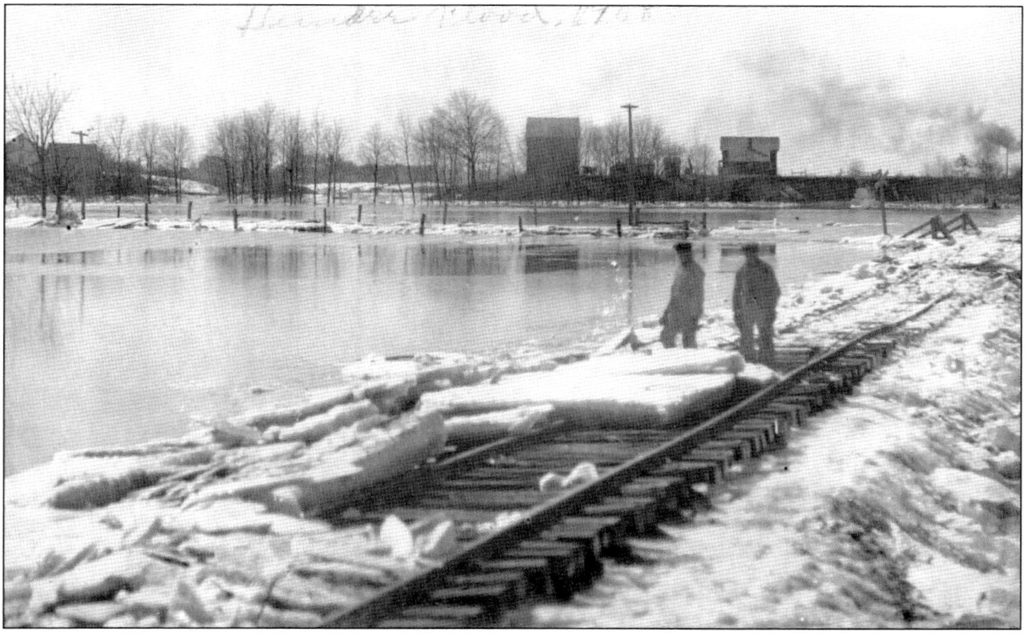

Henry Bigelow (left) and a companion clear the tracks after the 1908 flood. The *Dundee Reporter* wrote, "The DT&I bridge over the Saline near Bone Hill was stuck by a massive cake of ice early Saturday morning, breaking several of the piers, so that trains were unable to pass over the bridge for several days. The tracks of the Lake Shore west of town were all under water Saturday."

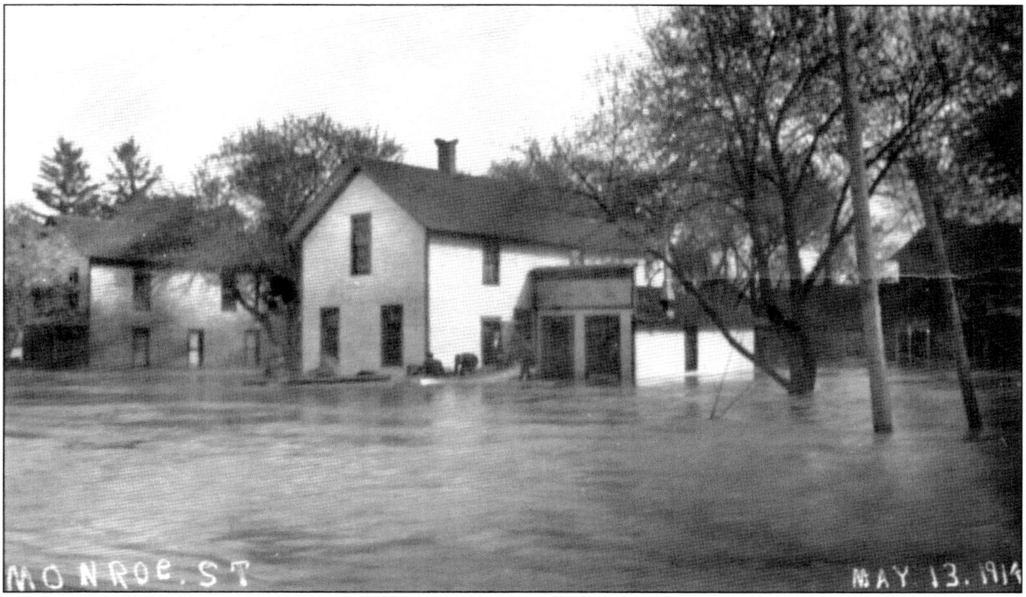

Another major flood occurred on May 13, 1914. A rowboat has pulled up to the house to offer help, and the water has reached the bottom of the windows here on Monroe Street. In every flood, homeowners on Monroe Street, from the downtown bridge to the railroad bridge, are inundated with floodwaters, occasionally to the depth of two feet.

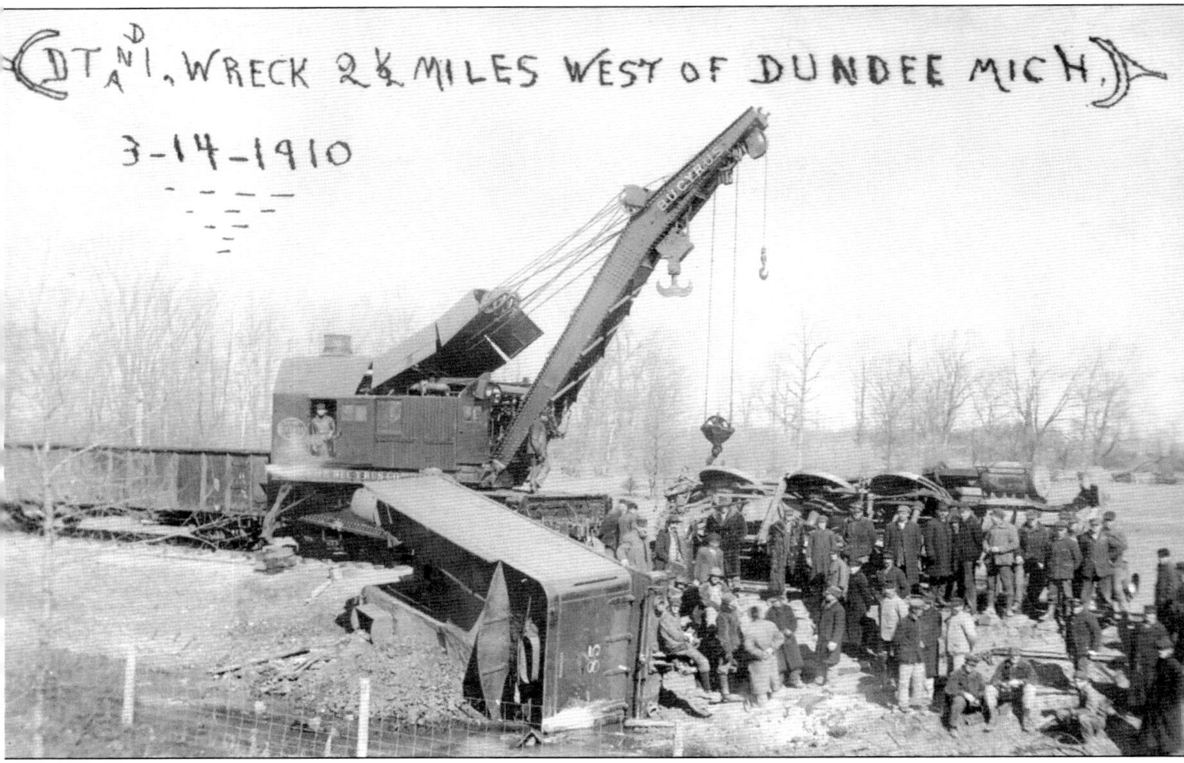

On March 14, 1910, a train wrecked 2.5 miles west of Dundee on the farm of Thurman Wiech on Rea Road. From the March 18, *Dundee Reporter*, "Monday last, a north bound freight on the DT&I . . . was found to be minus a portion of its train. The engine was dispatched in search of the missing cars. While backing, at a goodly rate of speed . . . just west of town, the rails spread, throwing the engine on its side across the track. The fireman and engineer were scalded and bruised, but not seriously." Here a heavy Bucyrus Company crane and a New York City work crew are preparing to lift the engine. A line of onlookers is aware of the camera.

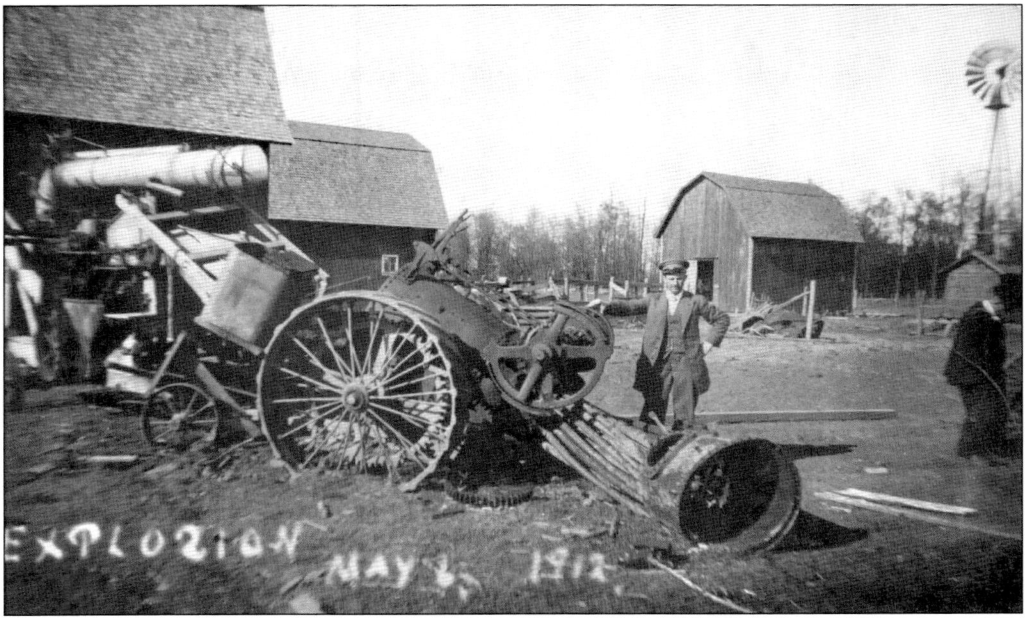

On May 6, 1912, John Stebbins, owner of a thrashing outfit, and his assistant Samuel Graves went to the Otto Drake farm, two miles west of Dundee. Stebbins's outfit had been stored there for the winter. Finishing repairs to the engine, the pair built a fire. Alas, there was an explosion that was so loud it was heard in town. The two men died in the accident.

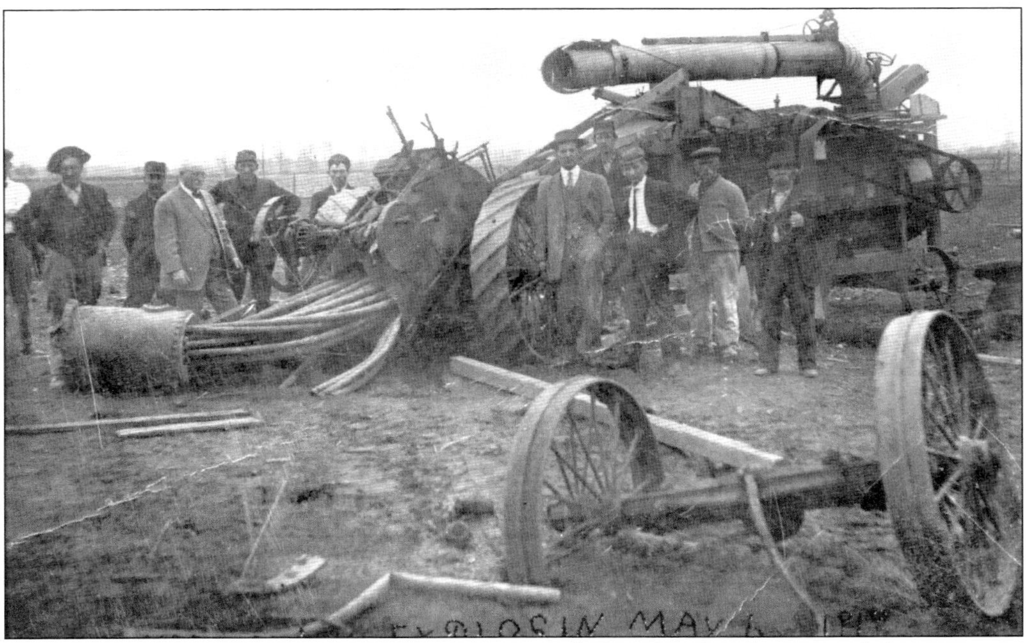

Dr. John B. Haynes, physician and mayor (center, in a light colored suit), pauses while examining the wreckage. The explosion blew off the front end of the traction engine, pulling out the boiler tubes. The doctor had been called to treat Stebbins and Graves, but, as the obituary noted, "They were so terribly injured" the men survived only three hours in the Drake home.

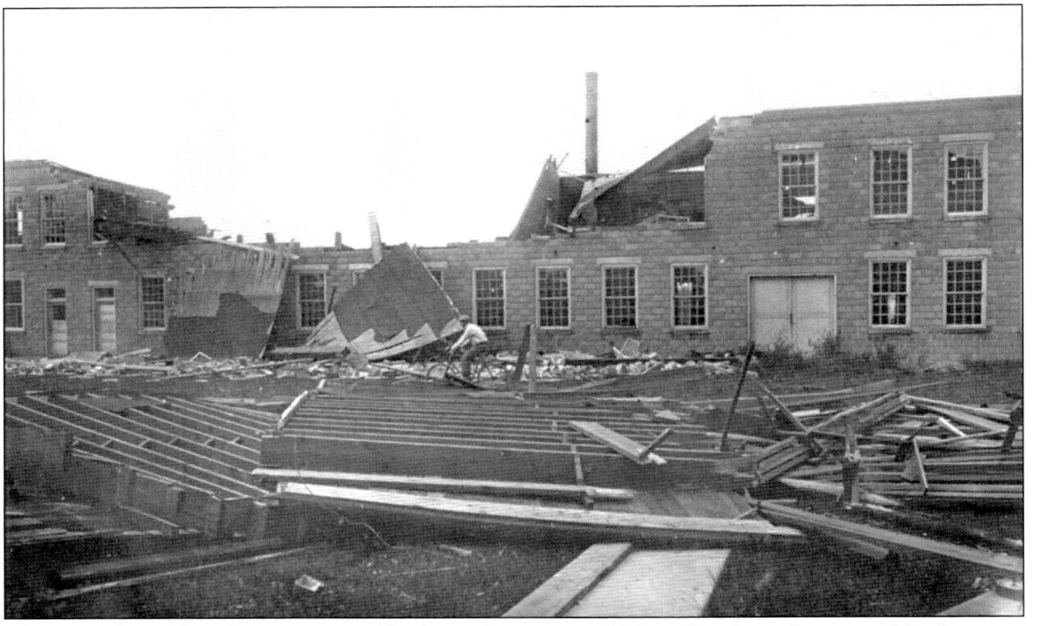

The DeVilbiss Plier Company, on Ypsilanti Street near Viking Boulevard, enjoyed high status among manufacturing plants in 1910, according to national magazine *Machinery*. But the very next year, the plant was hit by a tornado. The roof is upside down in the foreground, and cement blocks from the front wall are scattered about. A bicyclist nonchalantly peddles past the devastation. The structure was rebuilt and later became a suspender factory.

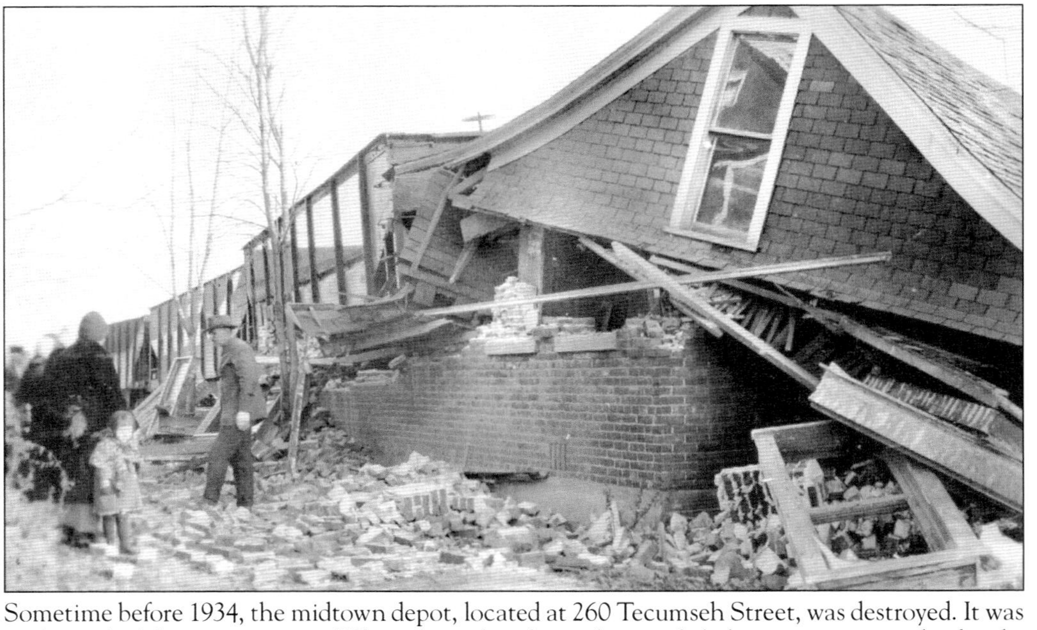

Sometime before 1934, the midtown depot, located at 260 Tecumseh Street, was destroyed. It was at the end of the turning wye. When the railroad switch crew failed to stop in time, the freight cars being backed into the spur ran through the stop and into the depot. Night watchman Tim Moor was injured. The station was never rebuilt.

In addition to floods from the River Raisin, Dundee has suffered its share of drownings. On July 14, 1951, two young men in their 20s, Calvin Tinsman and Charles Smith, were photographed as they paddled their canoe. Within minutes, the vessel capsized, and they were swept under by the treacherous undercurrent just below the dam. Rescuers are shown returning to shore with one of the bodies.

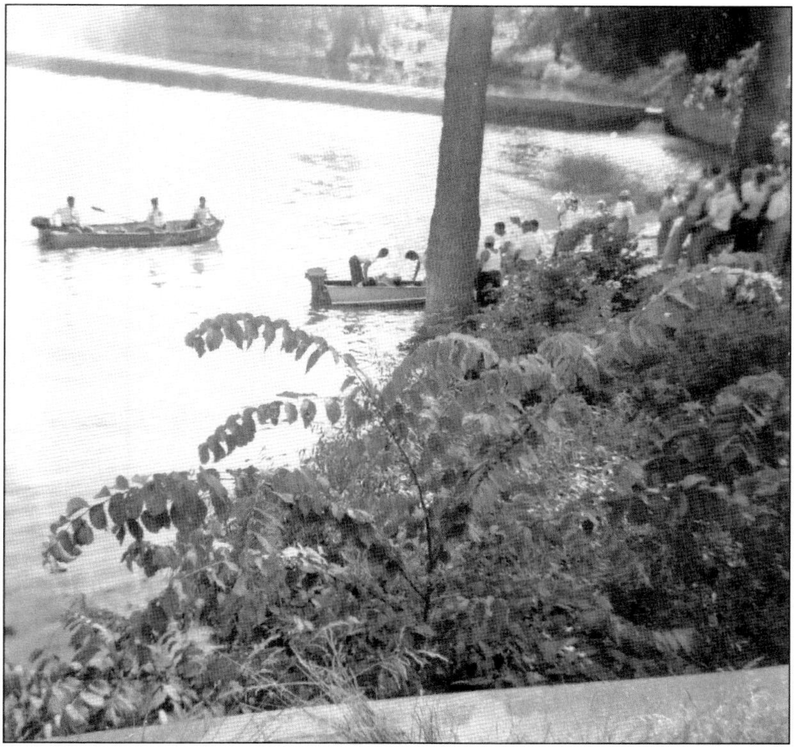

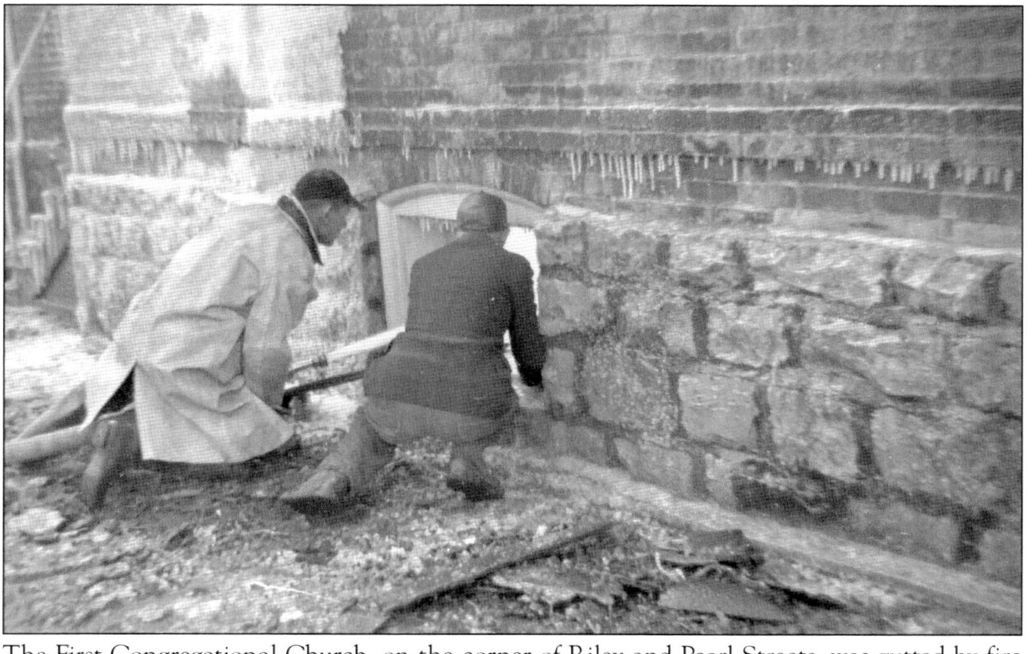

The First Congregational Church, on the corner of Riley and Pearl Streets, was gutted by fire on Sunday, February 1, 1953. The flames went from basement to roof, and water sprayed on the building formed icicles. Fire chief Clarence Rod, in a light coat, is seen here checking the basement while water is being directed into it.

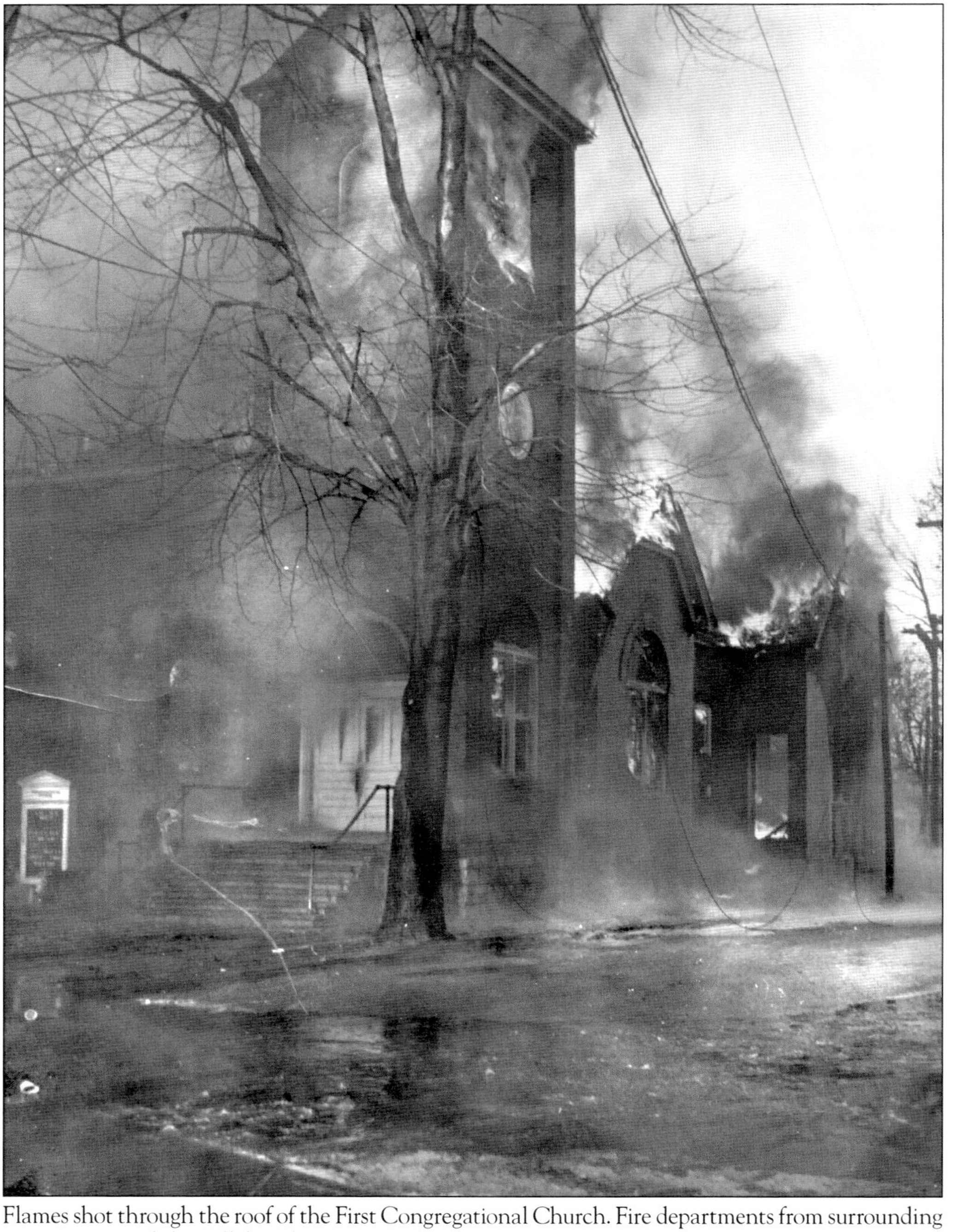

Flames shot through the roof of the First Congregational Church. Fire departments from surrounding towns answered the call, but they were unable to save the building. It must have been emotionally devastating to watch fire claim yet another beloved Congregational church. Betty Fairchild, who worked in the Coffee Cup Restaurant, recalled that the owners, Erma and Sid Fouts, sent urns of hot coffee over to the firemen. When the flames were finally quenched, the men were invited to the restaurant for a hot meal. When the firemen removed their rubber coats, the frozen coats stood by themselves in a corner. (Courtesy of Marilyn Rigel.)

Five

First Schools, First Churches

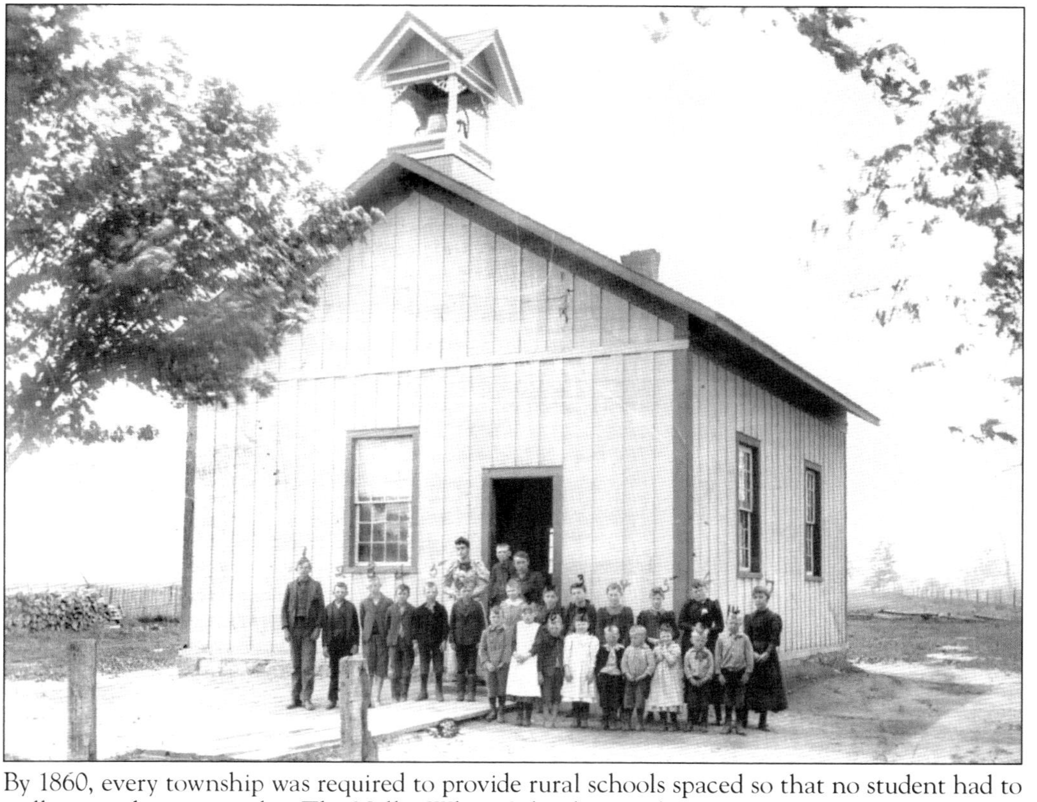

By 1860, every township was required to provide rural schools spaced so that no student had to walk more than two miles. The Nellie White School at Michigan Highway 50 and Petersburg Road was typical. Zelma Rankin is pictured standing outside the frame building with her pupils around 1893. Her brother Walter and sister Zada were also rural schoolteachers.

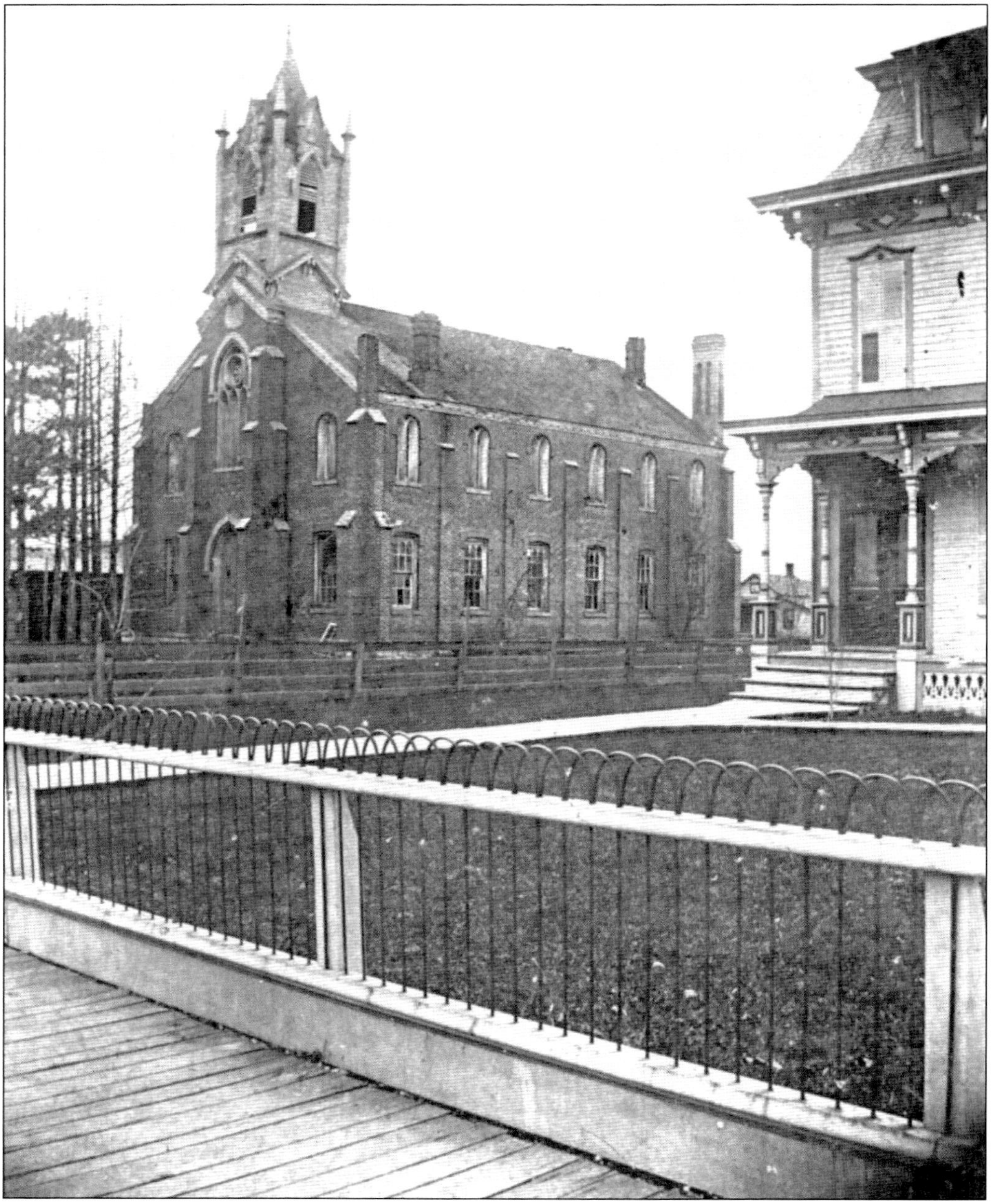

Dundee's first Union School, with its church-like appearance, was built in 1861 at 285 Main Street. It replaced the white frame school attended by children who lived north of Main and Tecumseh Streets and the red one for those who lived south. Children entered the grounds by climbing a stile. Unfortunately, the building was lost to fire around 1880. Perhaps the tall pine tree that is in this area came from this era. The mansard roof home to the right, with its wooden sidewalk and iron-and-wood fence, was still there in 1921, but now it is gone.

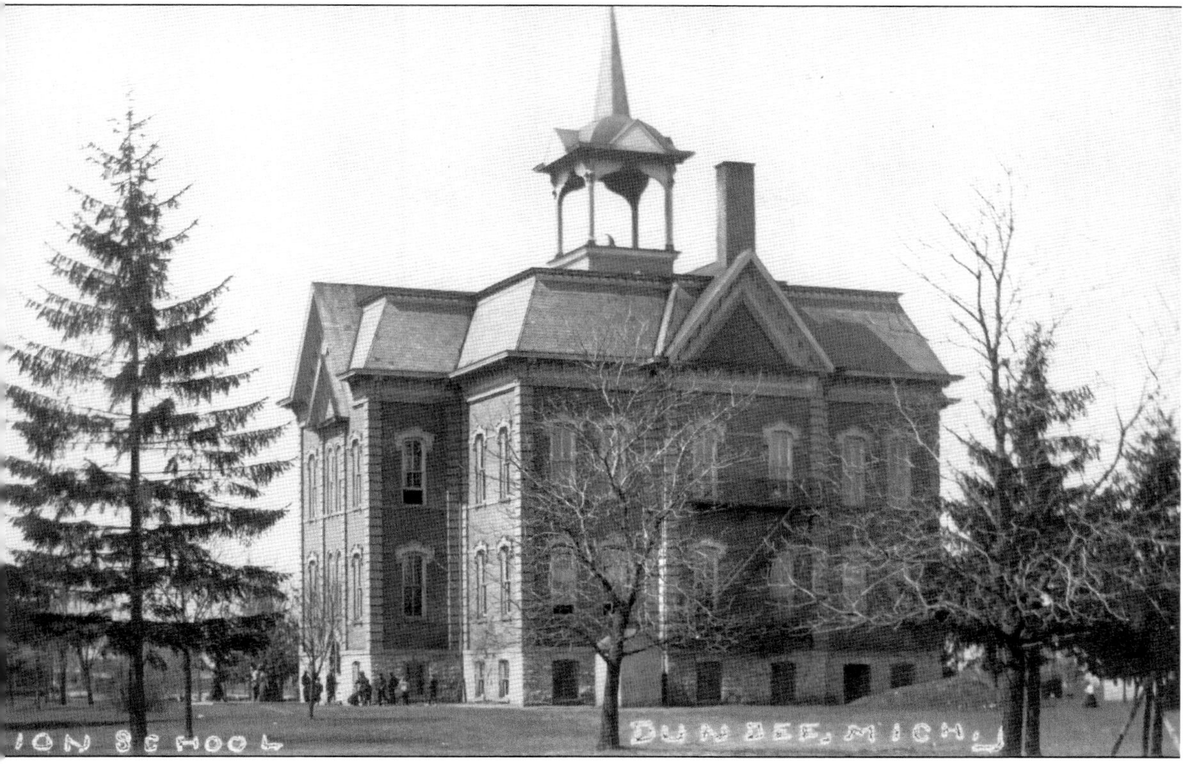

In 1884, this impressive school building was erected at Adams and Ypsilanti Streets. Called the Union School, it was to function as Dundee's center for education for 45 years. Many student groups and their teachers posed for their class and school pictures in front of the building. Originally, there was no indoor plumbing, cafeteria, or athletics—all of that changed. Eventually, the student population exceeded the capacity of the school. To alleviate overcrowding, two buildings were added: one called the "ag" building and the other a two-room building. Unfortunately, the main structure burned in 1929, which forced students to have classes in churches and lodges.

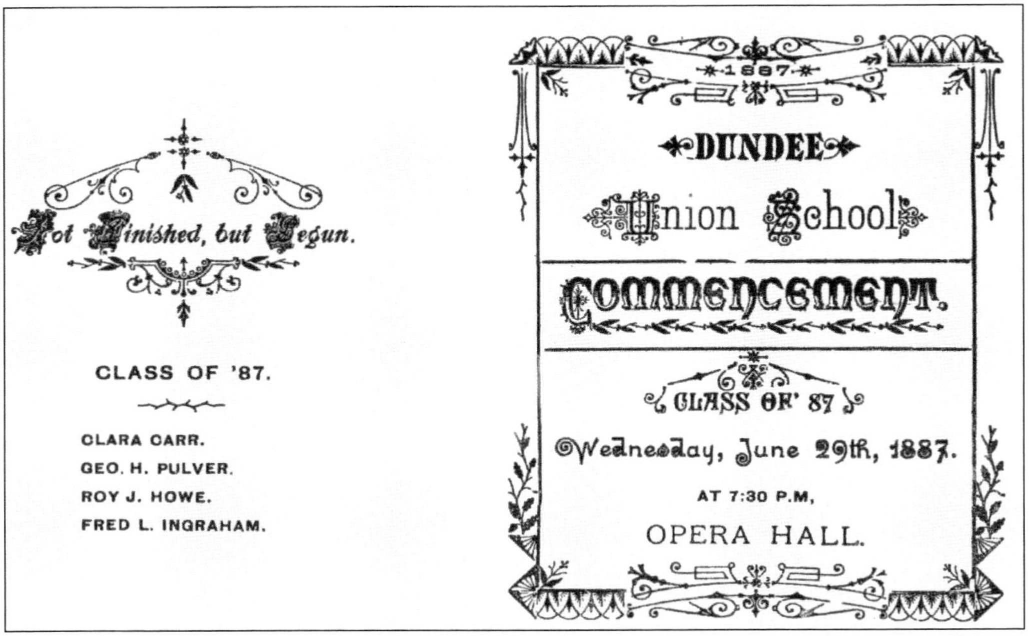

Not Finished, but Begun.

CLASS OF '87.

CLARA CARR.
GEO. H. PULVER.
ROY J. HOWE.
FRED L. INGRAHAM.

1887

DUNDEE

Union School

COMMENCEMENT.

CLASS OF' 87

Wednesday, June 29th, 1887.

AT 7:30 P.M,

OPERA HALL.

The first high school class graduated from Union School in 1887 with four students. One of them, Fred L. Ingraham, became a prominent lawyer in Yuma, Arizona, and helped write the state constitution of Arizona. Ingraham and Roy J. Howe, lifelong friends, rode to school on horseback. For many years, out-of-county students took the interurban to attend Dundee's high school.

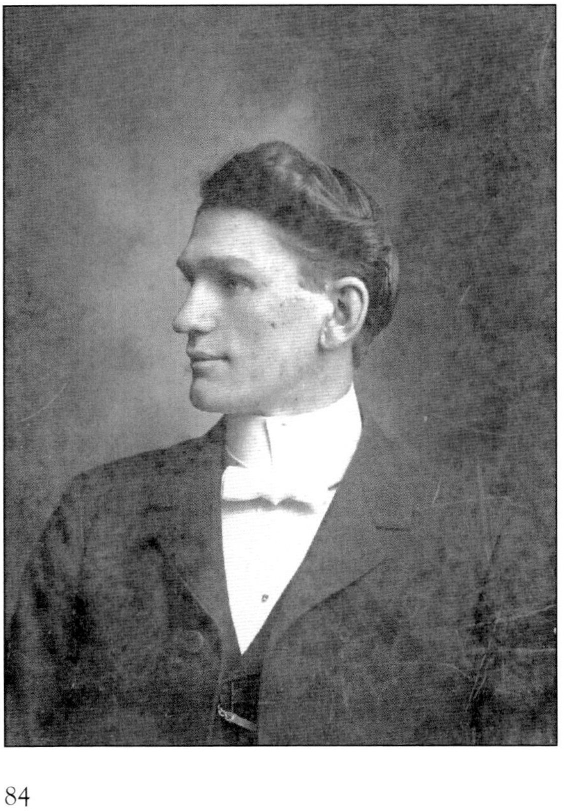

Walter Rankin taught for one year, in 1899, at the Rankin School on Michigan Highway 50, just north of Kimpton Road. He let the students play a schoolyard game, called Annie I Over, in which they threw a ball over the school's roof. In the schoolhouse, he relied on his older students to help teach the younger ones. Typically, when the students graduated from the eighth grade, they had finished all their formal education.

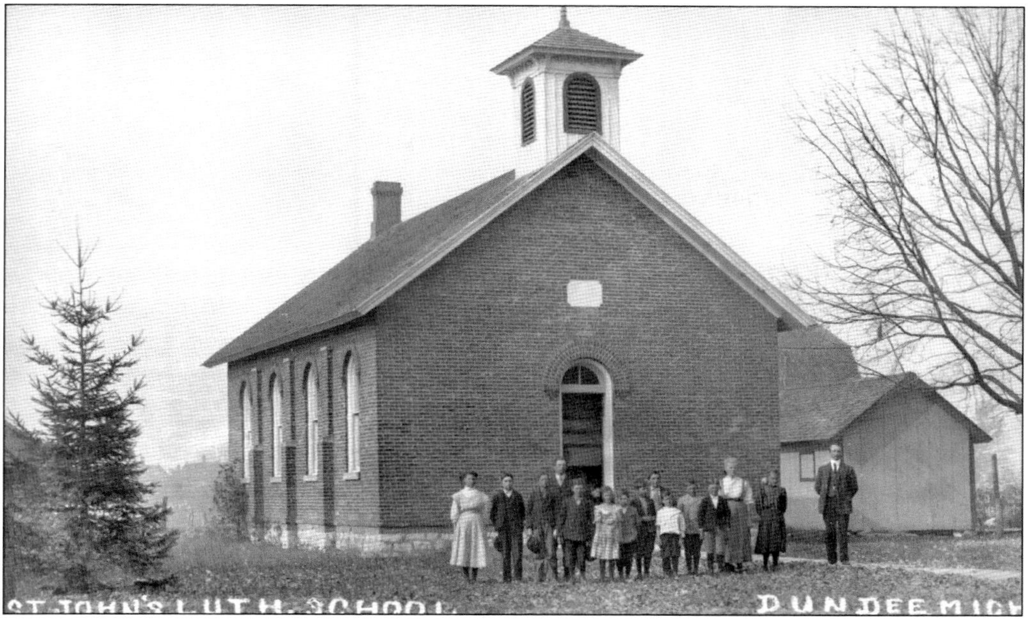

Many German families immigrated to the Dundee area. Their religious needs were served by St. John Evangelical Lutheran Church. The congregation built its first German school in 1867, replacing it in 1884 with this brick building. Classes were conducted in German. Many students passed through this school until it was discontinued in 1918 following World War I.

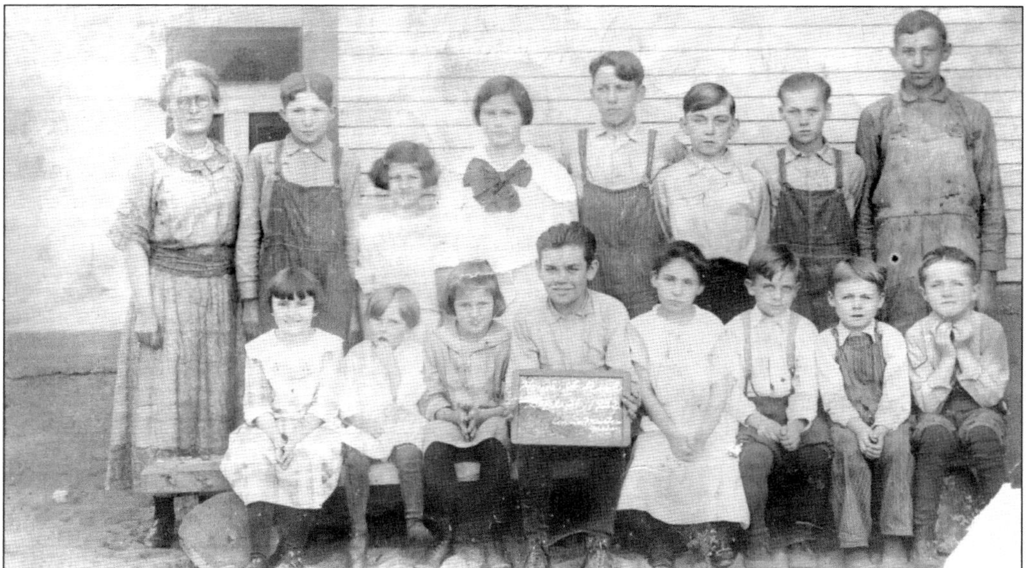

Ms. Anna Masten's students pose in 1929 at Howe School on Oelke Road, near Crowe Road, in Milan Township. Those pictured are, from left to right, (first row) Lucille Lamkin, two unidentified, Harold Miller, unidentified, Herbert Schultz, Wilmar Loss, and Oren Lamkin; (second row) Ms. Masten, Douglas Malkan, Popside ?, Alice Lamkin, John Wilson, Albert Tommlies, Orla Losses, and Ernie Howe. Students near township lines sometimes went to a "fractional" school in an adjacent township.

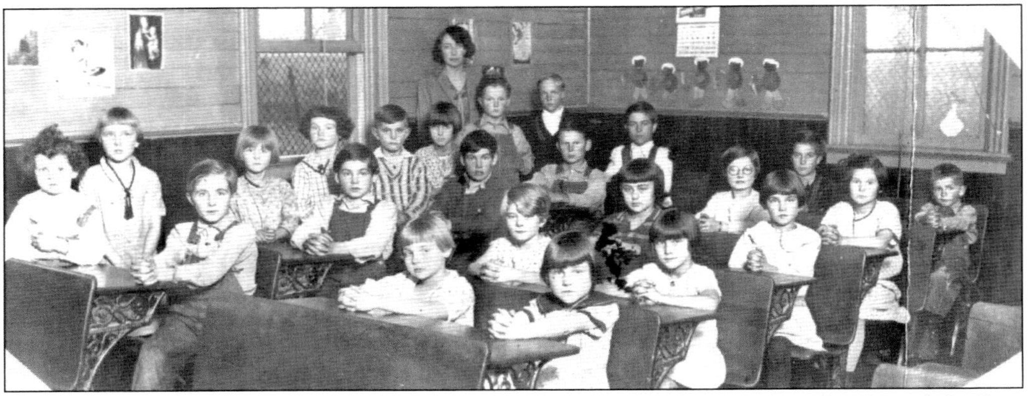

In Egypt School, at Day and Hiser Roads, in 1931 are, from front to back and right to left, (first row) Juanita Shilling, Dorothy Brockman, Margaret Robinson, Christine Abner, and Gerald Eyler; (second row) Eugenia Haystead, Doris Brockman, Helen Pilbeam, Margaret Craig, and Ivan Bame; (third row) Everett Bame, David Robinson, Donald Robinson, John Abner, and Raymond Bame; (standing) Audley Craig, Elinor Eyler, Audrey Bame, Norma Robinson, Harold Pilbeam, Virginia Bame, Marian Downing, Marion Koster, and unidentified.

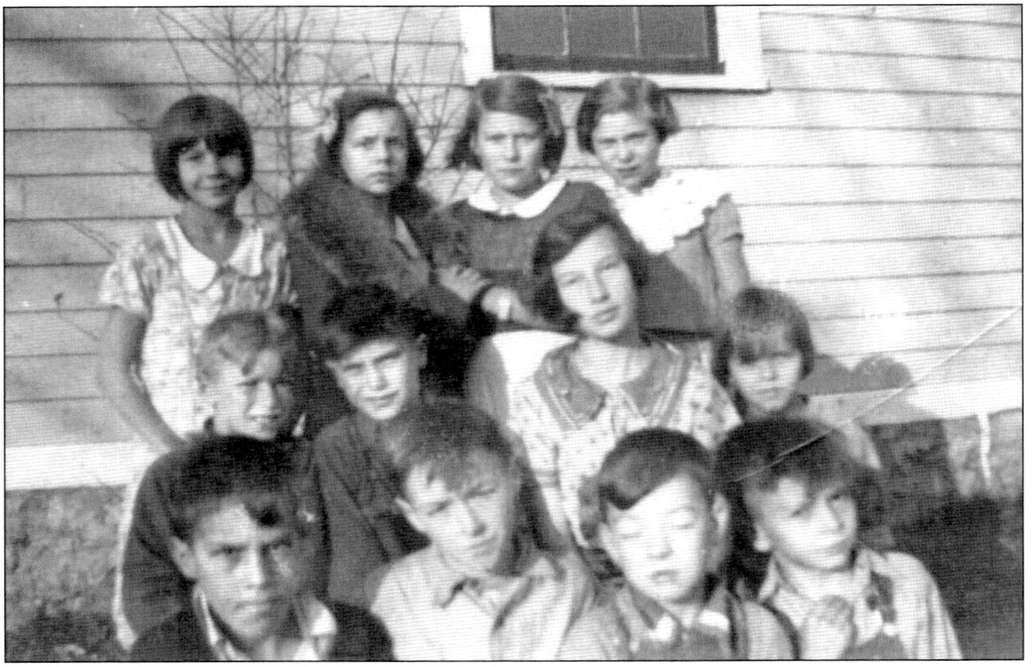

The whole population of Rea School, at Rea and Monk Roads, is seen posing here in 1936. Carol Robinson Wiech was in sixth grade when this photograph was taken. The students are, from left to right, (first row) Bill Welever, Charles Kingston, Tom Robinson, and Gordon Logan; (second row) Edward Baranowski, Ted Baranowski, Carol Robinson, and Audrey Logan; (third row) Marian Logan, Virginia Logan, Margaret Coleman, and Virginia Baranowski. Clara Ellis was the teacher. (Courtesy of Carol Wiech.)

LOCAL PHONE NO.	NAME			SEX
21	Mildred E. Rauch (Bartow)			F
DATE OF BIRTH	PLACE OF BIRTH	RACE	CITIZEN OF	
Jan. 2, 1890	Dundee, Mich.	W.	U.S.	

CHURCH PREFERENCE Protestant MEMBER Methodist

PHYSICAL DEFECTS none

PHONE NUMBER	DATE	HEALTH	MARRIED	CHILDREN	HEIGHT	WEIGHT
			yes	none		

YEARS	BUILDING	POSITION	YEARLY SALARY	MONTHLY SALARY	PAID TO RETIREMENT FUND
1912-13	Dundee	1st&2nd.	405.	45.00	
13-14	"	2nd&3rd.	450.	50.00	
14-15	"	2nd & 3rd	500.	55.00	
28-29	"	Second	1305.		
29-30	"	Fourth	1350.		
30-31	"	"	1375.		
31-32	"	"	1200.		
32-33	"	"	900.		
33-34	"	"	855.		
34-35	"	"	843.40		
35-36	"	"	916.65		
36-37	"	"	1100.		
37-38	"	"	1115.		
38-39	"	"	1200.		
39-40	"	"	1250.		
40-41	"	"	1300.		
1941-42	Dundee	Fourth	1300.		
1942-43	"	"	1450.		
1943-44	"	"	1600.		
1944-45	"	"	1687.		
1945-46	"	Fifth	1980		
1946-47	"	Sixth	2120.		
1947-48	"	"	2700.		
1948-49	"	"	3000.		
1949-50	"	"	3300.		
1950-51	"	"	3400.		
1951-52	"	Seventh	3800.		
1952-53	"	"	4000.		
1953-54	"	"	4200.		

Mildred Rauch taught over 40 years, most of them in the Dundee system. Rauch studied at Michigan State Normal in Ypsilanti from 1909 through 1911 before embarking on her teaching career. She was well educated for the time, as the law allowed high school graduates to sit for the teacher's exam without further preparation. Her annual salary began at $405, when a loaf of bread generally cost 5¢ and college graduates were averaging $720 per year. During the Depression, her salary was reduced by 25 percent. In 1949, Rauch received her bachelor of science degree. When she was hired, it was acceptable to ask teachers about their religion. Rauch was a devout Methodist, and she loved music. During the years she lived in Dundee, she was the director of music for the Dundee United Methodist Church.

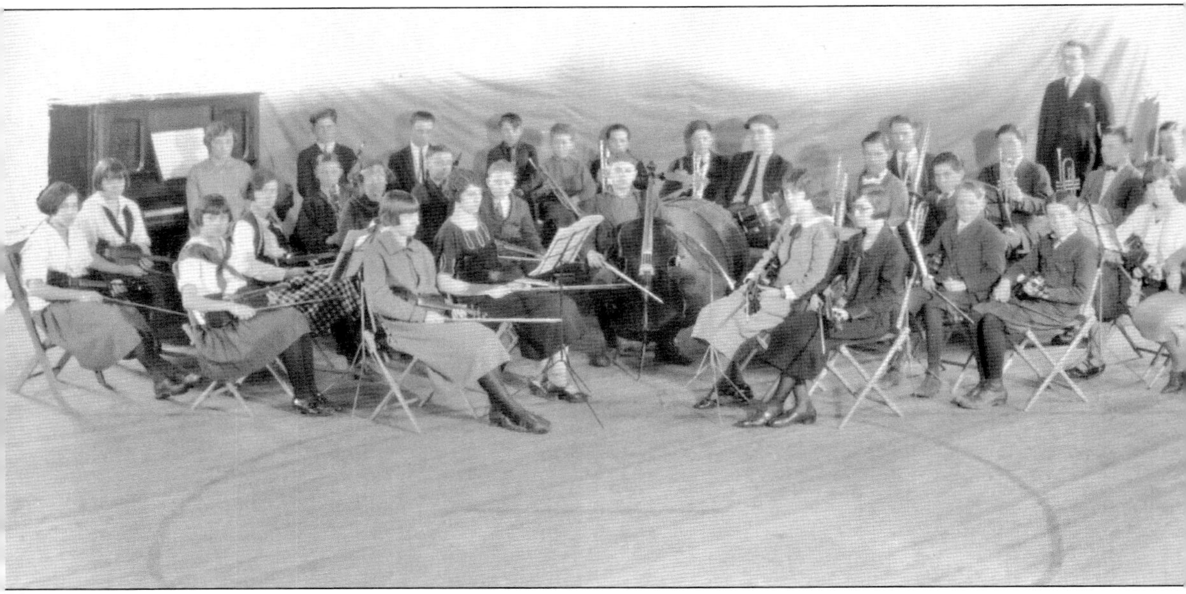

Music was an important part of the curriculum at Dundee High School, and these are the members of the 1924 orchestra. The violinists are in six pairs across the front; the last pair is on the left just behind the third pair. In that order the violinists are, from left to right, Dorothy Anderson and Doris Hanson, Iva Bordine and Margaret Wagoner, Mary Bigelow and Nellie Nieman, Alma Lincoln and Naomi Humphrey, Gerald Caldwell and Judson Oston, Wava Dorrell and Virginia Humphrey, and Isabell Roy and Otis Gloff. At the piano is Miss R. C. Winchell, the domestic arts teacher. The clarinets clustered at the top left are LaVern Weyher, Thurman Uhl, Wayne Hiser, Howard Waring, and John Stockberger. The cello player in the center is Joseph McMullen; next to him is drummer Mark Osgood. The brass across the back from center to the right are Karl Weyher, Lewis McBride, Shorty Spohr, Harold Swoverland, Merle Rigel, Lehr Barkenquast, Warren Benham, Clark Ford, and Foster Overmeyer. Mr. H. C. Klink, the director, is in the background on the right.

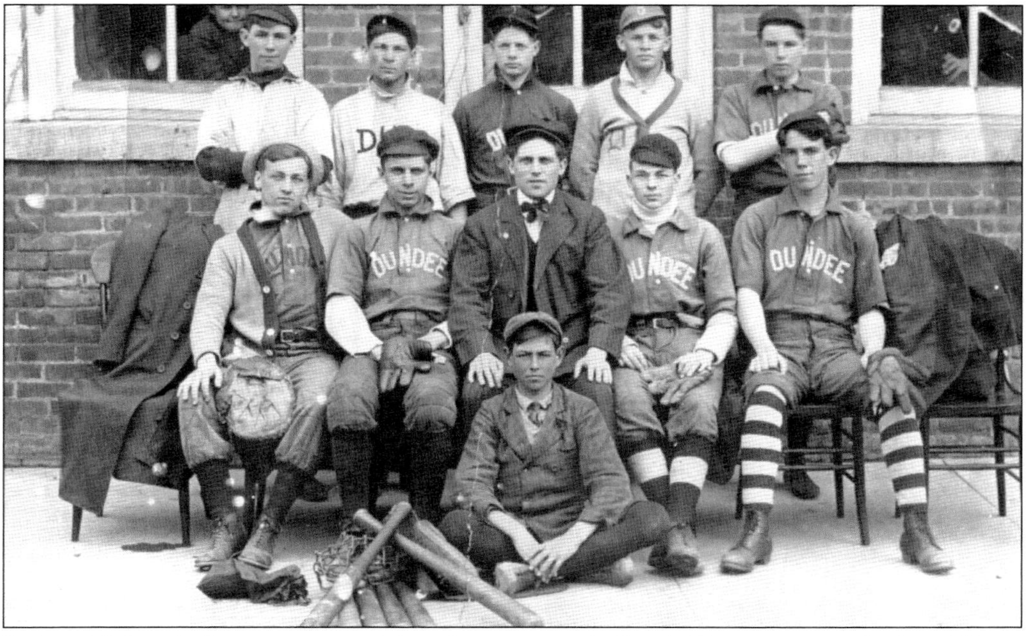

This 1908 baseball team poses with volunteer coach Frank Zimmerman, a barber. Those pictured include, from left to right, (first row) Max La Longe; (second row) ? Knoll, Harry Baker, ? Zimmerman, Russell Corkett, and Ivan Frear; (third row) Rolland Drew, Art Rinehart, Joe Sherwood, "Skinny" Miller, and Rolland Corbin. The message on the back of this postcard states, "I suppose you will recognize this crowd. They went to Tecumseh Saturday and did not get home until Sunday morning."

This solemn group of young ladies is the 1925 Dundee High School girls' basketball team. Middy blouses and half-court play characterized girls' teams of that era. Those pictured are, from left to right, (first row) Halcyon Lewis, Clara Nieman, Dorothy Rathbone, and Dorothy Anderson; (second row) Delores Spohr, Helen Brandt, Jane Shontz, Ethelyne Reum, and G. Woodward; (third row) Miss Pheterplace, Edith Rhora, Ada Raymond, Anna Haystead, Nellie Koster, and Miss Parker.

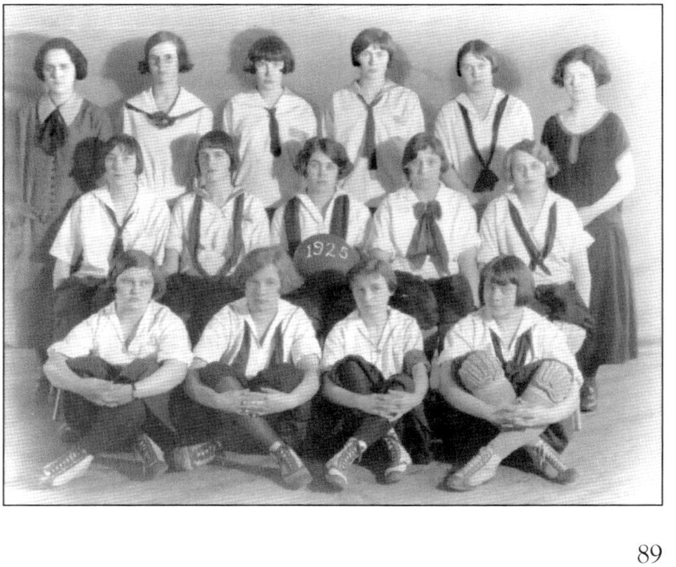

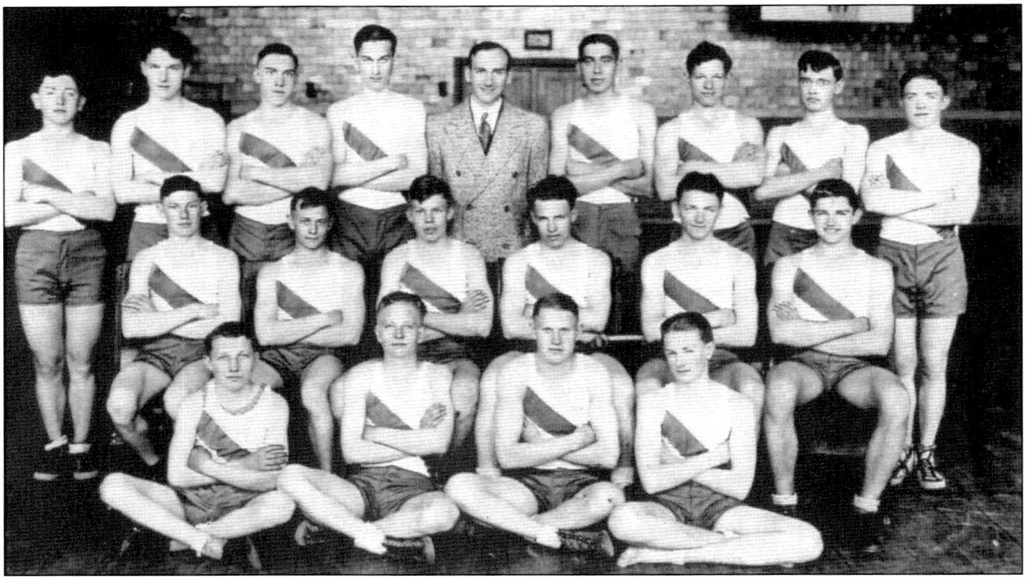

The Dundee High School track team of 1935 is pictured here. The members of that team are, from left to right, (first row) Wayne Hubbard, Wayne Lennard, Ed Regelin, and Jack Woodward; (second row) Norman Miller, Lloyd Russell, Leslie Grabsky, Truman Gee, Bud Pulver, and Gerald Verdon; (third row) Fritz Feldman, unidentified, Lucius Eyler, Russell Naus, Mr. Leroy Reames, Alex S., John Robinson, Warren Doughty, and Ben Laudy.

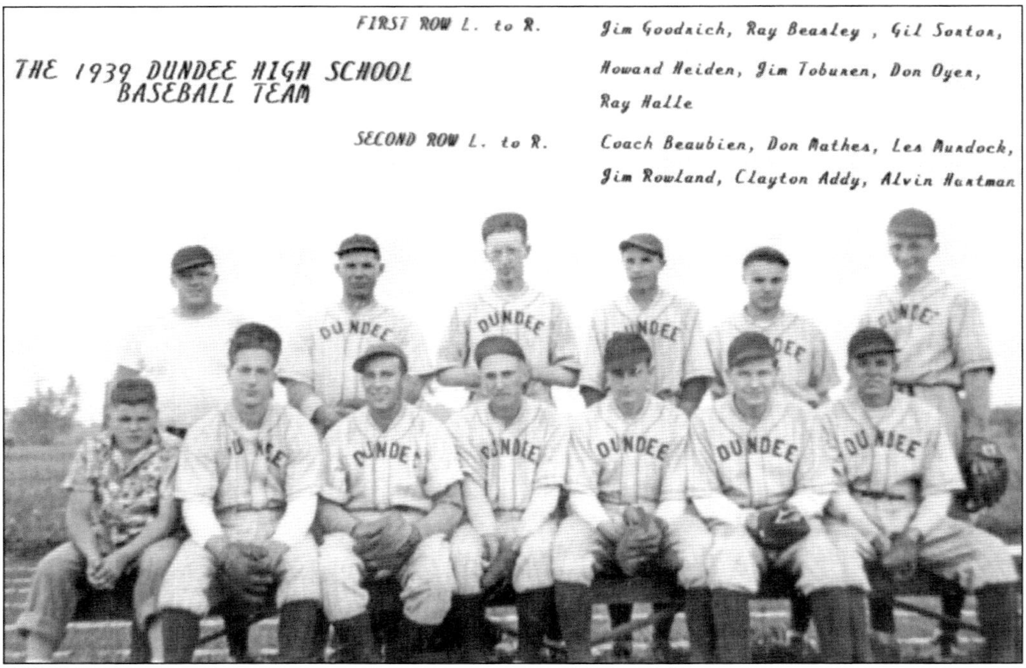

A few members of the 1939 Dundee High School baseball team are willing to smile. Those pictured are, from left to right, (first row) Jim Goodrich, Ray Beasley, Gil Sortor, Howard Heiden, Jim Toburen, Don Oyer, and Ray Halle; (second row) coach Beaubien, Don Mathes, Les Murdock, Jim Rowland, Clayton Addy, and Alvin Hartman.

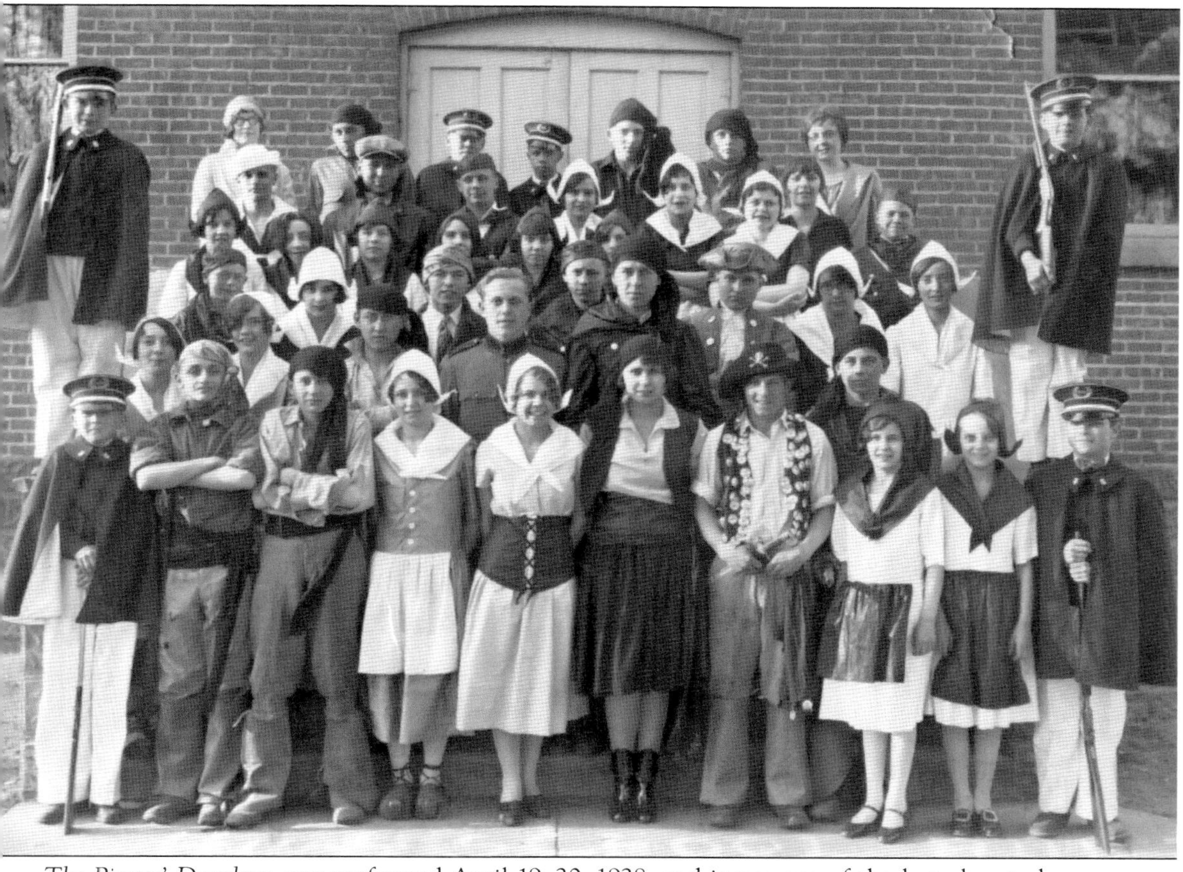

The Pirates' Daughter, was performed April 19–20, 1928, and it was one of the last plays to be presented in the Dundee High School Building before it was destroyed by fire the following year. The eager actors included in the production are, from left to right, (first row) Warren Benham, Billie Karner, Ed Ridge, unidentified, Ada Mae Stebbins, Marge Stowell, Doug Carver, two unidentified, and Delton Bigelow; among the others in the photograph are Dallas Rod, Tiny Spaulding, Rosie Waring, Cliff Tingley, Doug Brockman, Bub Hanson, Otis Gloff, Neva Uhl, Mary Williams, Edith Church, and Fred Noble. The happy faces and the "authentic" costumes add to the appeal of this picture.

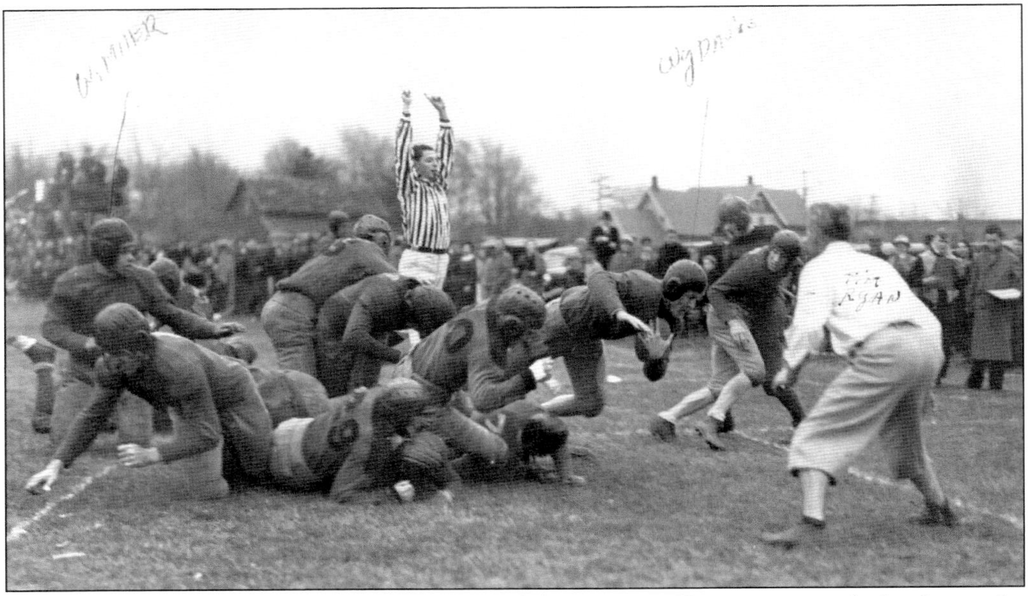

The referee appears to be anticipating this touchdown in a 1937 game—it might be due to the fame of the ball carrier. Wyman Davis and his twin brother, Wilford, were formidable football players. Wyman is fifth in all-time passing (1,173 yards in 1937) in the county, and Wilford is seventh in receiving (571 yards in 1937). Wilford became a quarterback at Michigan State and Wyman a halfback. Both men became veterinarians.

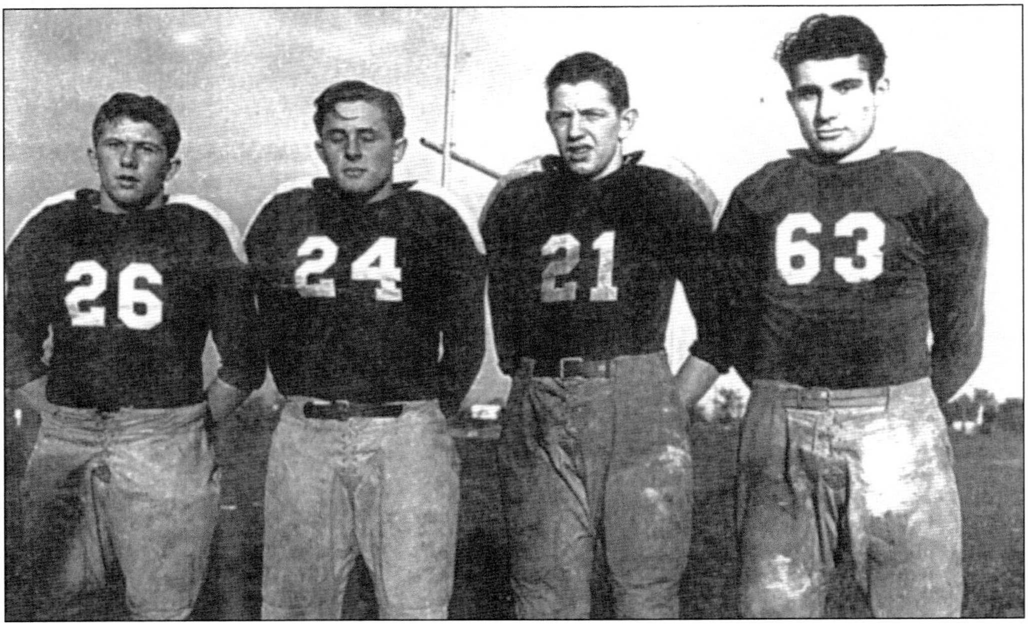

Four outstanding football players graduated from Dundee High School in 1943. Posing here for a photograph, they are Bill Siler, Harold Karner, Bill Busch, and Bob Corbin. Their feats gave the community something to smile about during the darkest days of World War II. All of the young men served in the armed services following their graduation. Siler later enrolled in Michigan State and became its quarterback until being injured in a Michigan–Michigan State game.

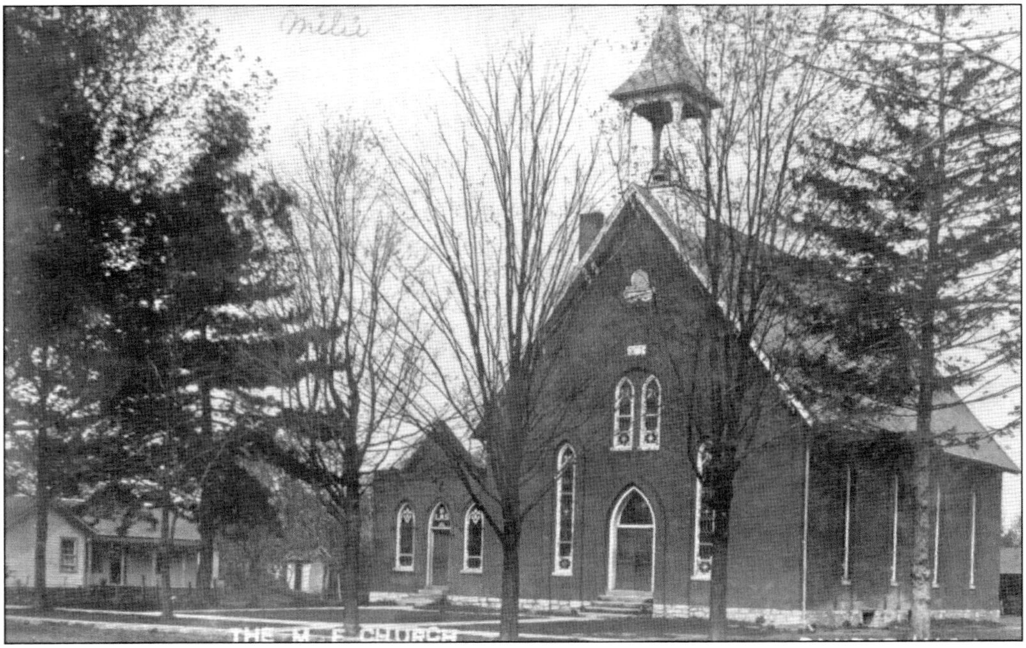

The first church to organize in Dundee was the First Methodist Episcopal Church of Dundee in 1826. Members met in homes and were served by a circuit rider from Monroe who came depending on the weather. In 1832, a parsonage was built at 231 Monroe Street, perhaps the oldest existing home in Dundee. This handsome building, the second Methodist church, was constructed at 318 Riley Street.

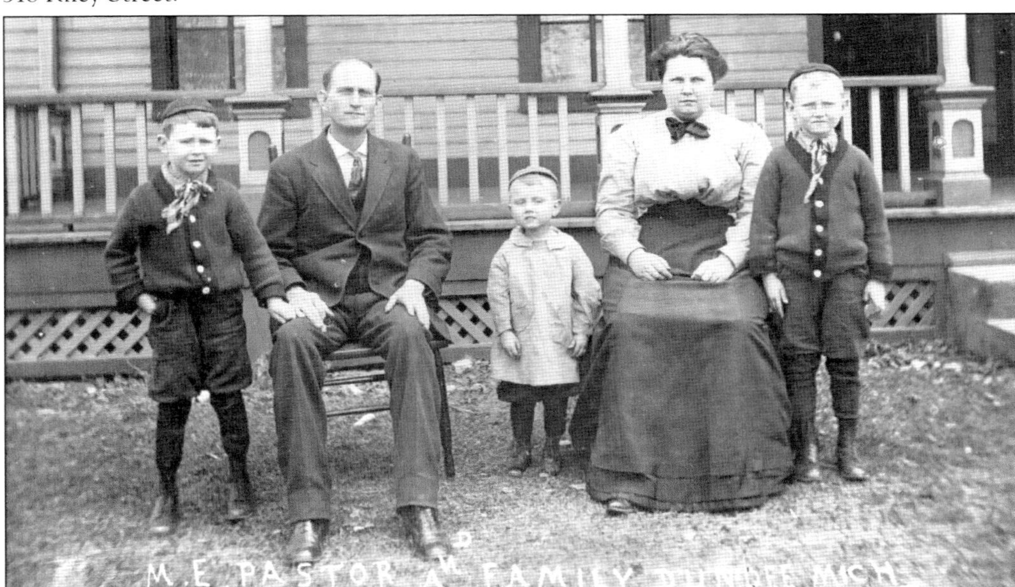

In 1880, the congregation bought a home across the street at 341 Riley Street for use as a parsonage. In March 1910, a parishioner sent this postcard showing Rev. H.R. Beatty and his family posing in front of the house. In May, the reverend was commended for the prayer he gave at the Memorial Day service. In June, Reverend Beatty was reassigned, and a new pastor took his place.

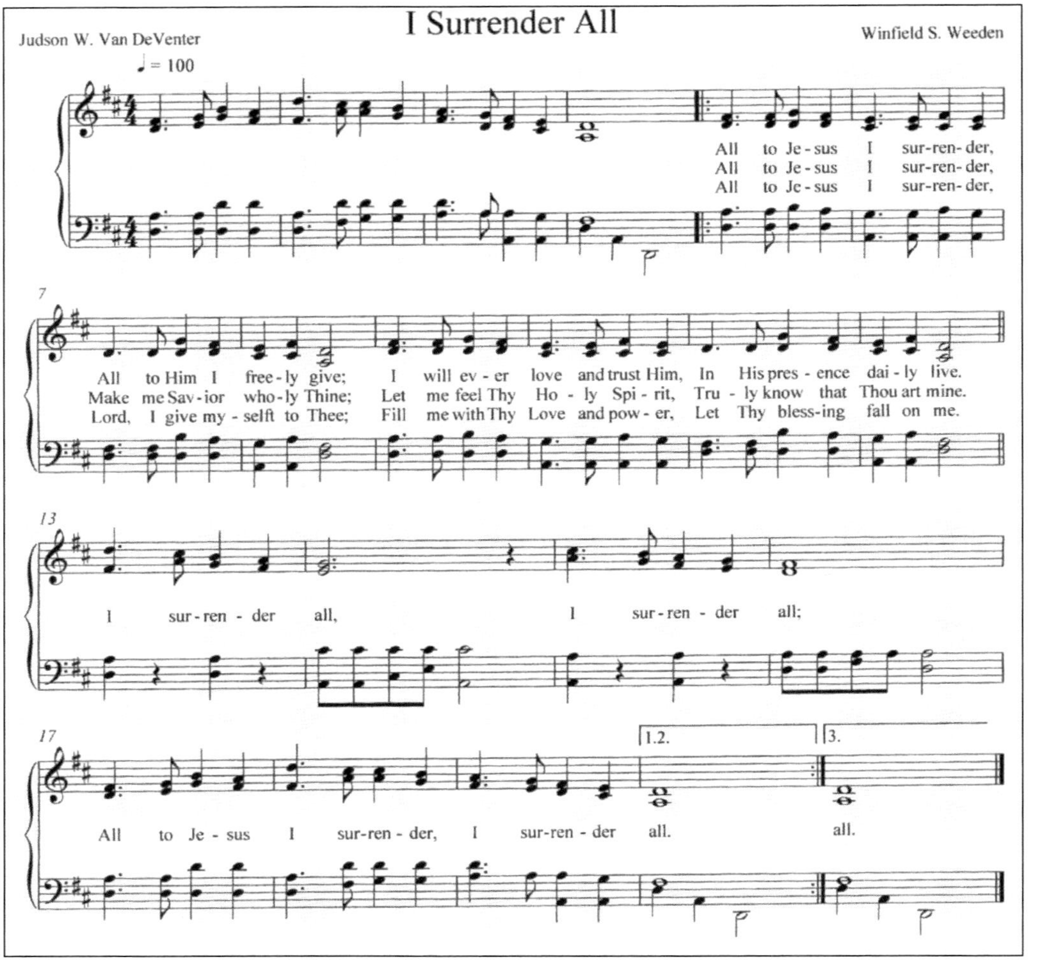

This beloved hymn, still sung in Methodist churches, was written by Judson W. Van DeVenter. "I Surrender All" was his second composition. Van DeVenter was born in Dundee in 1855 and educated at Hillsdale College. He taught at Rankin School in 1878 and wrote a delightful account of his experience. Later, he was persuaded to switch from his first passion, art, to one of music ministry. A prolific hymn writer, he gave performances singing his hymns accompanied by his wife on the piano. Through his evangelistic work, he became well known throughout the United States and Canada. Billy Graham acknowledged Van DeVenter's influence on him. At Judson Van DeVenter's funeral in 1939, Minnie Mott and Earl Stowell sang three of his hymns, "We Shall Shine as the Stars," "Eternity is Near," and "Looking This Way." Van DeVenter is buried in Maple Grove Cemetery in Dundee.

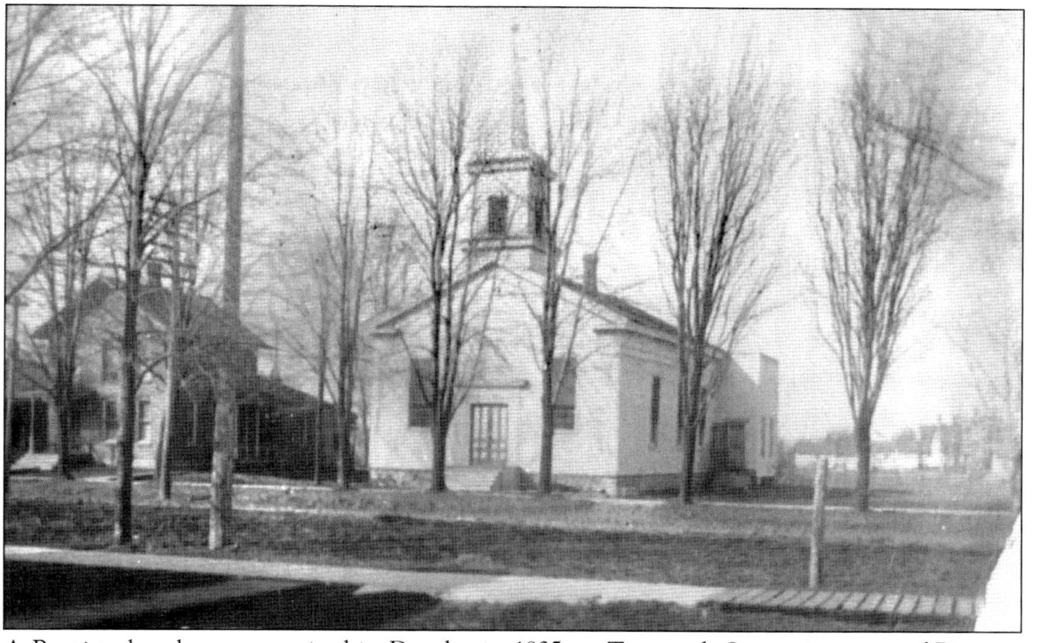

A Baptist church was organized in Dundee in 1835 on Tecumseh Street, just west of Barnum Street. It contained a built-in, waist-deep baptistery. The church flourished in the early 1900s until its congregation aged. Eventually, the building was sold to the Farm Bureau, which converted it into a feed and fertilizer store. Later, the Waterstradts replaced the building with a gas station. (Courtesy of the Monroe County Historical Museum.)

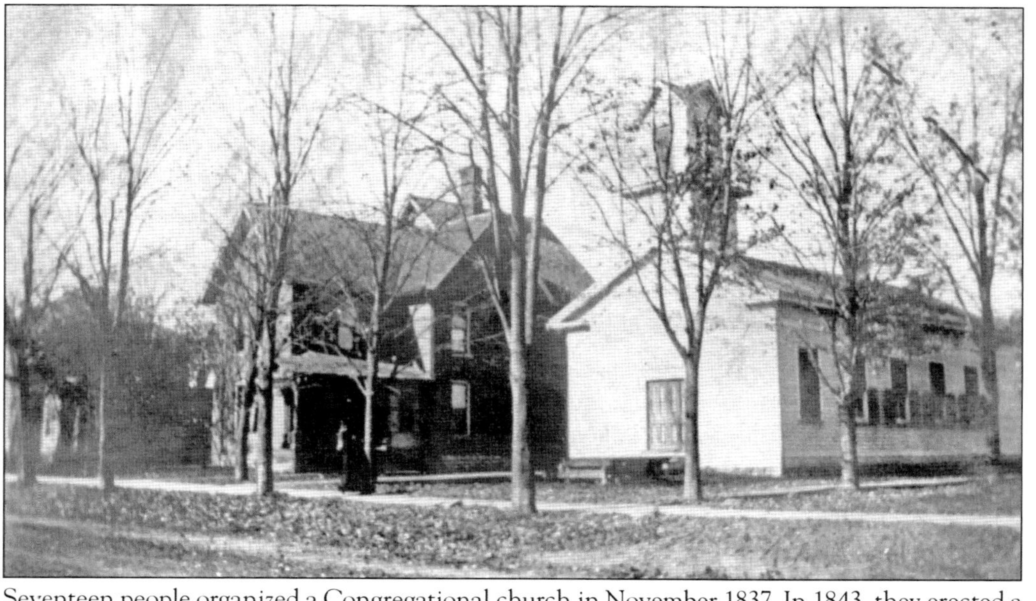

Seventeen people organized a Congregational church in November 1837. In 1843, they erected a white frame building at 224 Riley Street. For a number of years, the church struggled financially, perhaps even closing from 1858 to 1863. In 1867, a bell was hung, and a parsonage was constructed in 1890. The last service in this church was held on March 24, 1901, with Daniel Spaulding, an original member, in attendance.

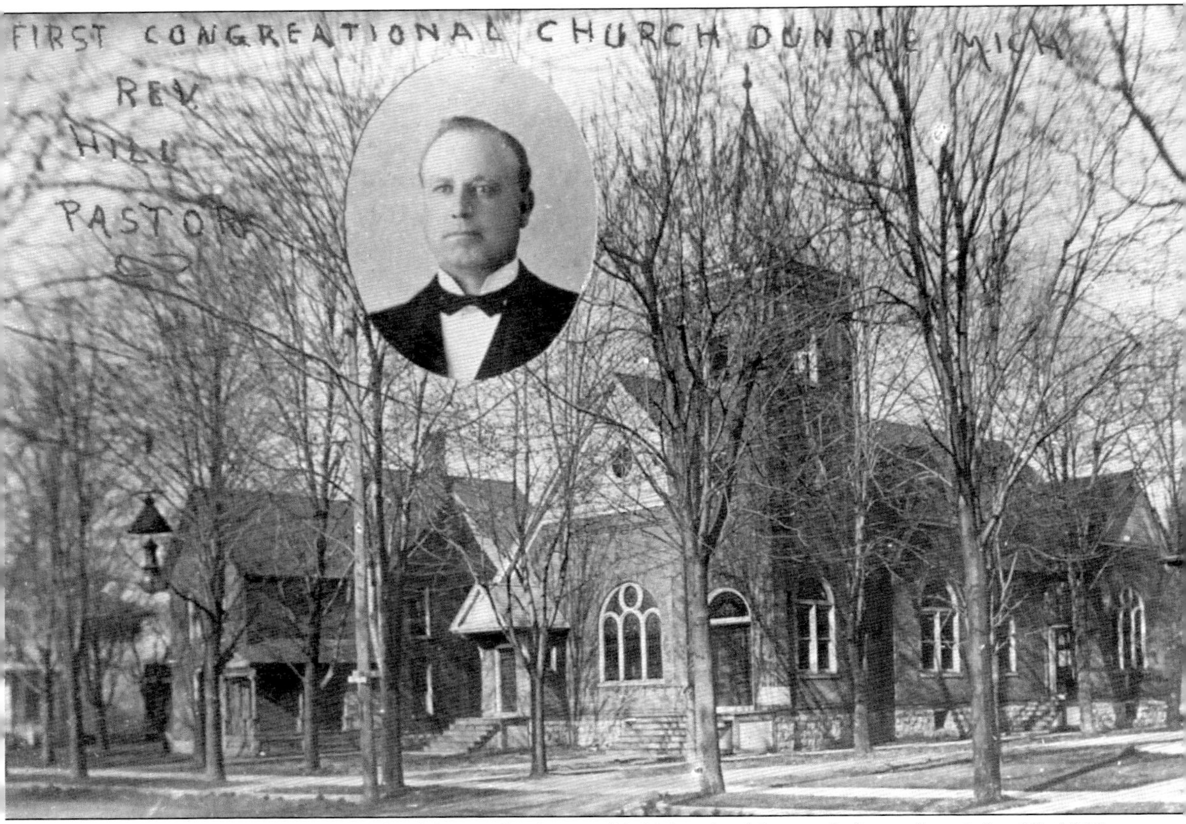

This distinguished brick building, which cost $3,500 to build, was dedicated on May 18, 1902, at 224 Riley Street. It replaced the white frame structure. Although the building spoke of prosperity, the congregation continued to experience financial difficulties. In 1907, the pastor, Reverend Hill (pictured) was quite discouraged. A visiting minister, Reverend Steward, helped him to abolish the congregation's debt. Under Reverend Prestidge, the membership increased, and the Good Fellows Club was inaugurated. This latter group served popular fish suppers and New Year's dinners. Just as the pastor and congregation were experiencing stability, the church burned in November 1921. (Courtesy of the Monroe County Historical Museum.)

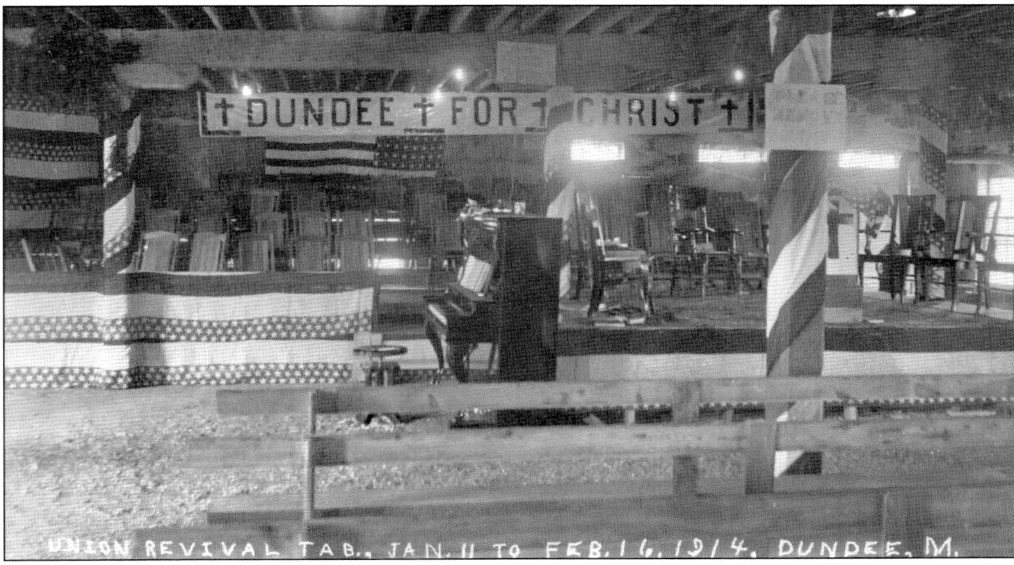

Dundee had a winter revival in 1914 that was probably held indoors at the roller-skating rink at 127 Barnum Street. From January 11 to February 16, the Union Revival Tabernacle held services. The sponsors set chairs on the skating platform, put a piano on the dirt floor, and unfurled a banner, "Dundee for Christ," across the room. Pictured is the dimly lit room as it awaits the preacher, pianist, and worshippers.

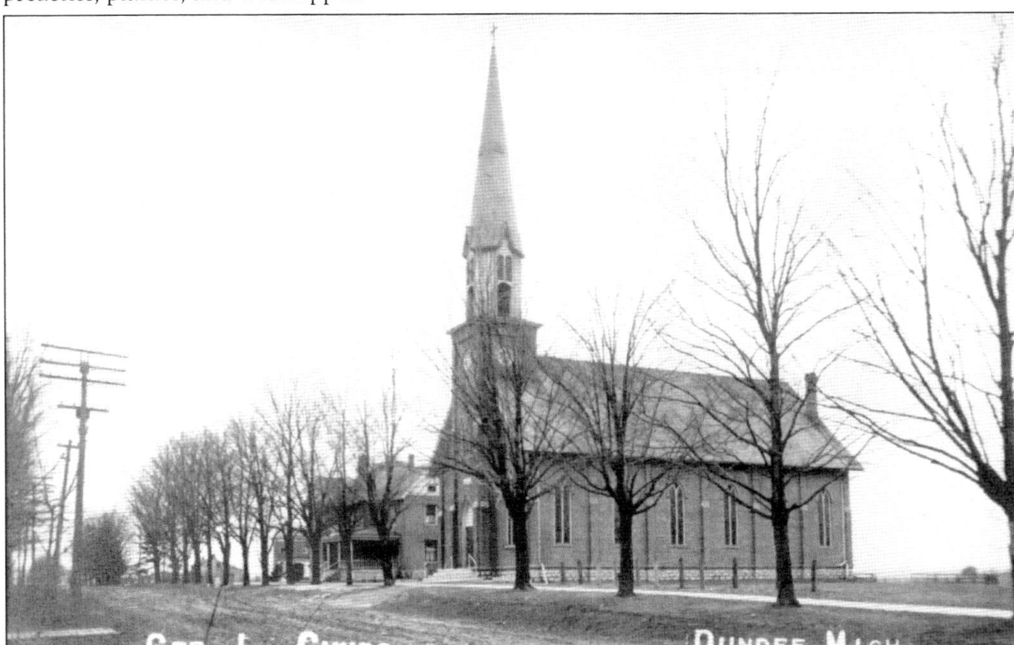

Twenty-two German speakers founded St. John Evangelical Lutheran Church in 1862. Their first church was dedicated in 1863, minus a steeple, altar, and pews. Things were financially difficult for a while; however, in 1890, this lovely building, with its 125-foot steeple, was erected at 460 Riley Street. The c. 1905 view shows the church with no close neighbors to the east, but a parsonage, school, and barn are just to the west.

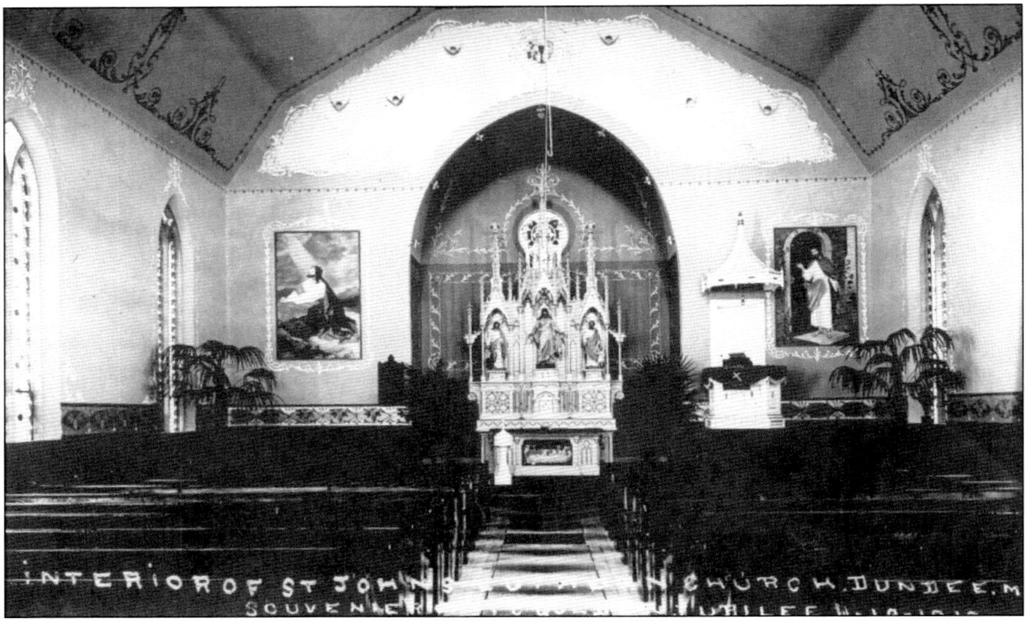

This 1910 photograph shows the interior of St. John Evangelical Lutheran with its magnificent gilt and white wooden altar. The altar, imported from Germany in 1904, was shipped in pieces and reassembled at St. John. In 1911, the minister conducted a bilingual service the last Sunday of the month. By 1945, all services were in English. Revs. Phillip Diehlman and Fred W. Cesler were beloved longtime pastors.

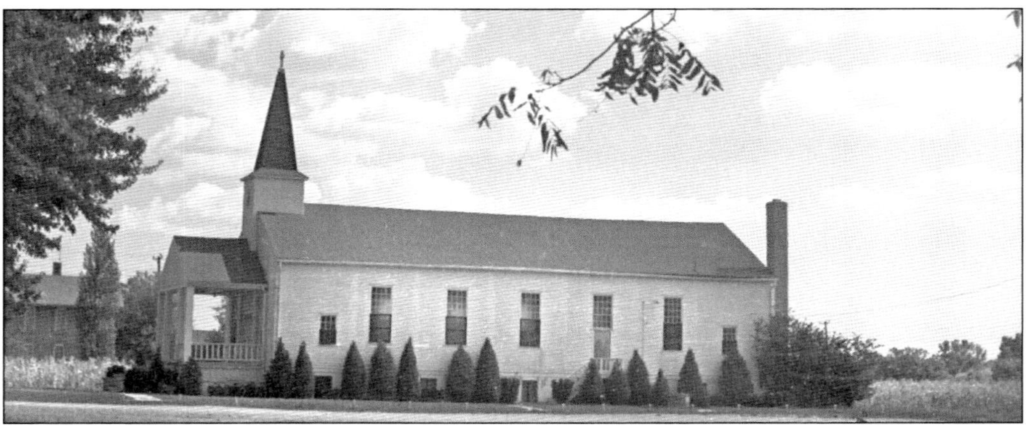

In 1944, St. Irene Catholic Church was organized as a mission of St. Joseph Catholic Church in Ida, Michigan. The first meeting place was above the bank in the old opera house on Riley Street. In 1947, St. Irene successfully bid to purchase the Willow Run Airbase chapel for $635. The building was sawed into eight-foot sections and trucked to Dundee, where it was reassembled at 568 Main Street. (Photograph by L.T. Harris.)

Six

The Old Mill and Dam

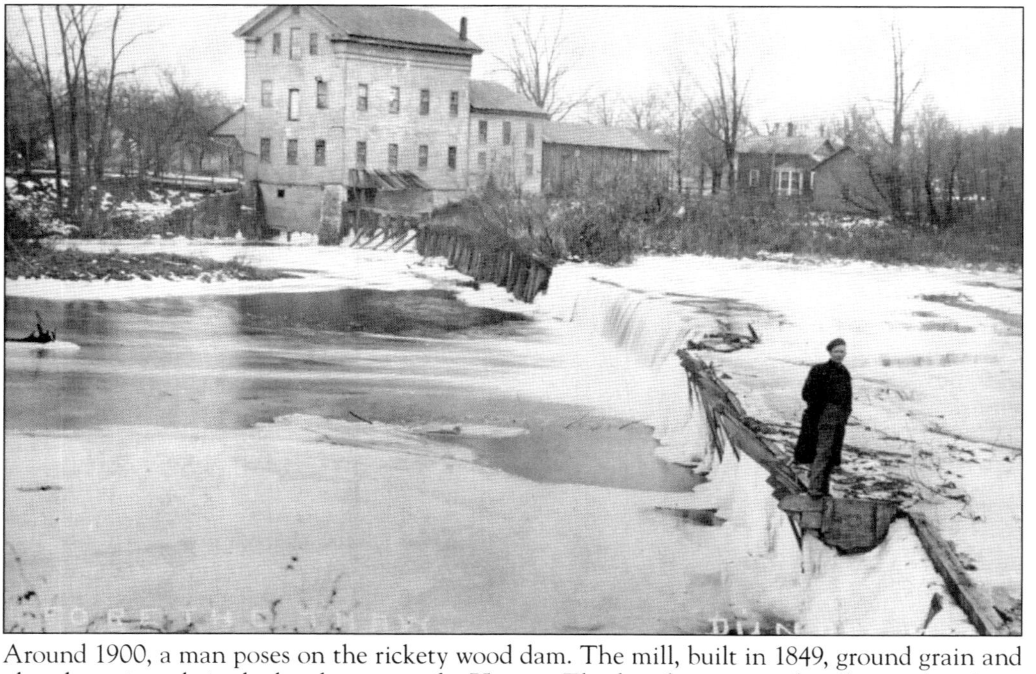

Around 1900, a man poses on the rickety wood dam. The mill, built in 1849, ground grain and played a major role in the local economy for 75 years. The first dam was made of logs and timbers. The dam seen here, a rafter dam, used salvaged timber from a railroad trestle upstream. The mill is starting to show its age with the shed over the water intake deteriorating.

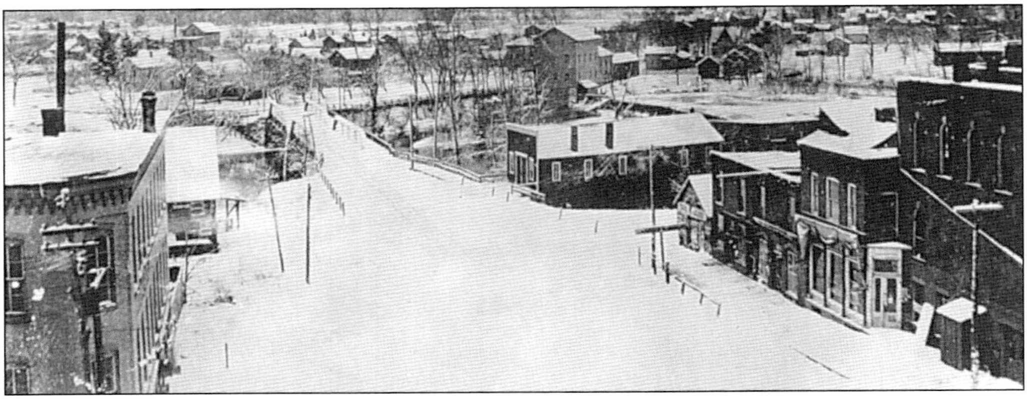

The blacksmith's shop, with its two chimneys, is on the right side of the street with the water-powered mill and dam directly above it. Along the top, on the left, is a two-story wood building with a peaked roof. This is a competing steam-powered gristmill, making this a rare photograph with both mills. The image, taken around 1900, shows the steam mill with its shed and tall chimney.

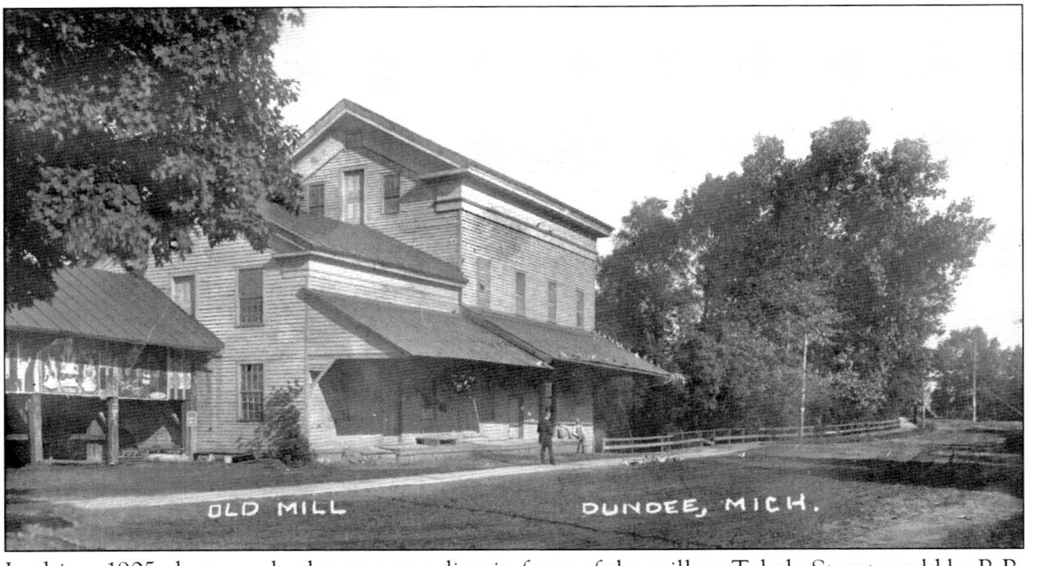

In this c. 1905 photograph, the man standing in front of the mill on Toledo Street could be R.B. Davis, who owned it for 25 years. The overhang was designed to protect the grain from weather while unloading and loading. Note the pigeons on the shed roof waiting their chance for a spill. The Greek Revival mill was built in a style popular in the early and mid-19th century.

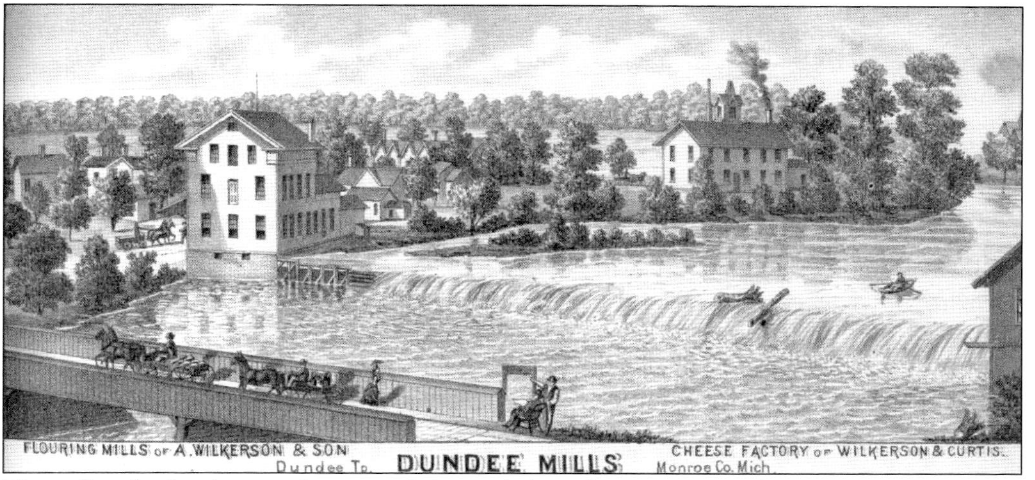

The mill and rafter dam are shown in a lithograph from the 1876 *Beers Atlas*. The cheese factory, to the right, is some distance away from the mill. Locals were proud of their cheese. It is said the factory had a standing order for cheese from the president—only no one knows which president.

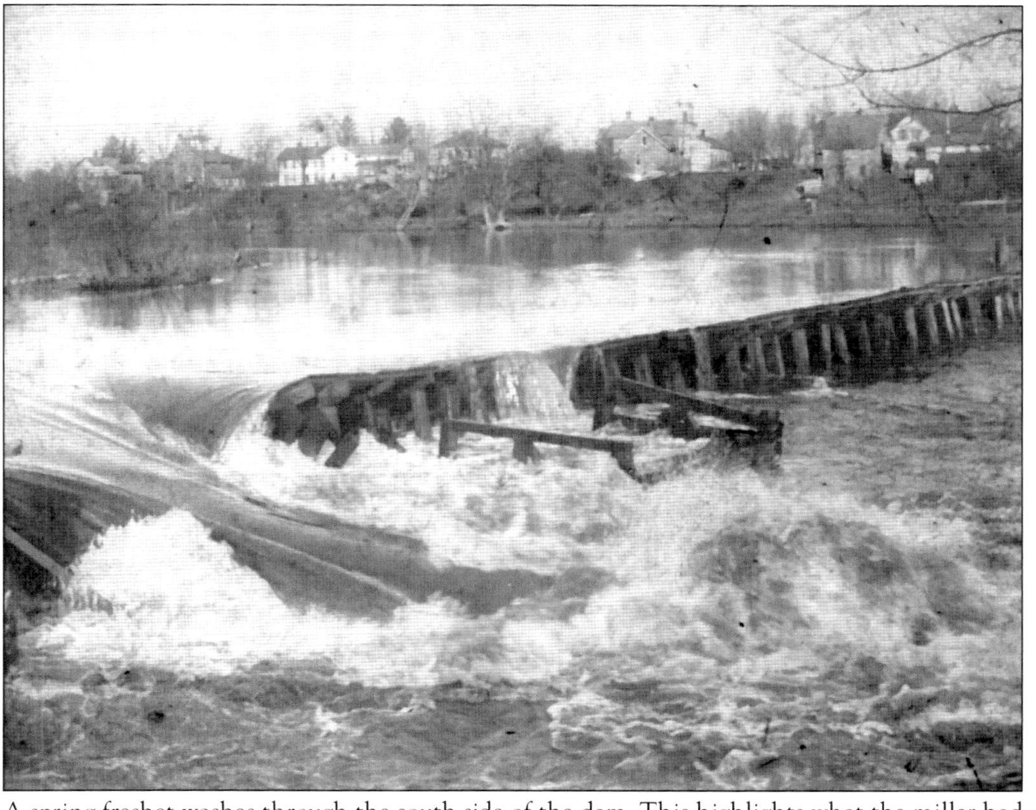

A spring freshet washes through the south side of the dam. This highlights what the miller had to contend with; once the dam gave way, the miller no longer had power. The old wood dam was a source of constant headaches for the mill's operation. Scenes like this were a common sight until 1911, when a concrete dam was built. The houses seen here are on Riley Street.

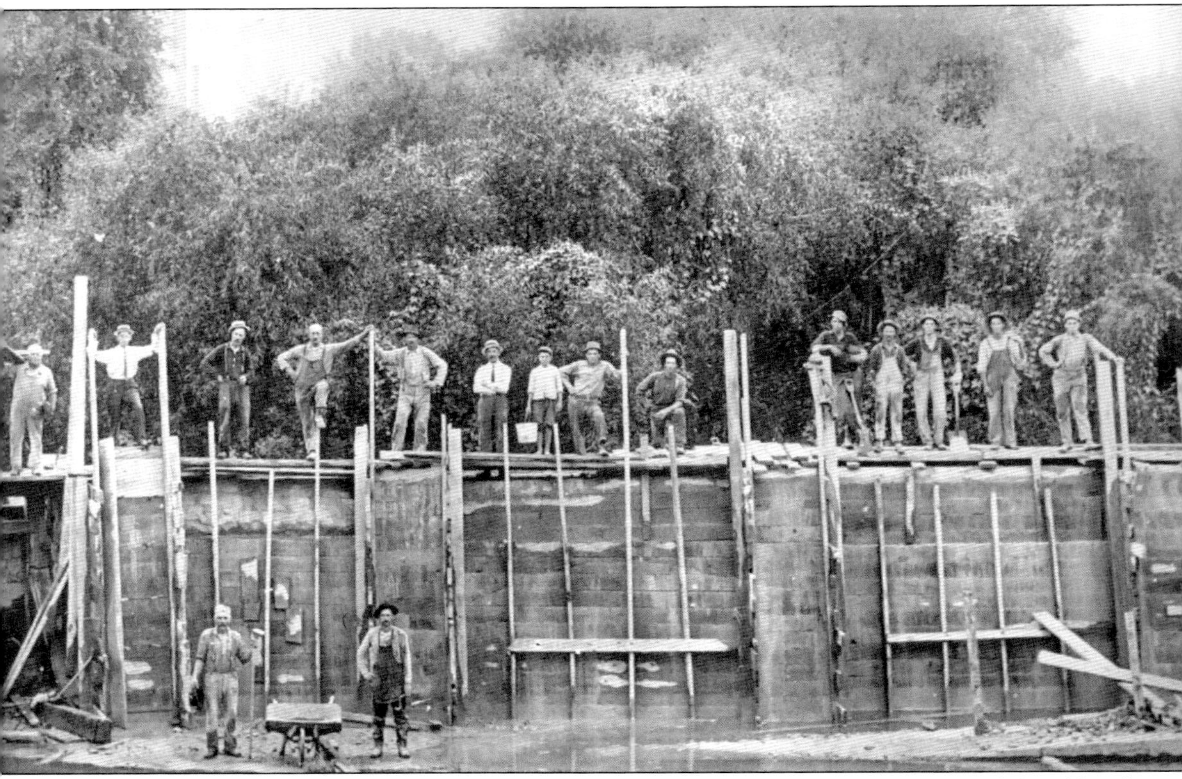

The following is from the *Dundee Reporter* of February 24, 1911: "About 100 feet of the old mill dam gave way from the sheer pressure of water, during the forenoon of Wednesday last. This means a most vexatious inconvenience to those depending on the water power for electric motor power. The lighting of the town will be taken care of, as of yore, by the old plant. The Hydraulic Company is certainly having troubles of its own." This news report referred to the old steam plant on Main Street that took over electric power as a backup during the outage. Workers for the new concrete dam are seen taking a moment for a photograph in 1911. They had to divert the river and build wood forms to pour concrete. The new concrete dam cost about $40,000.

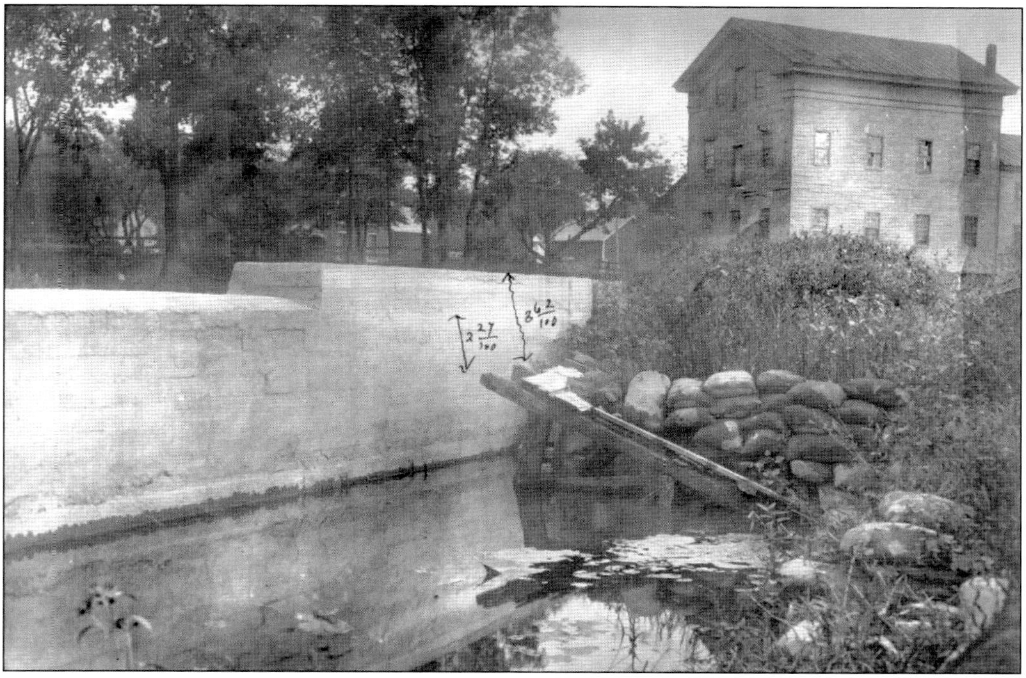

The farmers upstream claimed the new dam was higher and filed a lawsuit in 1912 pointing out that it was flooding their properties. The farmers won their case in county court. When the dam owners appealed in state court, the farmers won again. As a result, the dam owners had to cut back the height of their new concrete dam. This picture with handwritten notations was part of the state trial evidence.

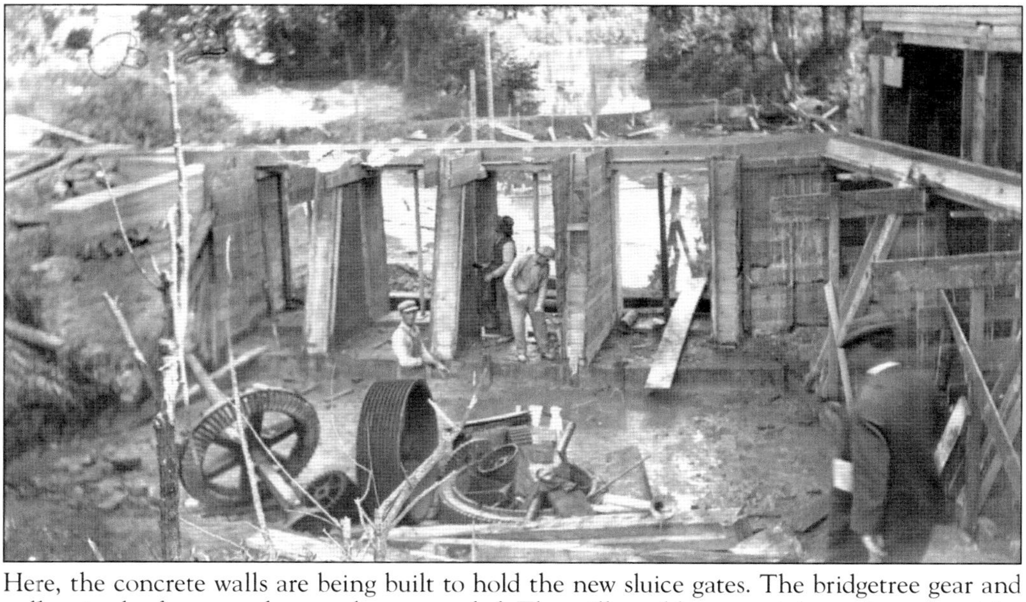

Here, the concrete walls are being built to hold the new sluice gates. The bridgetree gear and pulleys in the foreground are no longer needed. The mill would now mainly produce electricity and some feed for farmers. Over the new gates, a temporary dam can be seen holding back the River Raisin from the work area.

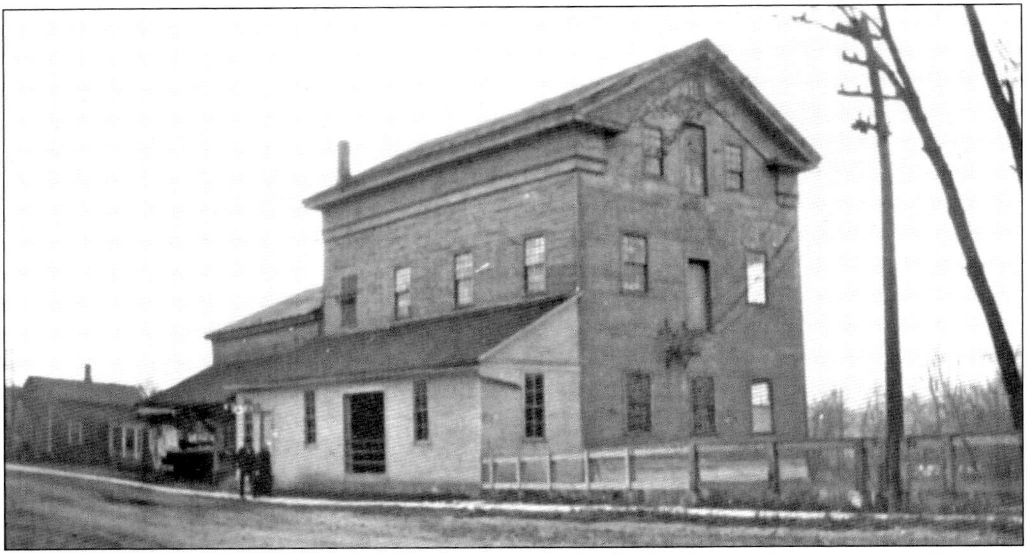

Just after 1911, the mill is shown functioning primarily as a hydroelectric plant supplying electricity to the village of Dundee. Wires connect the front of the building to an electric power pole, but the electricity was unreliable. Town wags remarked that if the lights suddenly went out, a fish was caught again in the turbine.

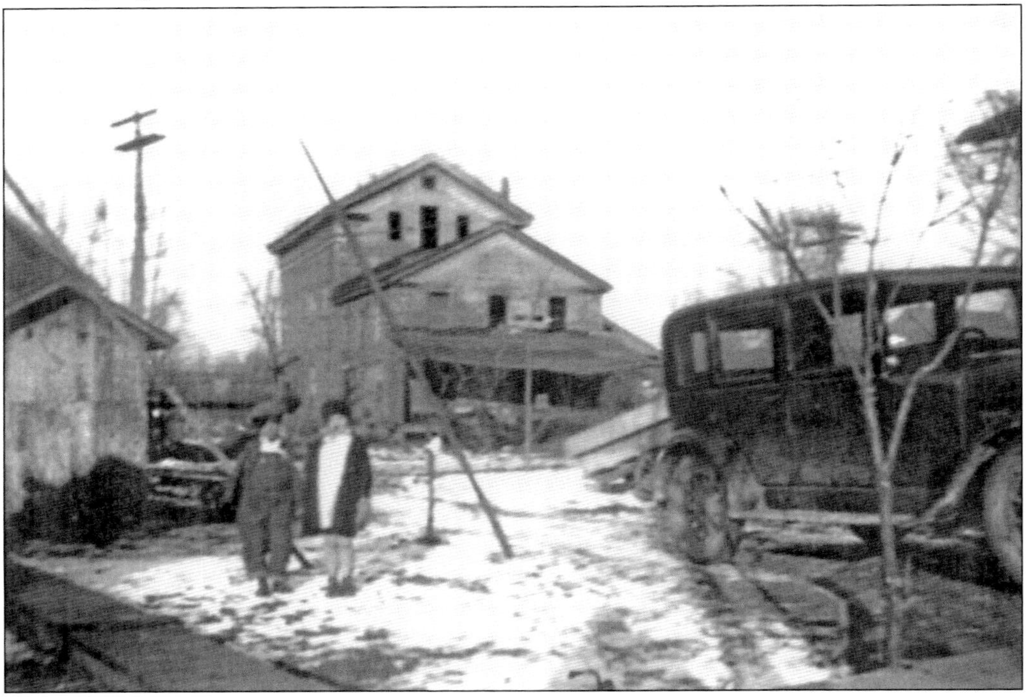

Madelyn Berns, a longtime Old Mill Museum archivist, poses with her twin brother, Wyman, behind their home around 1931. In the background, the mill has fallen on hard times and has been abandoned for seven years. The Dundee Village Council considers it a fire hazard and an eyesore and has contacted the state fire marshal about having it demolished. To everyone's surprise, the fire marshal discovers that Henry Ford is the owner.

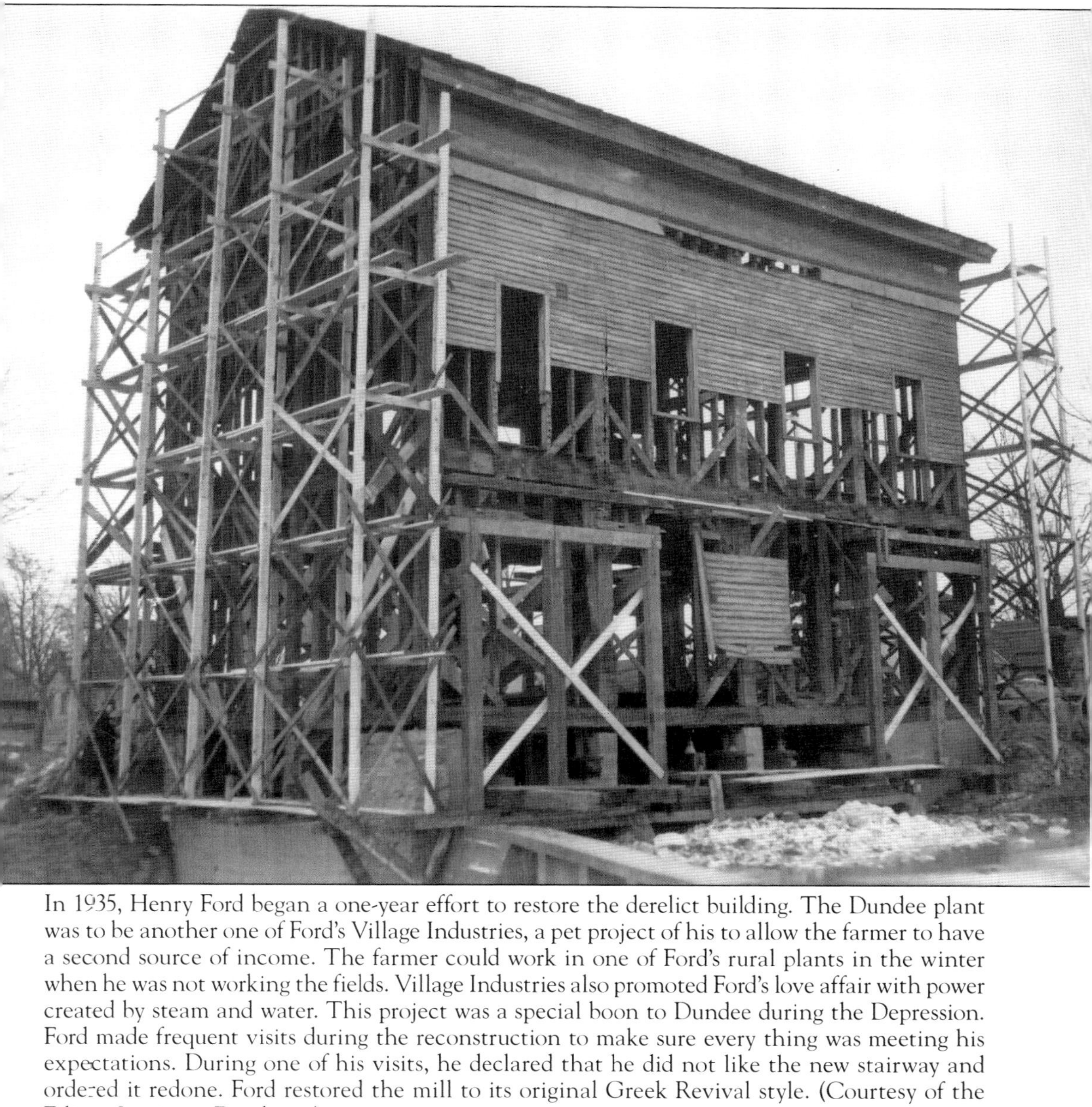

In 1935, Henry Ford began a one-year effort to restore the derelict building. The Dundee plant was to be another one of Ford's Village Industries, a pet project of his to allow the farmer to have a second source of income. The farmer could work in one of Ford's rural plants in the winter when he was not working the fields. Village Industries also promoted Ford's love affair with power created by steam and water. This project was a special boon to Dundee during the Depression. Ford made frequent visits during the reconstruction to make sure every thing was meeting his expectations. During one of his visits, he declared that he did not like the new stairway and ordered it redone. Ford restored the mill to its original Greek Revival style. (Courtesy of the Edison Institute, Dearborn.)

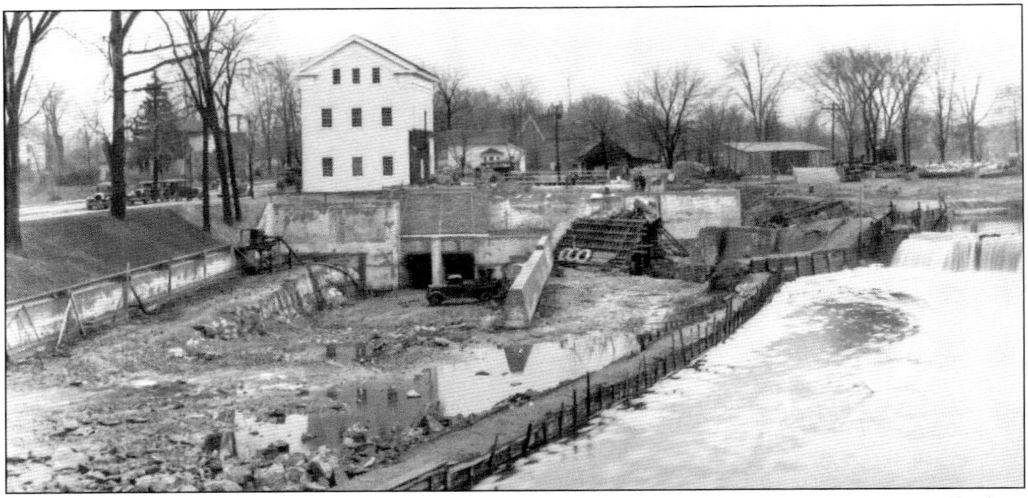

Here work proceeds on the limestone addition and the dam area in 1935. A temporary cofferdam has been constructed so that the limestone base of the river is laid bare. A tailrace for the new turbine has been blasted out of the limestone, lowering it nine feet. Master craftsman Larry Sharp used quarried limestone to build a stone addition to the mill. (Courtesy of the Edison Institute, Dearborn.)

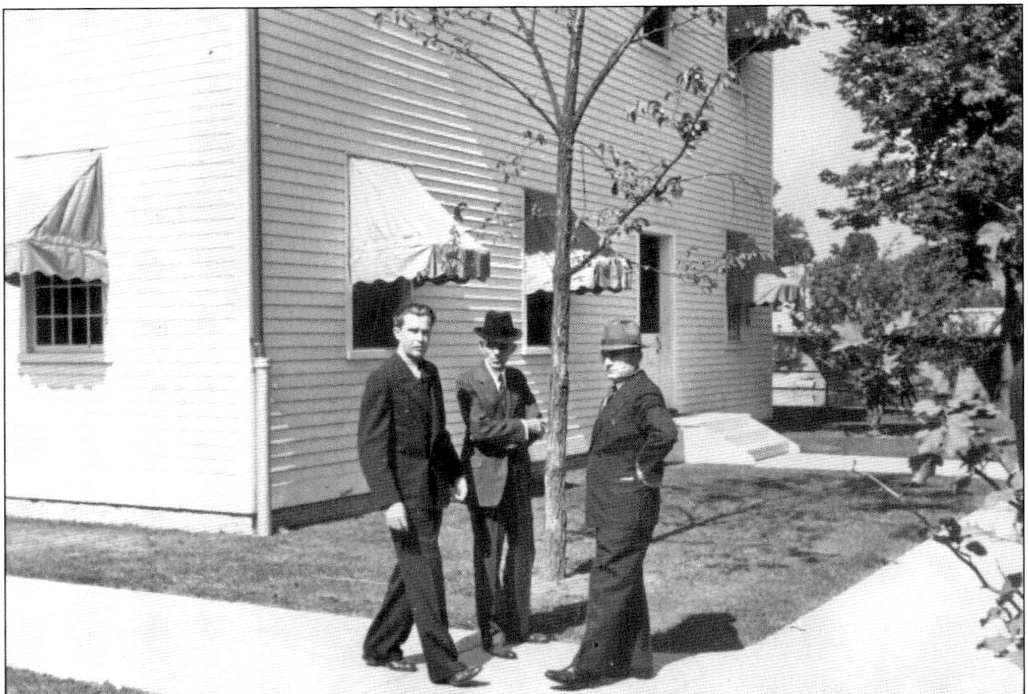

Henry Ford (center) stands in front of the refurbished mill with his entourage. This photograph was probably taken before the mill's grand opening in 1936. Ford brought along his grandson William Clay Ford on some of his later visits. Ford was idealistic about building factories in farm territory. He said, "With one foot on the land and one foot in industry, America is safe." (Courtesy of the Edison Institute, Dearborn.)

Bill Ellis pours molten brass into forms for spot welding tips. He is working in the foundry in the limestone addition at the Dundee Ford factory. The copper welding tips, which were shipped to the Ford River Rouge plant, were the Dundee's main product. The limestone addition also housed two large, coal-fired boilers that provided steam for heat and a steam-powered generator. (Courtesy of the Edison Institute, Dearborn.)

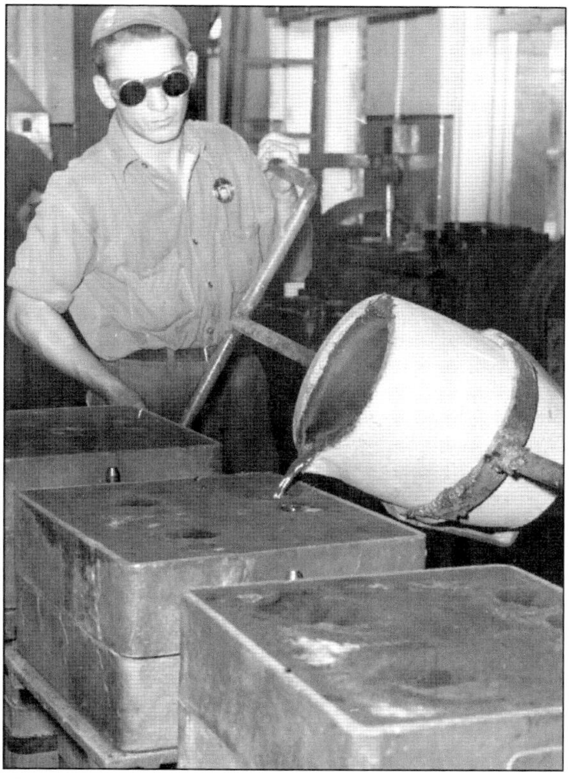

Ace Diver is operating a turret lathe. The turret could be turned to bring a drill and other tools into position to shape the welding tips. The metal shavings in this picture came from metal cut from the welding tips. Spot welding was first introduced to the automobile industry around 1920. (Courtesy of the Edison Institute.)

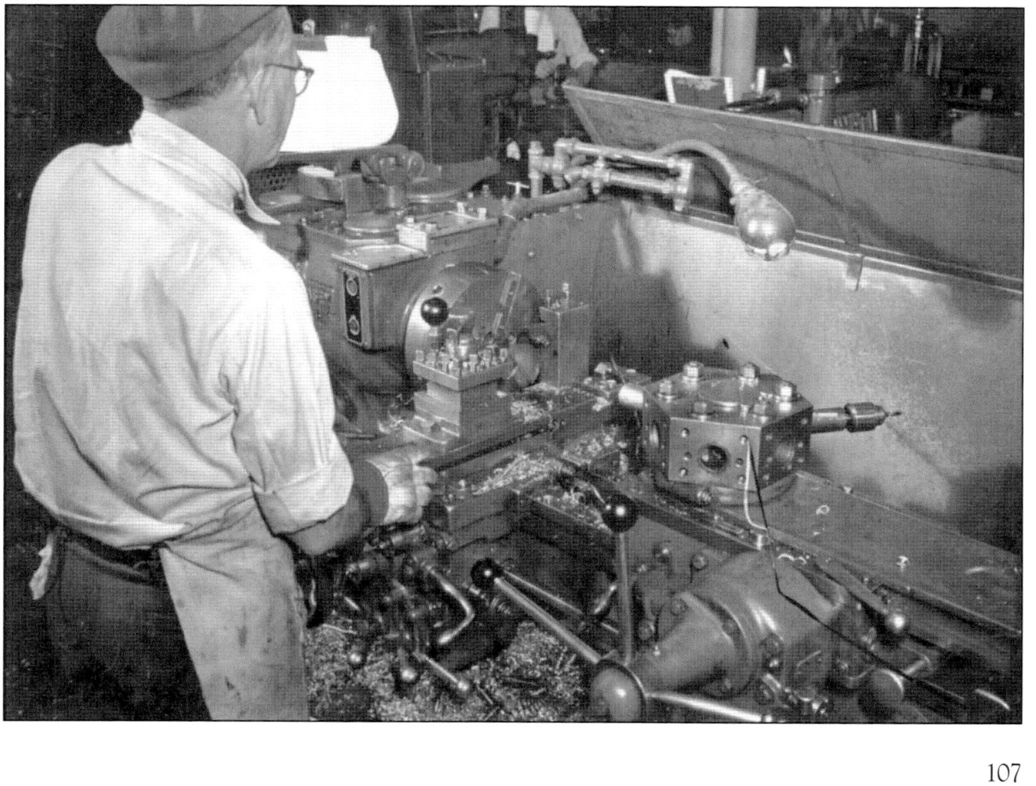

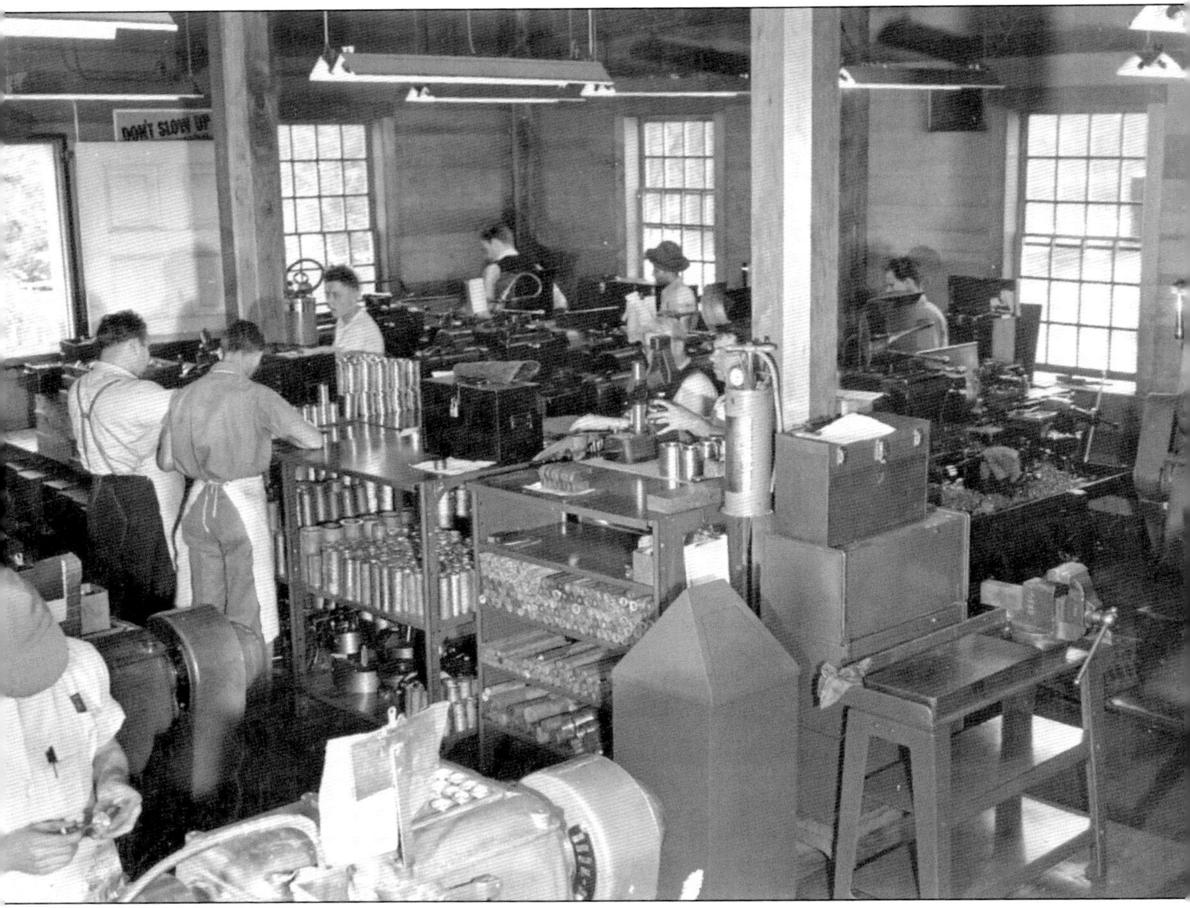

On the second floor, the old gristmill employees used machine tools to finish the cast welding tips. Electricity came from a combination of sources: Ford's steam and water-powered generators and Edison lines. In the 1800s, the second floor of the mill would have had flour-producing machinery, driven by water-powered turbines in the basement through a system of shafts, pulleys, and belts. After Ford's death in 1947, Ford Motor Company began selling Village Industries holdings. The Dundee plant was purchased by Wolverine Manufacturing in 1954 to produce paper gaskets for automobiles. In 1970, the Village of Dundee purchased the property for $1. The Ford part of the current complex serves as a museum and kitchen area for the community center (the Wolverine addition). (Courtesy of the Edison Institute, Dearborn.)

Seven

THE NEWFOUND FIFTIES

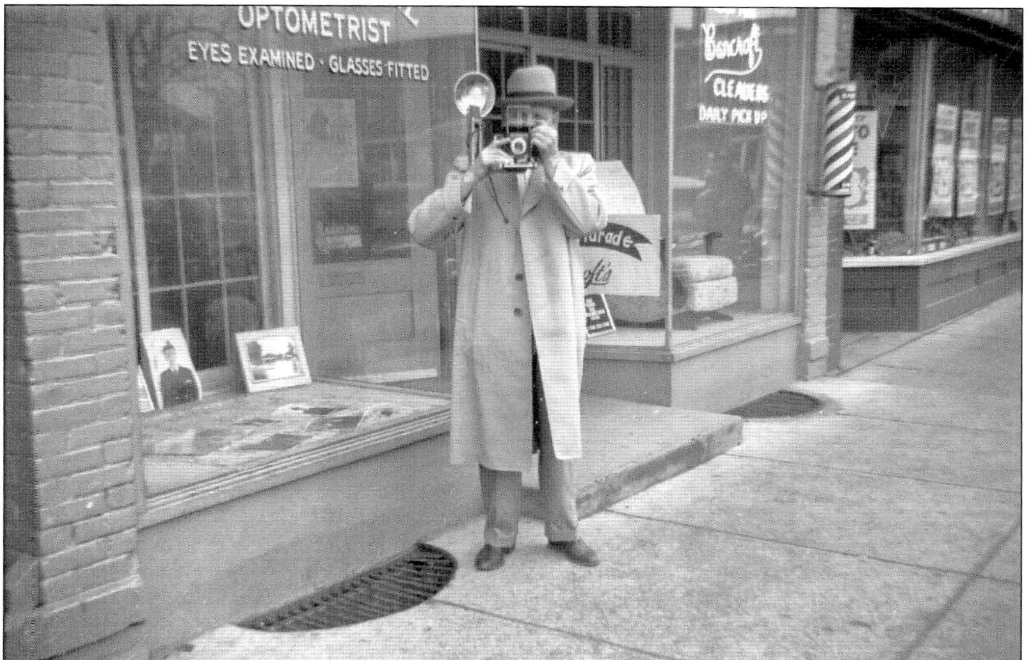

Lloyd T. Harris was a respected photographer and artist. A treasure trove of his negatives was recently discovered. L.T. Harris documented Dundee happenings in the 1950s through his photography. He is shown here on Riley Street. His body of work is eclectic and includes Memorial Day parades, youth activities, and the opening of limited-access US 23. Unless otherwise noted, Harris took all photographs in this chapter.

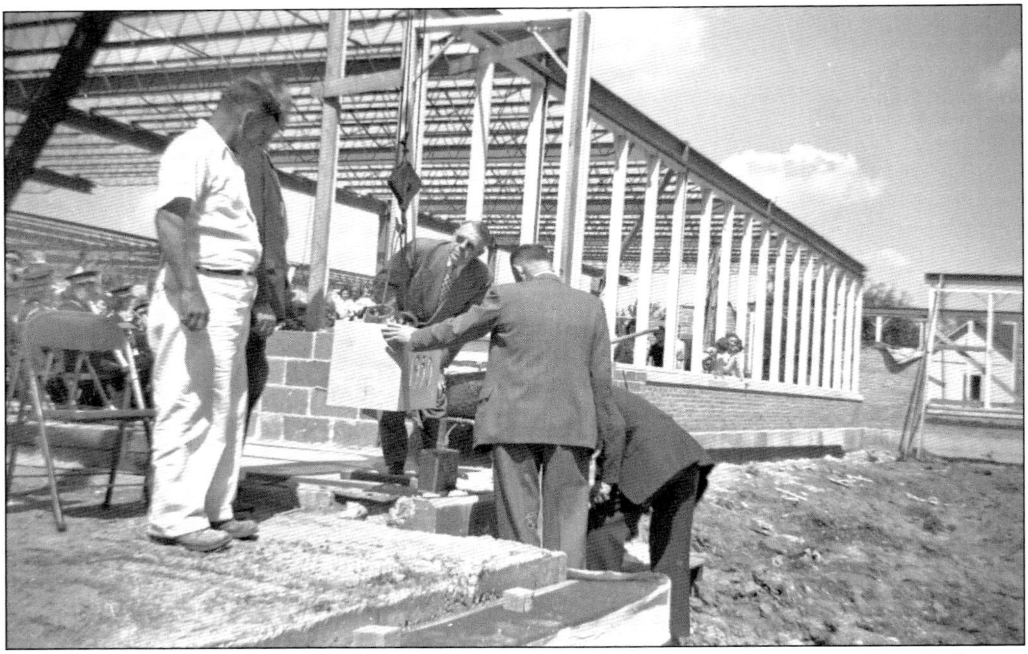

After consolidation in 1947, Dundee Community Schools needed more room to accommodate its pupils. In 1950, it laid the cornerstone for an addition to its present elementary building on Adams Street. A block and tackle assists board members, including Ernest Waterstradt, Edward Rath, Carlyle Kay, Harry Coleman, Harry Busch, and longtime Supt. Frank Ayres, lay the stone.

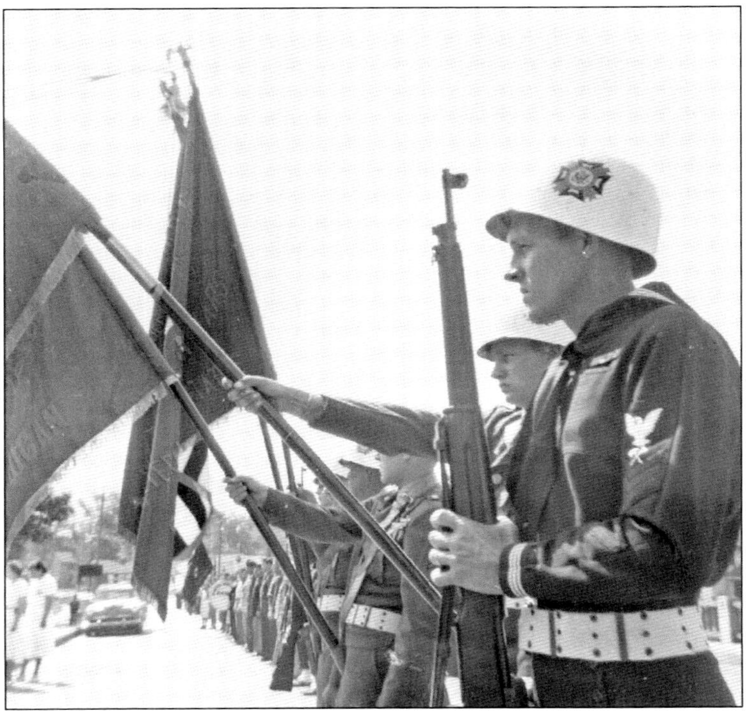

An honor guard, including Navy man Wyman Hanson (right) with Maynard Miller next to him, stands at attention on the Dundee Bridge during this 1951 Memorial Day parade. Barely seen on the left is a line of the veteran's auxiliary. The ladies line the bridge. When given the signal, they would toss a wreath into the river commemorating those lost at sea.

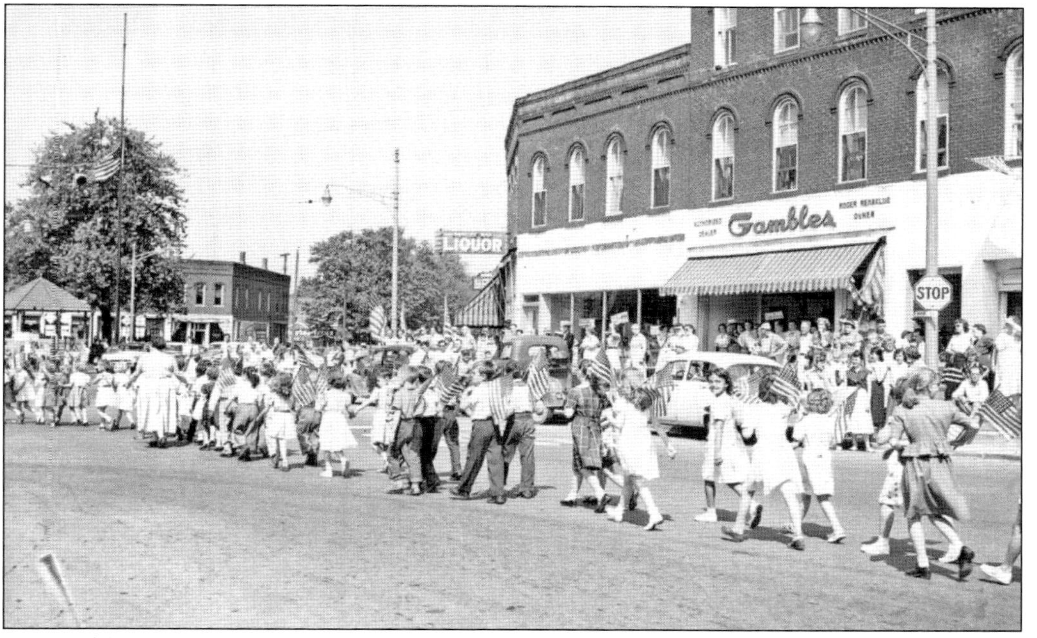

A crowd has gathered in front of the Main and Tecumseh Streets stores to watch the 1953 Memorial Day parade. A long line of schoolchildren marches in front of the crowd. The students are turning left toward the bridge and the wreath-tossing ceremony. Almost all of them are carrying American flags.

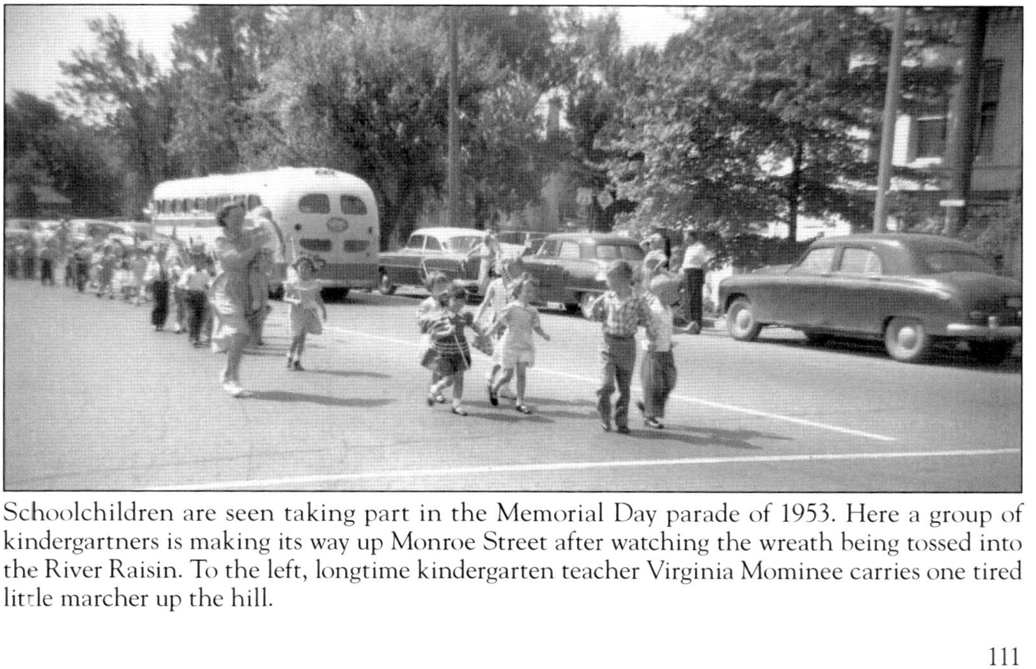

Schoolchildren are seen taking part in the Memorial Day parade of 1953. Here a group of kindergartners is making its way up Monroe Street after watching the wreath being tossed into the River Raisin. To the left, longtime kindergarten teacher Virginia Mominee carries one tired little marcher up the hill.

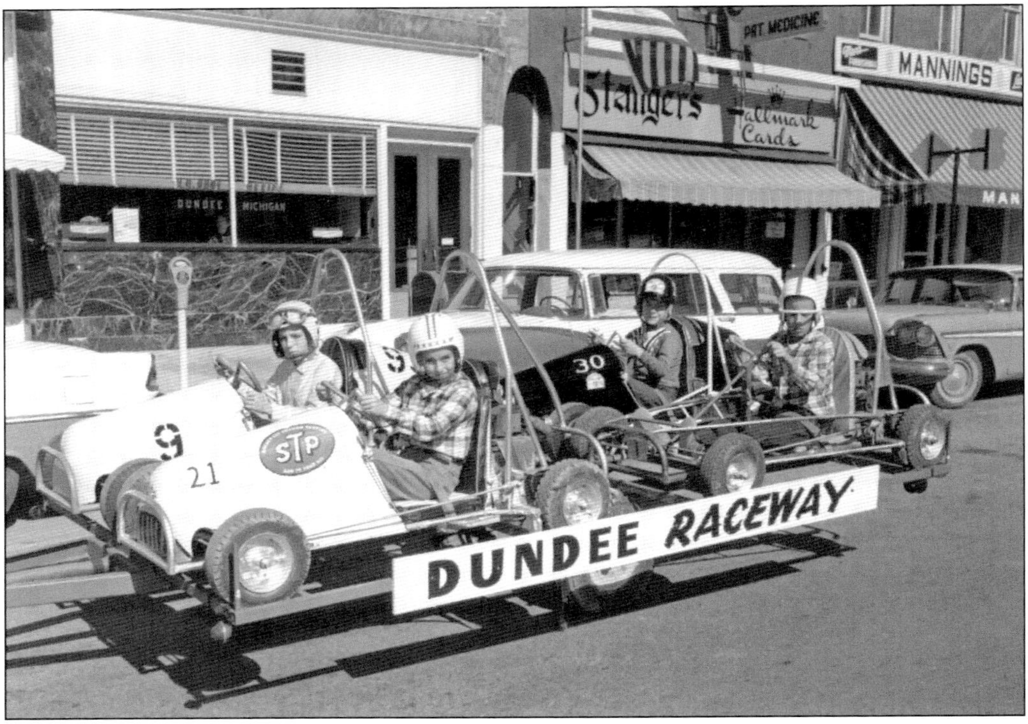

These youngsters, all under 10 years old, enjoyed driving their go-carts in parades. They are called "Track Rabbit Racers." The drivers are, from left to right, Bob Bazzell, Mike Curley, Douglas Jennings, and Wayne "Butch" Williams. They were probably all the envy of their classmates, and their mothers were most likely very grateful that they had roll bars.

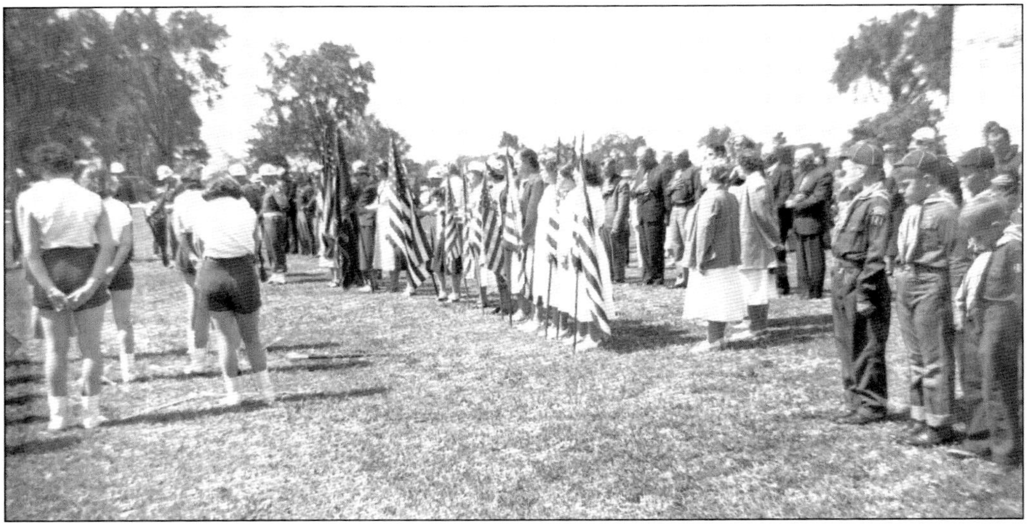

A crowd pauses in Maple Grove Cemetery during the 1952 Memorial Day observance. High school band members stand respectfully on the left, with Boy Scouts on the right. Typically there was a benediction before high school students read the Gettysburg Address, Gen. Logan's Orders, and Joyce Kilmer's "In Flander's Fields." The program closed with "Taps" before some moved on to Oak Grove, the pioneer cemetery, on Summerfield Road.

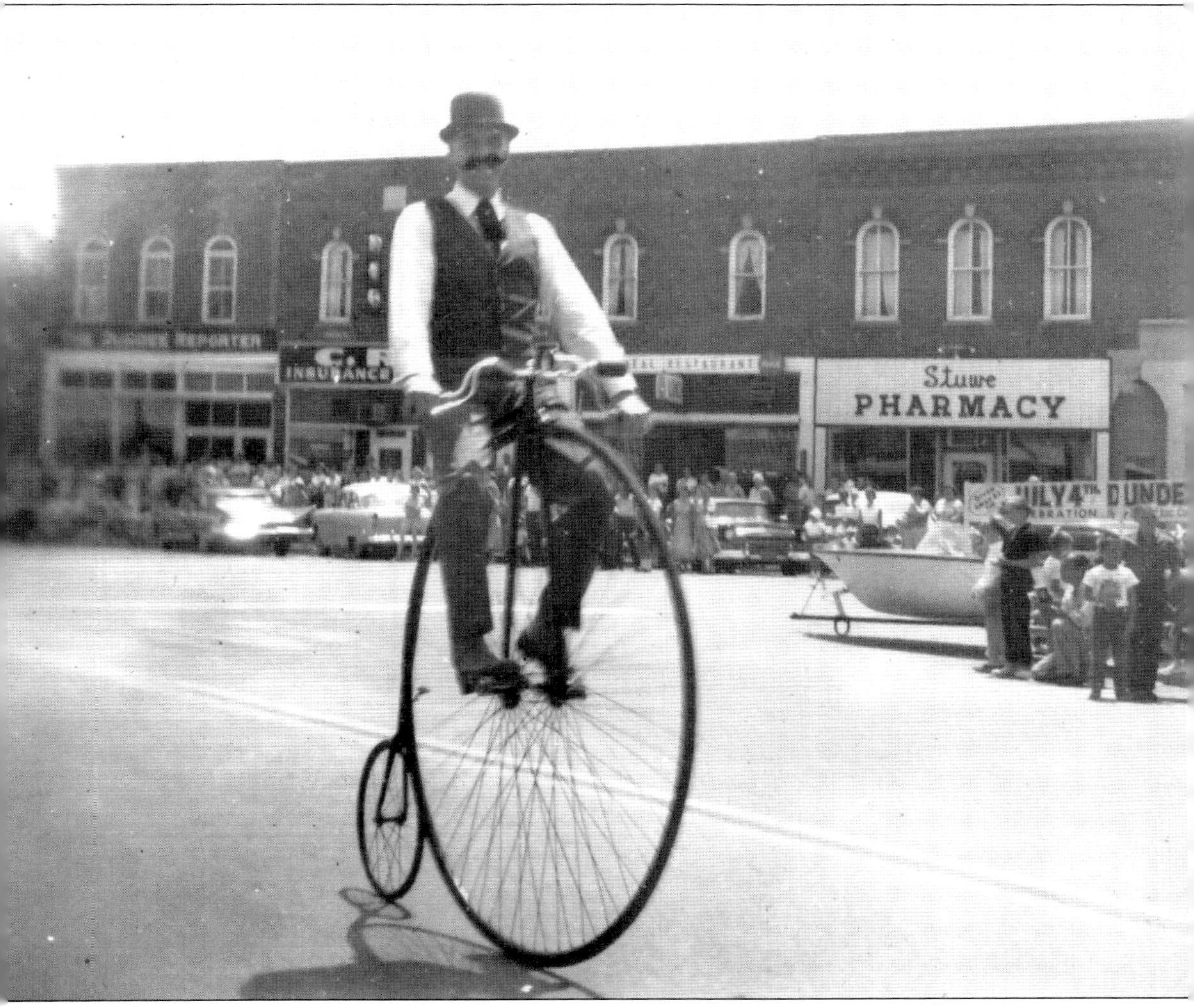

Everyone loved watching Rene Crombez ride his high-wheel bike in Dundee parades. Beaming, Mr. Crombez is seen peddling down Tecumseh Street in a Fourth of July parade. In addition to his bicycle-riding ability, Crombez was also known as Dundee's last blacksmith. The story is told that he saw a woman taking his picture, so Crombez struck a pose, lost his balance, fell, and declared that it was his last parade. In the background, a boat, which was a raffle prize, appears to be "moored" at the point of the triangle.

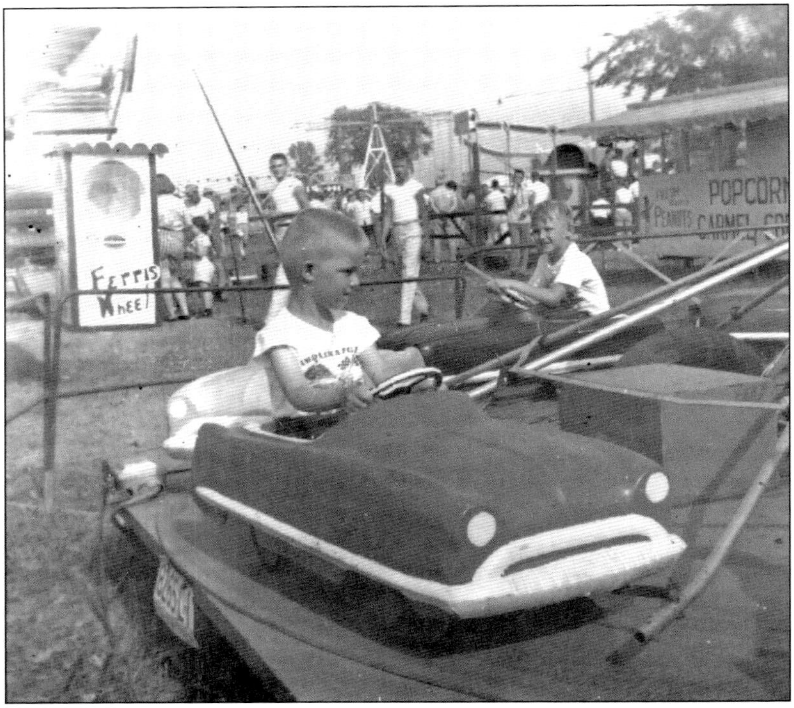

These little guys are enjoying one of the Fourth of July carnival rides. In the background, parents and kids wait their turn on the Ferris wheel. In the right background is the track for the roller coaster. Popcorn and caramel candy, always crowd-pleasers, are for sale. The carnival was set up at Penfield and Van Nest Streets.

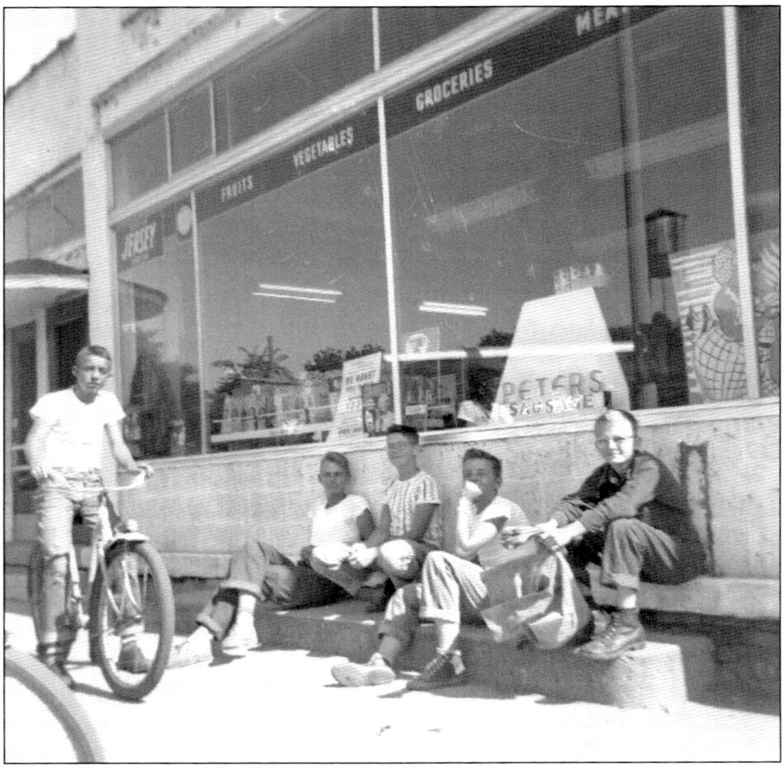

These five newspaper boys sit in front of Iott's Market on the very step where the Civil War Stonewall Regiment posed in 1908. The boys are waiting for their deliveries of the *Monroe Evening News.* They are, from left to right, Dale Goetz, Bill Dean, Dean Sheldon, Paul Dean, and Jack Ingall.

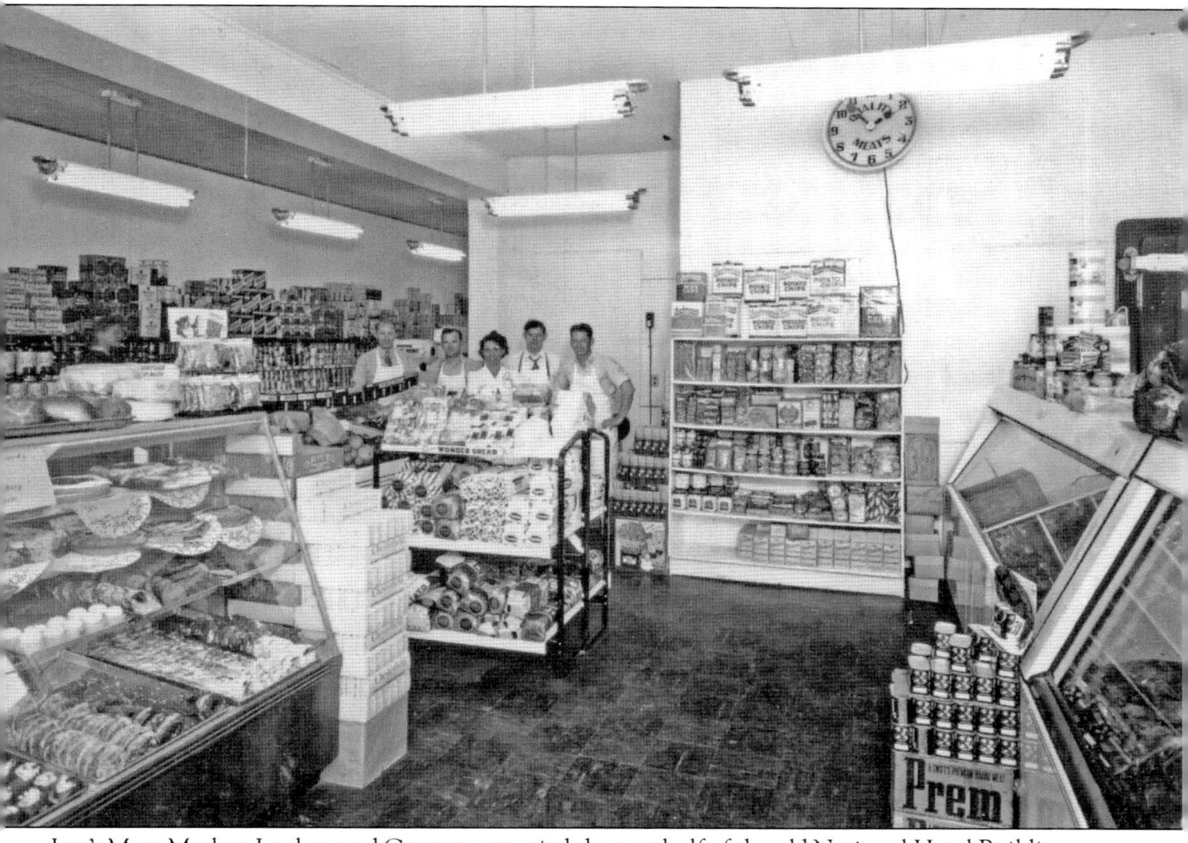

Iott's Meat Market, Locker, and Grocery occupied the east half of the old National Hotel Building at 112 Main Street. Around 1950 are, from left to right standing behind the bread display, Otis Gloff, who will soon buy the store, Bunny Iott, Clara Furrow, Walt Rawley, and Leon Schultz. This photograph highlights the back of the store with its refrigerated locker. At this time, some people only had iceboxes, cooled by almost-daily blocks of ice. To store large quantities of meat and vegetables, Iott rented shelves in his locker to customers. The door to the locker is on the extreme right. A large stack of Chesterfield cigarettes sits on the floor next to the pastry case and in front of the racks of bread.

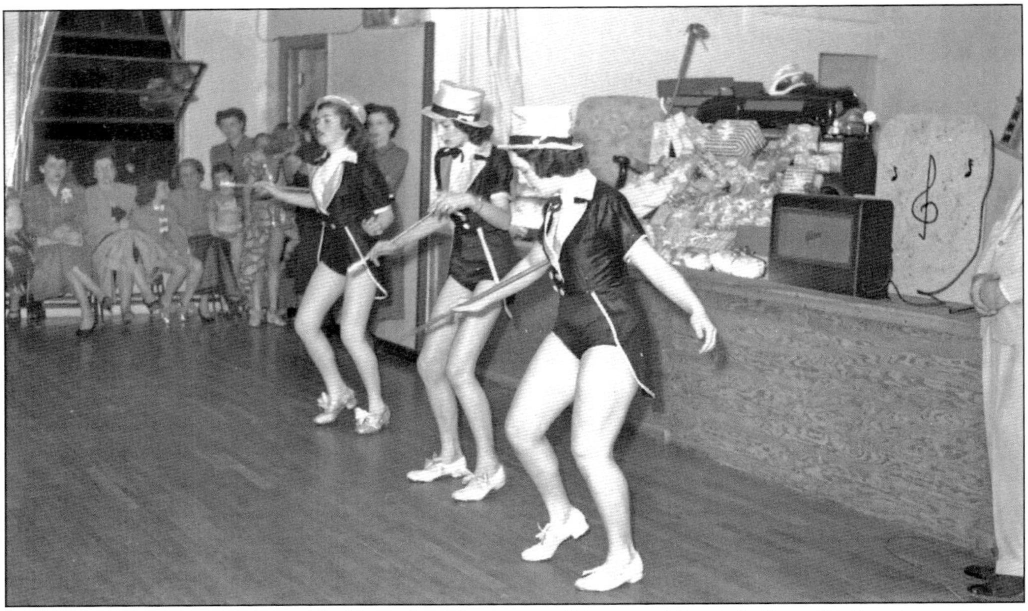

The 1952 Fireman's Ball was held in the Veterans of Foreign Wars Hall at 418 Dunham Street. Entertainment was provided by these three teenage tap dancers. This was a time when dancing was not always confined to recitals. The girl in the center is probably Barbara Ralston. The VFW hall was frequently used for community affairs.

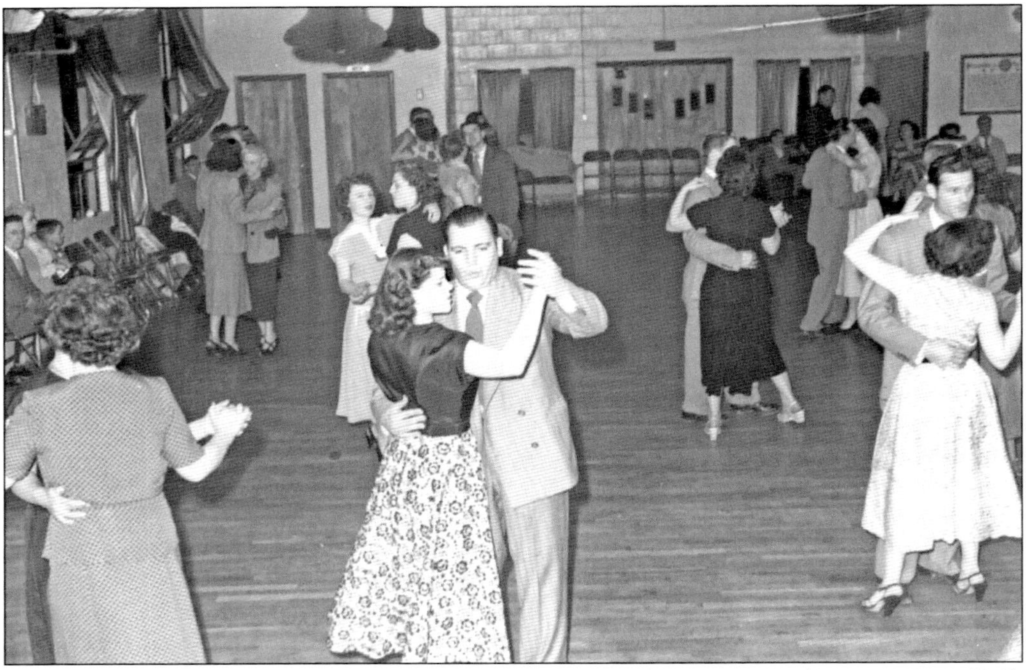

Couples dance at the 1952 Fireman's Ball held at the popular Veterans of Foreign Wars Hall. Although most couples are composed of men and women, it appears that at least two sets of women are doing the fox trot in the background. The bell decorations on the ceiling suggest it is Christmastime.

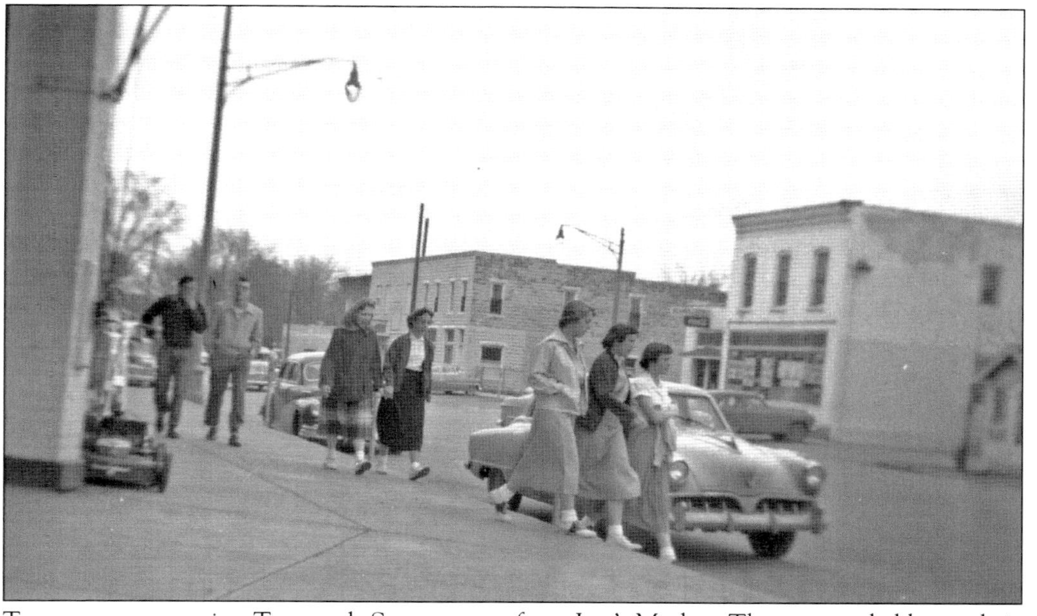

Teenagers are crossing Tecumseh Street across from Iott's Market. They are probably on their way from school for a quick lunch at Mitch's (Spero Mitchola) Ideal Restaurant, which was for many years a favorite hangout for area teenagers and the town fathers. When students arrived at the restaurant, they would find a row of 50¢ hamburgers waiting for them, the local version of fast food.

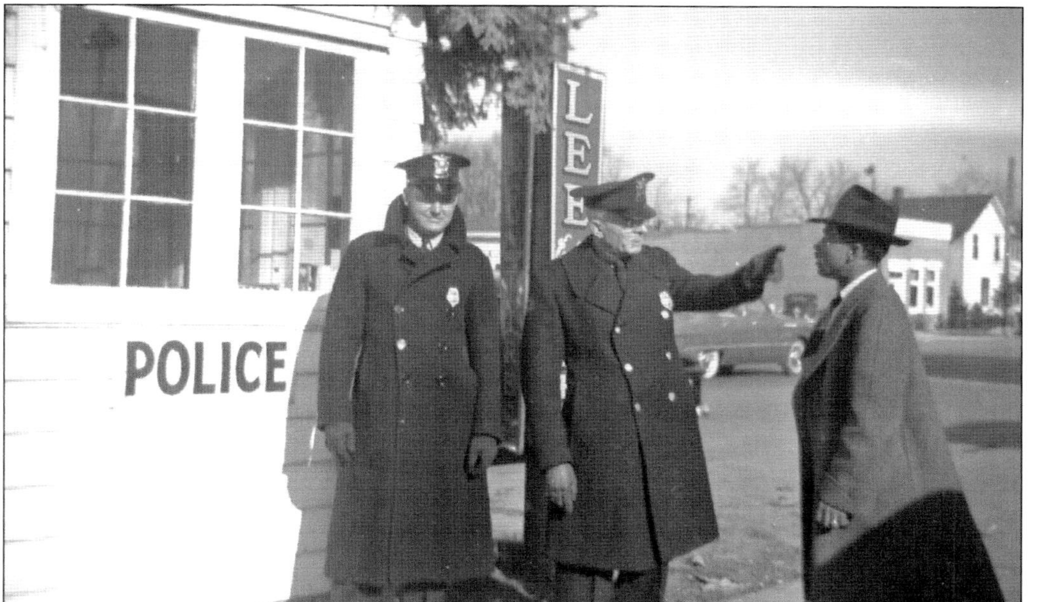

Lyle Goodridge (left), and his partner stand in front of their police shack, a little building located on Main Street in front of the gas station. From time to time, the village has maintained its own police force. In the background is the Dundee Branch Library. Considering the heavy coats and the evergreen garland, it is probably December.

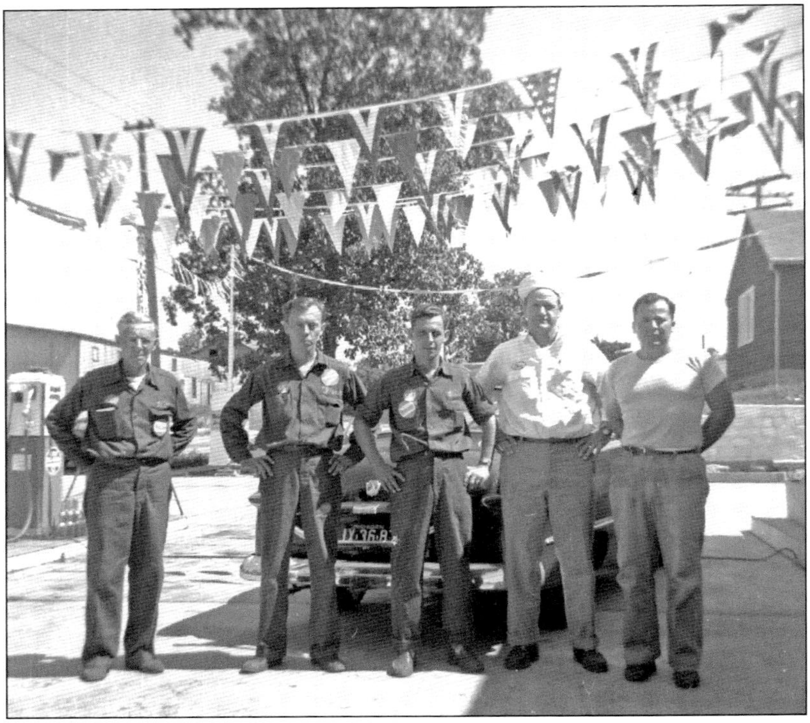

These gentlemen are lined up at the grand opening of the Gulf gas station on Monroe Street. From left to right, owner Bill Kuhlman and his sons Frank and Bill pose with customer Chas Jennings and noted race-car driver Iggy Katona in the bright sunshine. The Van DeVenter tomato cannery can be seen in the left background on the bank of the River Raisin.

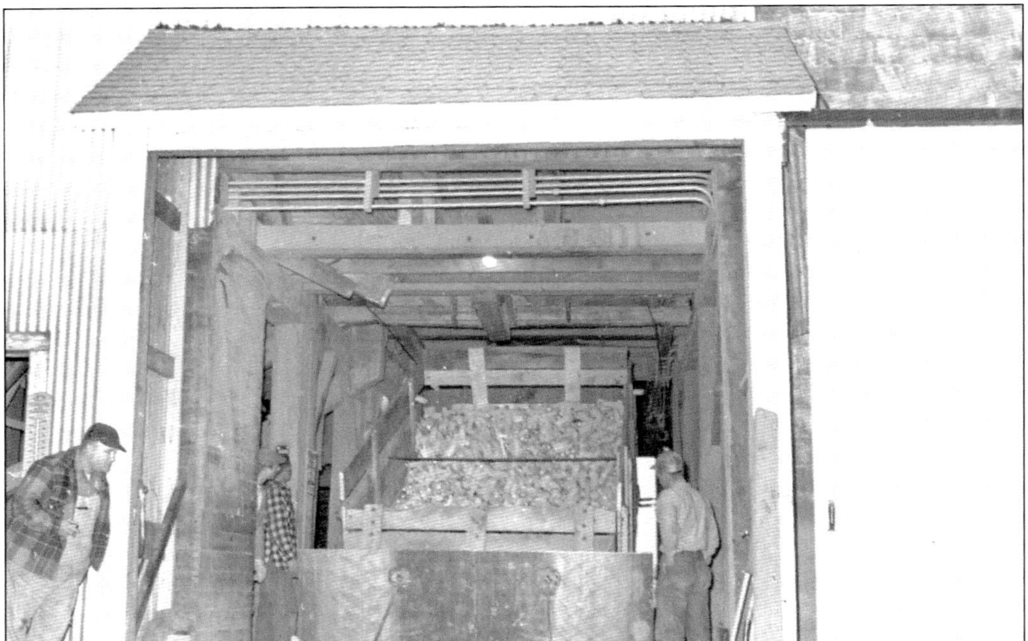

Corn is being dumped at Karner's grain elevator at 607 Main Street. The elevator structure was located beside the railroad with space in the rear of the property for community auctions. Corn is one of the major crops of Monroe County. During the fall, grain dryers can be heard whirring day and night. Richard Karner, the owner, played many civic roles, including school board president.

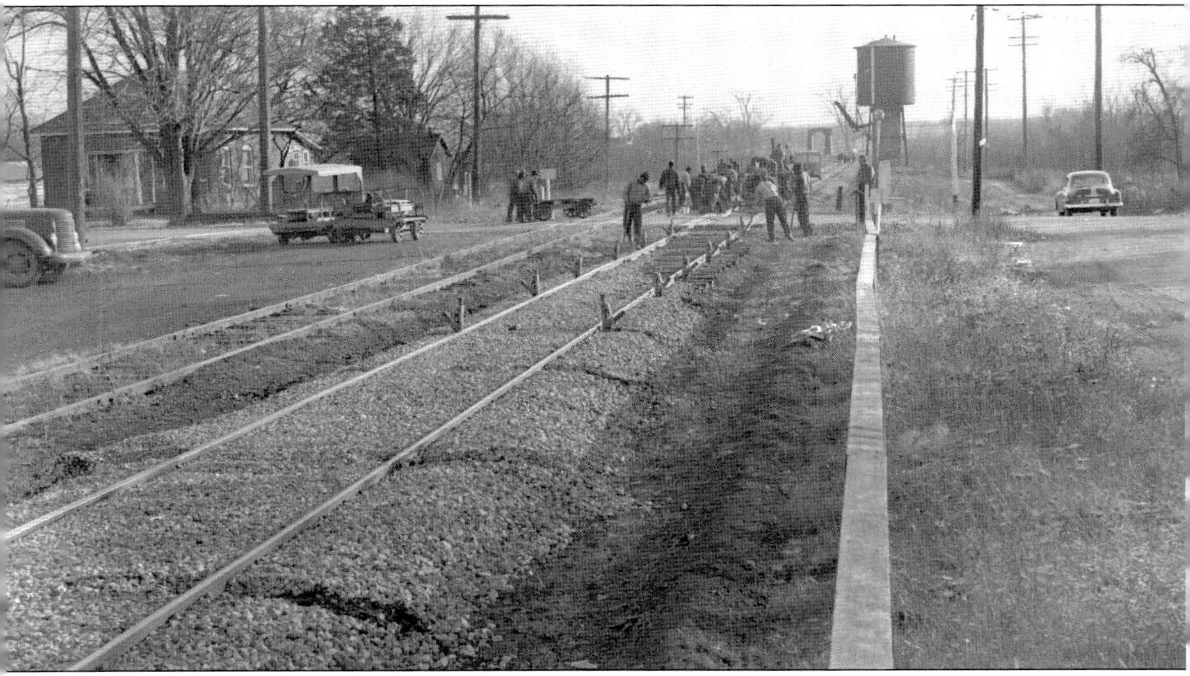

The date is November 11, 1952, and a railroad section crew is improving the Ann Arbor Railroad roadbed in preparation for heavier diesel trains. Jacks hold up the rails, while the men level off the bed. No crossing gates have been installed on Main Street at this time. The last passenger train left Dundee two years before. The water tower is visible on the other side of Main Street, but it disappeared when steam trains were phased out. Darrell Powell remembers watching the work crew and playing ball with them after hours. The crew slept in cars on their work train as they traveled the length of the system.

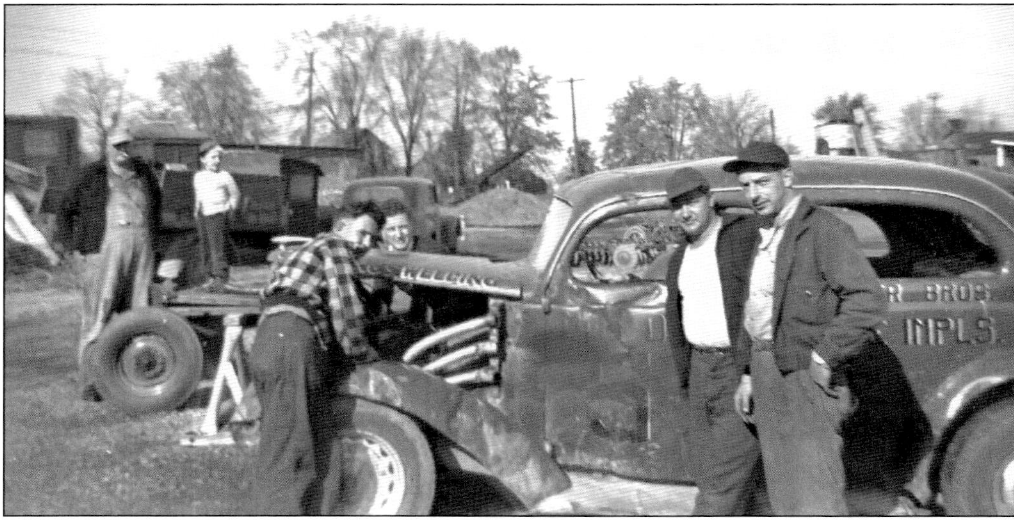

Hot-rod lovers work on a car in a lot next to the Karner elevator. Hot-rodders loved the speed, and they loved turning an old wreck into a winning car. They were often backed by a business, such as Karner Bros., which sponsored this car. It helped with expenses and put the firm's name in front of the public.

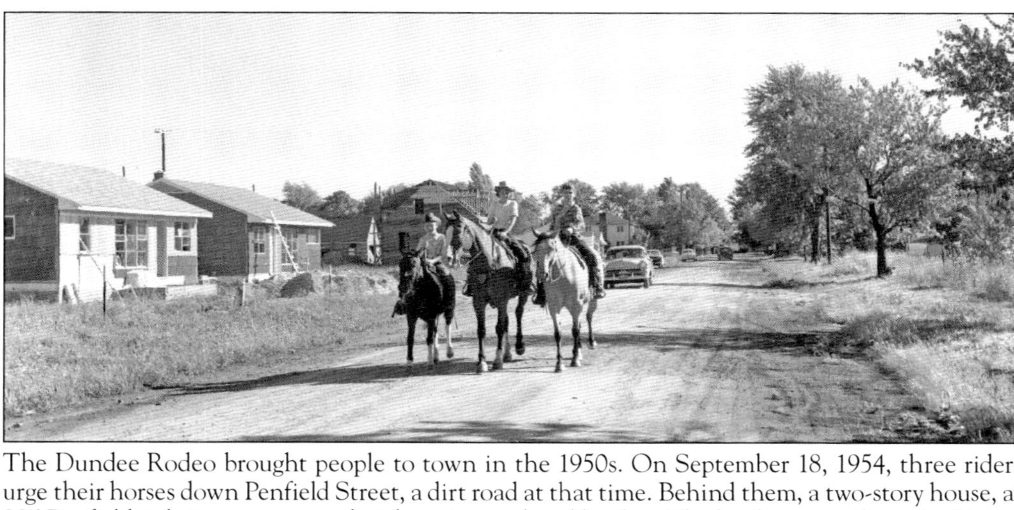

The Dundee Rodeo brought people to town in the 1950s. On September 18, 1954, three riders urge their horses down Penfield Street, a dirt road at that time. Behind them, a two-story house, at 286 Penfield, is being constructed with various colored lumber. The lumber came from the Union Station after it was torn down. Steven Lipka, the last stationmaster, was building the home.

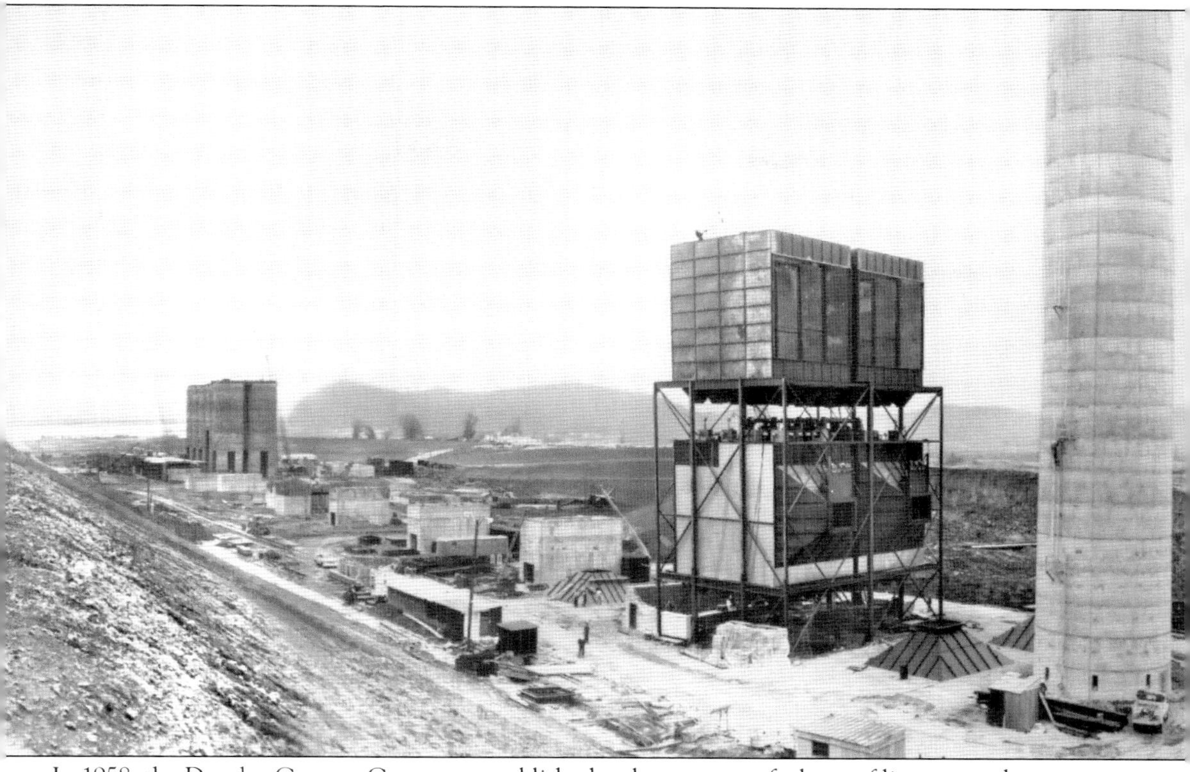

In 1958, the Dundee Cement Company established a plant on top of a layer of limestone close to the surface at Dundee. This site, pictured under construction, also provided ease of transportation, as it was located between US 23 and a railroad. One of the first employees, Gary Brockman, had to go to Canada for training. He asked his girlfriend, Jeanette Helle, to go with him. She said yes if they were married, so they had a Friday wedding presided over by Rev. Fred Cesler. As it turns out, the Brockman marriage has lasted longer than the cement plant, which closed in 2010. During its 50 years of production, the plant played a major economic role in the community. For many years, it was the largest taxpayer. At the time of its closing, it employed 160 workers. (Courtesy of Gary Brockman.)

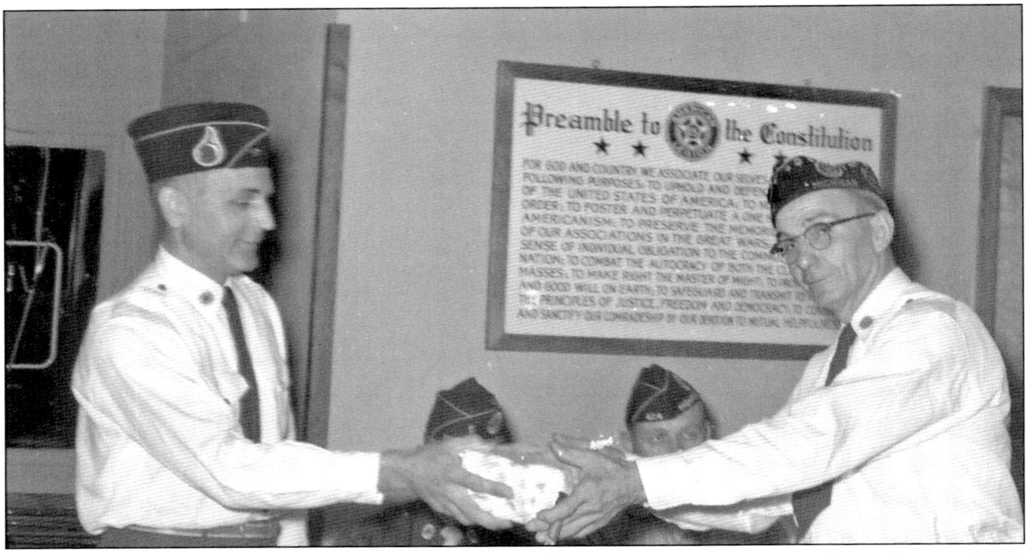

Harold "Heinie" Hanson (right) installs Steven Lipka as VFW post commander in August 1957. Dundee's Grand Army of the Republic William Bell Post No. 10 was one of the first in Michigan when it was founded in 1879. The Veterans of Foreign Wars, the American Legion, and the Disabled American Veterans posts have formed the Veterans Memorial Corporation, which maintains the veterans' building on Dunham Street where this installation took place.

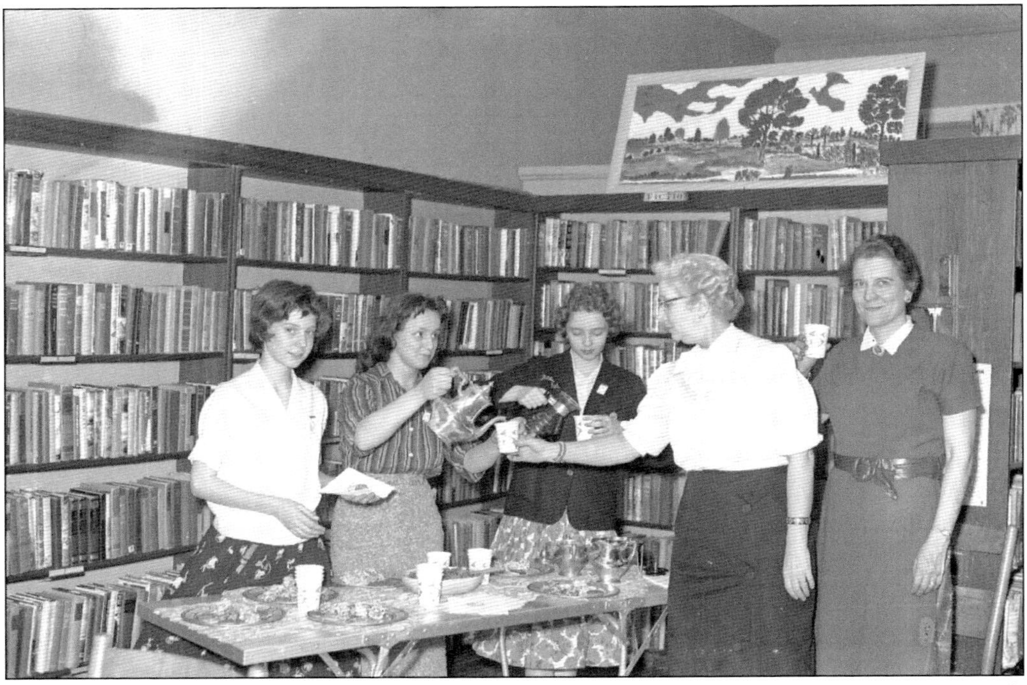

In 1934, the Tuesday Club of Dundee set up a library on a shelf in the back of the Ford Dry Goods Store on Main Street. Linda McLean is seen in May 1959 pouring tea for township librarian Hallie Eckert and high school librarian Charlotte Timm. The library was located at 139 Main Street. Marilyn Riter and Eckert were longtime public librarians who inspired the next generation of readers.

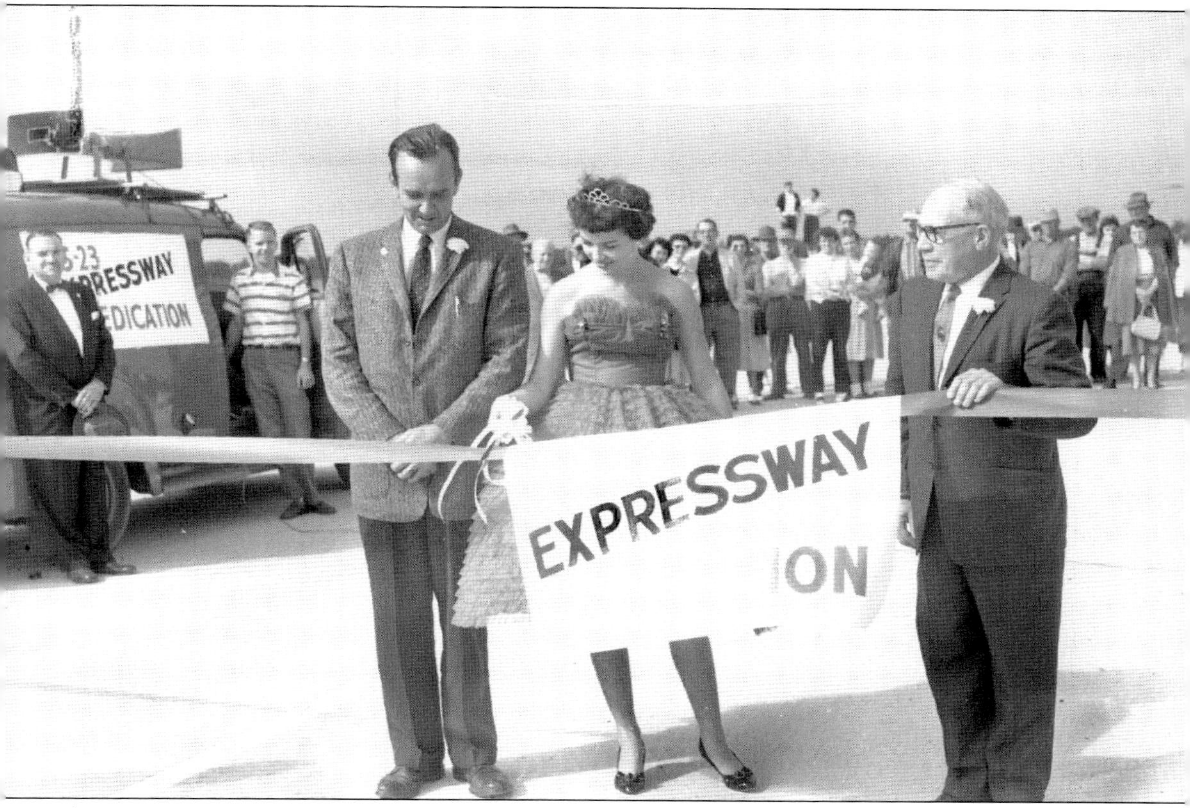

The new US 23 was dedicated on October 1, 1959. Barb Kahley, queen of Dundee High School, stands next to John C. Mackie, Michigan state highway commissioner, to cut the ribbon. Bert Lutz, former Ford Plant superintendent, is on the right. Floyd Wilson, a local businessman, leans back next to the van in a dark suit, while Dale Williams stands in a striped shirt. Wilson was known for driving through town using his loudspeakers to announce important events. Before the new expressway, US 23 followed local roads from Toledo to Dundee. At one time, it went north on Dunham Street through Azalia, Milan, and on to Ann Arbor.

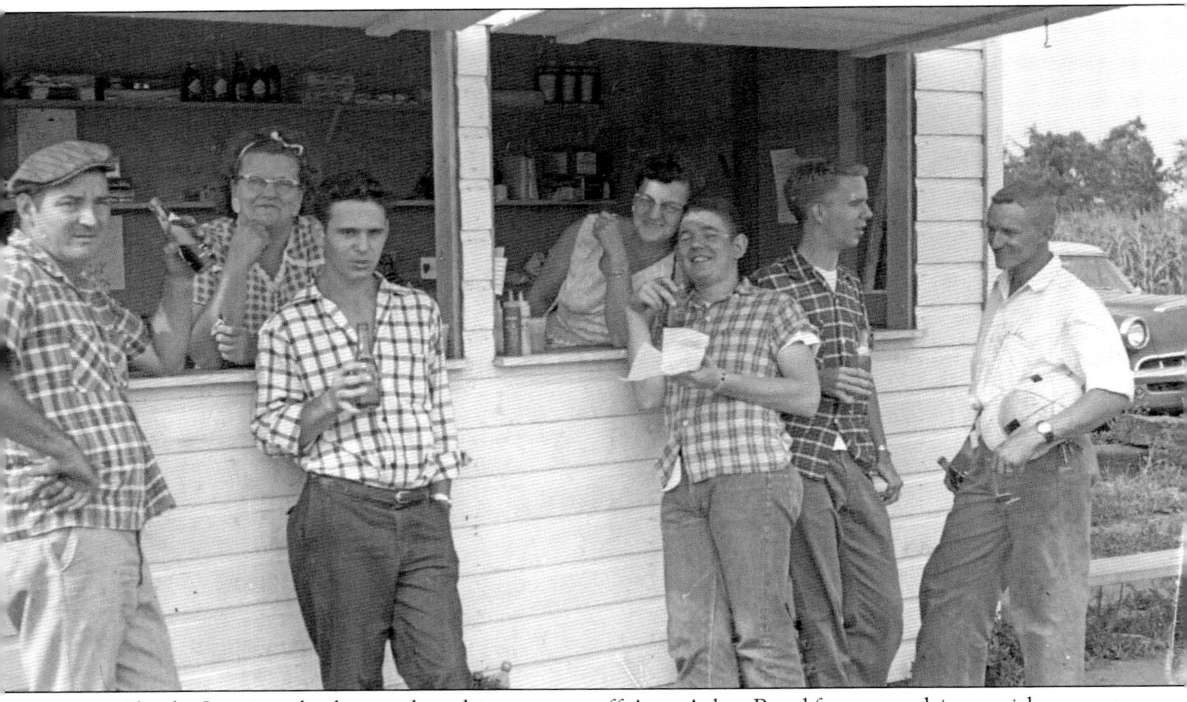

Charlie Jennings built a track on his property off Ann Arbor Road for young drivers with go-carts. Many Dundee boys and their dads participated in this activity. The boys were part of a circuit of racers that held meets in places such as Adrian, Dexter, and Jackson. Besides the racetrack, Jennings provided a snack bar run by his wife, Irene. She is leaning on her elbow (left) in a checkered dress. Her friend Helen Prielipp is behind the counter on the right. Those enjoying drinks are, from left to right, two unidentified, Gary Brewer, Dale Williams, and John Eicholtz, who often served as race announcer.

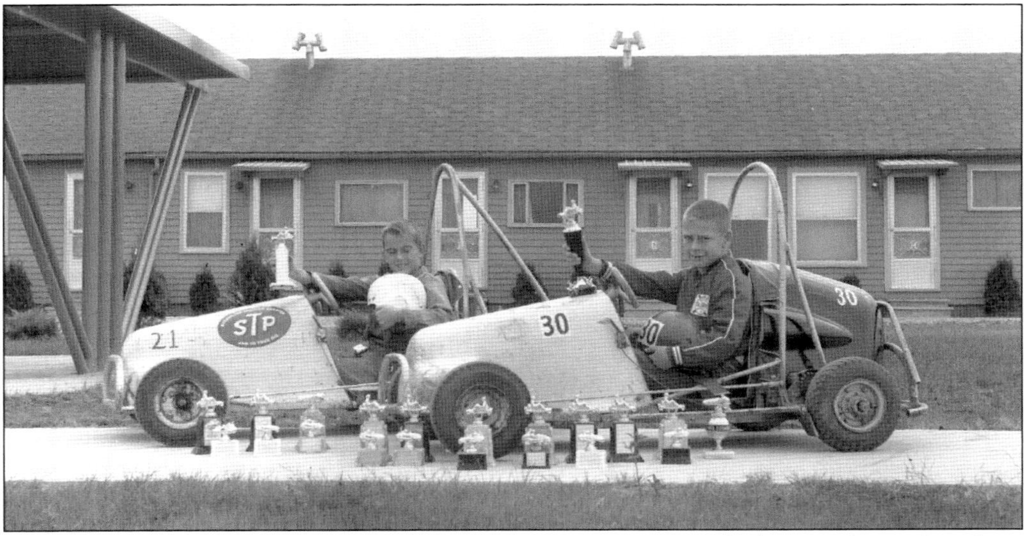

Prizewinners Mike Curley (left) and Doug Jennings pose in 1959 with their trophies. These boys raced until they entered middle school and became involved with school sports. Doug's cowl shows a partially mended hole that was made when another car clipped him on the track. The young drivers are particularly proud of their customized helmets.

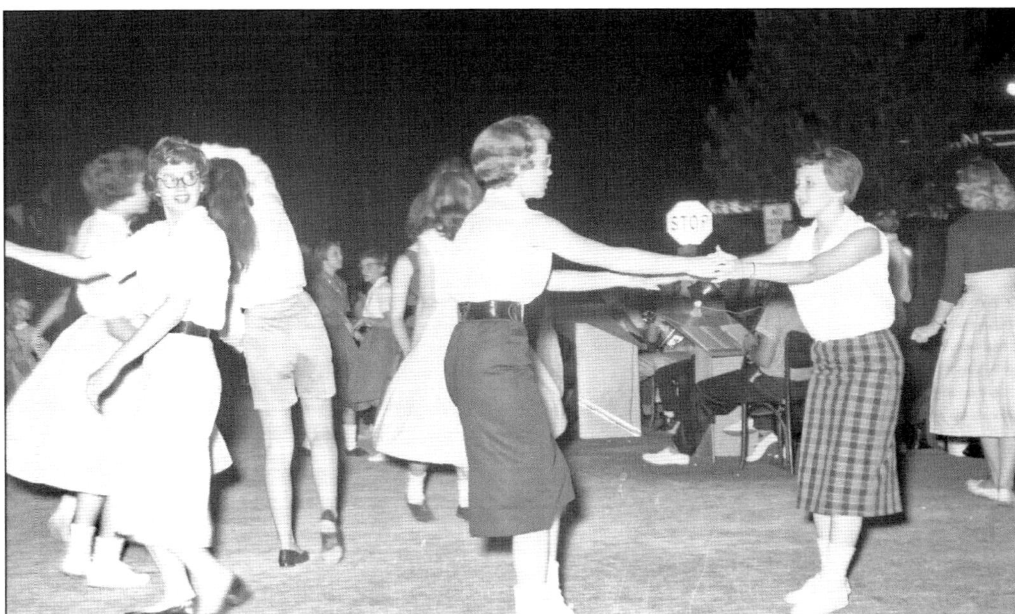

Kay Wilson (center, with the dark skirt), jitterbugs with Bonnie Winans at a street dance June 19, 1959. Rosie Waring often served as the announcer. Dundee had a long tradition of sponsoring events around the triangle. For years, stores would stay open late on Saturdays to allow for shopping. Residents would mingle in the open air while listening to music. As Dundeeites became more mobile, these communal gatherings happened less often.

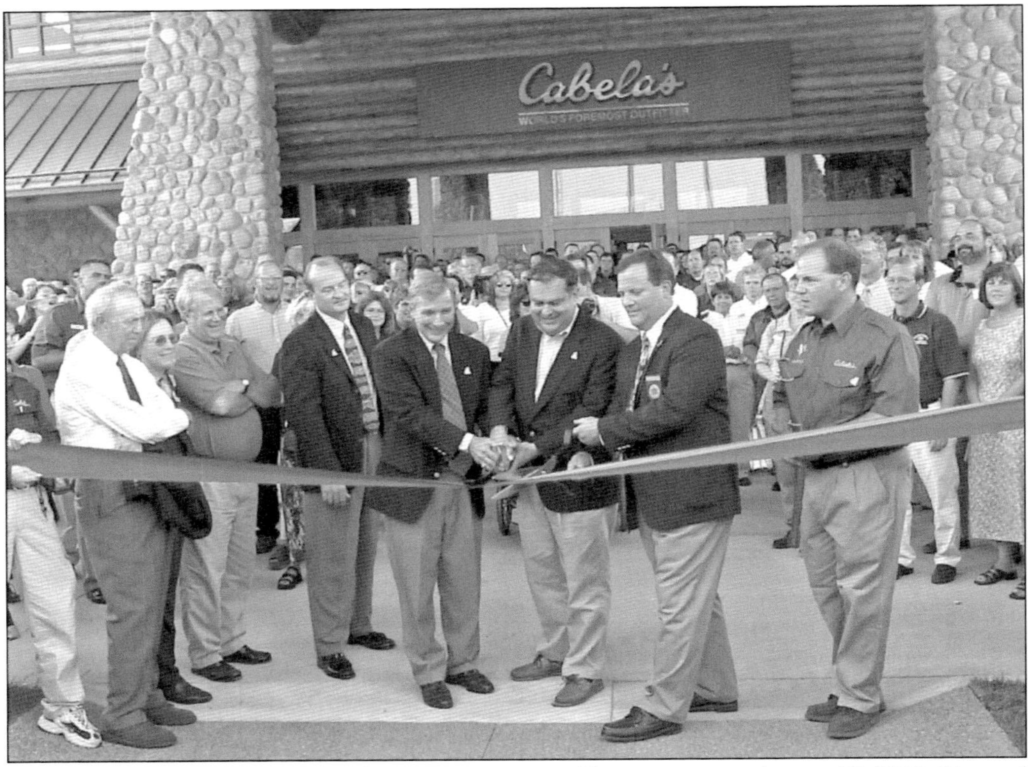

Cabela's, the world's foremost outfitters, is seen at its ribbon cutting on August 29, 2000. Pictured from left to right are, starting with the man in the dark blazer, unidentified; Michigan lieutenant governor Dick Posthumus; Michigan senator Spencer Abraham; Tim Holland, Cabela's director of retail; and Greg Golab, the Dundee store's general manager. This was Dundee's first "destination" store, where customers could come from far and near to shop in an environment with museum-quality wildlife displays and a broad retail selection. (Courtesy of *The Independent*.)

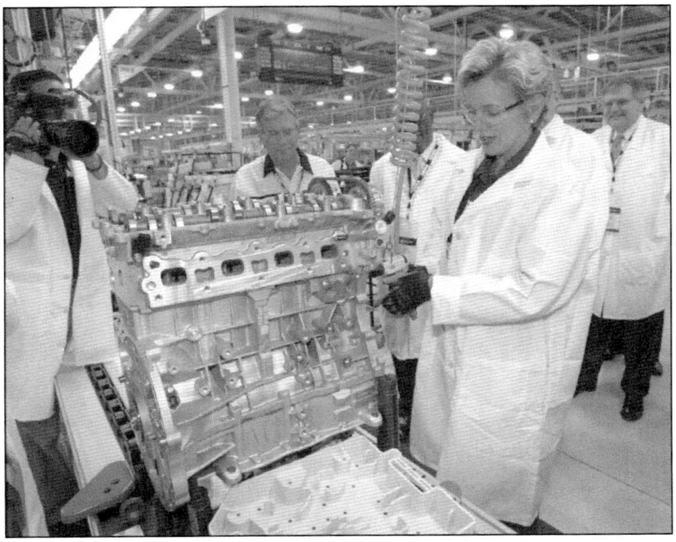

On October 3, 2005, the new Global Engine Manufacturing Alliance (GEMA) World Engine Plant began mass production of its four-cylinder World Engine to be used in Chrysler, Dodge, and Jeep vehicles. Michigan governor Jennifer Granholm helps celebrate by joining the assembly line at Dundee. The plant's main product in 2011 is the 1.41-liter, 16-valve FIRE (Fully Integrated Robotized Engine) for the North American Fiat 500. (Courtesy of Chrysler Group LLC.)

EPILOGUE

By the time the 1950s came to a close, Dundee had already been serving as the commercial hub for the surrounding agricultural community for over 100 years—locals traded with locals. Transportation was the key to the village's original success. Pioneers traveled by water on the River Raisin and by land on converted Indian footpaths. In the 1860s, the village waited for the railroad to find it after enduring the snub that Ida beat it to claim the first railroad line. Soon enough, a freight and mail train came three times a week. Then, in 1873, the Canadian Southern ran the first passenger route through Dundee. Eventually, the New York Central, the Detroit, Toledo & Ironton (DTI), and the Ann Arbor Railroad all made stops in Dundee.

With the dawn of the 1960s, Dundee was poised on the brink of change. Another form of transportation was about to transform Dundee's self-sufficient way of life. In the 1950s, Pres. Dwight Eisenhower had inaugurated the interstate highway system. In 1959, US 23, which had originally meandered its way through little villages, became a limited-access highway. Using it and Interstate 94, Dundeeites could easily commute to the automotive factories of Ypsilanti and Dearborn. Rural living was combined with city employment.

Now the little village was no longer required to meet all the material needs of its citizens who could drive to the "big cities" of Detroit, Ann Arbor, and Toledo. Citizens traded with the wider world. This impacted the dress shop, hardware store, grocery, and shoe store, among others, on the triangle. Traditional shops closed, and restaurants and gift shops opened in their place.

Meanwhile, industries began to look favorably at Dundee with its easy access to both a major highway and a railroad. To accommodate them, the Dundee Village Council opened four industrial parks in 1983, 1990, 1994, and 2004. Tecumseh Products R&D was followed by Mac Valves, Dundee Wire, Diamond Electric, Swann's, Carpenter Textiles, Axis Engineering, Aries Engineering, and Young's, Inc. These and the two enterprises presented on the opposite page are bringing the 21st century to Dundee. Onward!

Recording and preserving Dundee's history is the Village of Dundee's Old Mill Museum, which opened in 1986. It welcomes visitors Friday through Monday from noon unto 4:00 p.m. Patrons can reach the museum at 734-529-8596 or museum@dundeeoldmill.com.

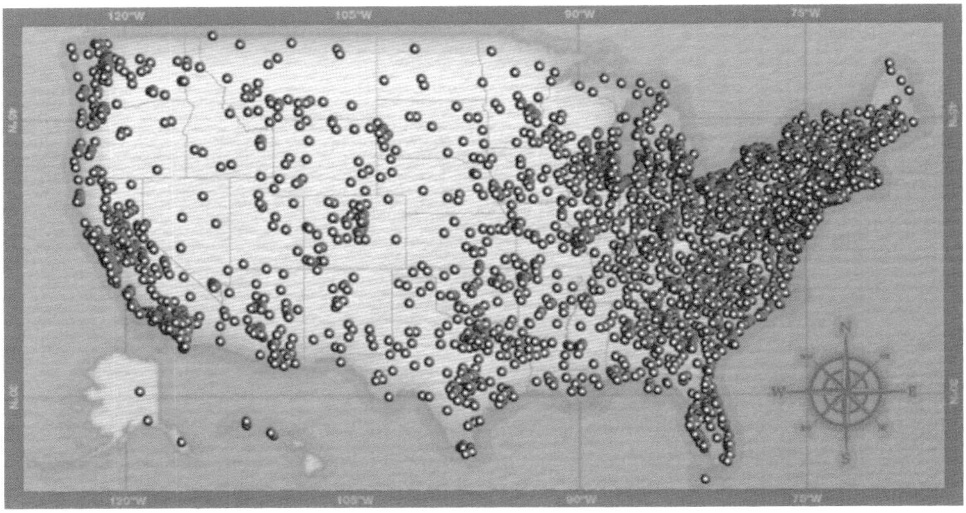